DIRT

THE QUIRKS, HABITS,

and PASSIONS

of KEEPING HOUSE

Edited by

MINDY LEWIS

SEAL PRESS

Published by Seal Press
A Member of the Perseus Books Group
1700 Fourth Street
Berkeley, California 94710

Library of Congress Cataloging-in-Publication Data
Dirt : the quirks, habits, and passions of keeping house / edited by
Mindy Lewis ; foreword by Penelope Green.
    p. cm.
 ISBN-13: 978-1-58005-261-0
 ISBN-10: 1-58005-261-4
1. Women. 2. Family. 3. Housekeeping. I. Lewis, Mindy. II. Green,
Penelope.
 HQ1155.D57 2009
 648'.50922--dc22

                        2008051788

Cover design by Kimberly Glider Design
Interior design by Tabitha Lahr
Printed in the United States of America
Distributed by Publishers Group West

"Few tasks are more like the torture of Sisyphus
than housework, with its endless repetition:
the clean becomes soiled, the soiled is
made clean, over and over, day after day."

—Simone de Beauvoir

CONTENTS

Foreword

Penelope Green

*O*n a bright Sunday afternoon in the fall of 2008, on one of those preelection weekends when the Dow had taken a near-vertical dive on the preceding Friday, a curious scene was being enacted in a specialty shop in Manhattan's Chelsea neighborhood. At the Container Store on Sixth Avenue, lines of shoppers snaked through the building. True, it was during the store's annual shelving sale, but the people in the lines didn't seem to be loaded up with much in the way of shelves. Instead, their carts were filled with cedar sock organizers, bamboo CD holders, plastic sweater bags, and other esoterica (like linen-covered boxes that were $69 and not on sale that day) that had been created under the premise that people will pay top dollar for objects that purport to make their lives tidier. Oh, the poignant promise lurking in a plain linen box!

I can tell you what was in those carts because I was one of the shoppers (my cart held plastic file tubs, a clutch of wooden hangers, and, though I'm embarrassed to admit it, one of those $69 linen numbers). My daughter's college fund had been eviscerated, yet I was buying pricey organizing supplies. You didn't need a PhD to analyze my behavior or that of the other shoppers: The world was in chaos, but if our mail could be stacked properly and our shoes lined up just so, perhaps the center would hold.

"Where's the recession?" I asked the woman who rang up my purchases. She shrugged eloquently.

"It's not in here," she said. "It's been crazy like this every day."

No matter what the economic climate is, Americans have always been enraptured and ensnared by the metaphor of the clean (or dirty) house. And marketers have long found success in mining that conflict. From Mrs. Beeton's early household guides to Martha Stewart's late-twentieth-century media empire or the creation of the National Association of Professional Organizers—otherwise known as NAPO—whose 4,300 members are ever poised to de-clutter the lives of some 135,000 anguished clients annually, the business of clean and the abolition of mess have flourished through good times and bad. Last fall was not a happy time to be a retailer, by any measure, but the organizing systems business, as it is called, was holding steady, according to *Closets* magazine, which tracks that sort of thing—indeed, last fall it was still a $3 billion industry that includes the ministrations of the NAPO folks as well as the offerings at the Container Store, the fetish-worthy tools in the Homekeeping line at Williams-Sonoma (which sells things like Australian lamb's-wool dusters for $135), and the organizing systems sold by closet designers and makers of office supplies.

The reasons behind this particularly American phenomenon—an anxiety, really, that plays out in a tidy versus messy dialectic that pits spouse against spouse, parent against child, ego against id—could and should fill a book. And at last they have, in this anthology! How we think about our messes, who wields the vacuum and why, and what our cleaning styles—or lack thereof—reveal about our innermost selves are a few of the potent emotional engines for the essays collected in the following pages.

Katy Brennan looks deep in her muddled closet and finds a reflection, as she writes, "of who I've been and who I am, not who I'd like to be." How many of us would recognize ourselves in Brennan's clear-eyed diagnosis: "I am sentimental, confused, and conflicted." Julianne Malveaux takes pride in living with dust bunnies the size of tumbleweeds and explores racial history in her own cleaning ambivalence: "Perhaps in utter rebellion against the historic roles of African American women, I cultivated a studied indifference to housework," she writes. "I used to joke that I had a dust ball that had grown so tall I might date it one day." On the other side of the broom is Louise Rafkin, who decodes the emotional life of a house's inhabitants as she cleans the objects in it, tracking the breakup of a marriage, noting the empty spaces in the house of a lonely man.

In cleaning a house . . . ," Rafkin writes, "I am part of the rightful order of things. I contribute to the continuation of the story."

Finally, consider the emotions surrounding Laura Shaine Cunningham's relationship to the pumpkin-pine floorboards in a beloved farmhouse. Twice a year she enacts a ritual obeisance toward those floors, crawling on hands and knees, classical music blaring, rubbing Butcher's floor wax into each honey-colored plank. It is an act born from memory—of a long-dead mother—and the sort of house pride an adult orphan takes in joyfully putting together her own home. Cunningham's floor waxing is a celebration of a relationship that has lasted for decades, one that is still, as she puts it, "charged with erotic overtones and undertones of subjugation, drudgery, and ecstasy. I confess—my floors have brought me to a place no man has ever done: my knees."

Pledge, anyone?

DIRT: AN INTRODUCTION

*T*hree things in life are certain: death, taxes, and dirt. No matter how hard or frequently we clean, we can't escape the dust, soot, grime, soil, crumbs, and clutter that are bound to besmirch our homes. Domestic cleaning is among the most humbling and recurrent of all human conditions. *For dust thou art. Set thy house in order. Cleanliness is next to godliness. On your knees, humans! Amen.* And so were invented Mr. Clean, the washing machine, the dishwasher, the self-cleaning oven, the vacuum cleaner, the DustBuster, the Swiffer, the HEPA filter, the cleaning woman/person/service/housekeeper/nanny, the legal and illegal immigrant day worker, the stay-at-home dad, the housewife, and various other time- and labor-saving devices.

Our housekeeping styles express who we are on the most intimate psychological level. In cleaning (much as in writing) we make sense of our lives, sort our messes, restore order to our psyches, work out our anger and frustration, rediscover the beauty in our lives, and express our love for (and resentment toward) others. Housecleaning is the daily/weekly/monthly—or in some cases, quarterly, semiannual, or way-long-overdue—necessary ritual of restoration. For many, it's an ongoing, constant occupation; for others, an easily overlooked distraction.

In these pages, thirty-eight talented writers come clean on how they deal with dirt in their physical, psychological, and relational environments. Male and female, spanning generations, our contributors are journalists, essayists, memoirists, novelists, and short story writers who also happen to be hoarders and tossers, clutterbugs and neatniks, slackers and dust-busters.

Following our authors from bathrooms to kitchens, living rooms to bedrooms, nurseries to studies, we peer through their streaky or spotless windows while they empty their closets, vacuum the rugs, wax their floors, gather their dust bunnies, load their dishwashers, scrub their sinks, all the while confronting their spouses, children, parents, roommates—and their own habits. Reading their stories, we learn about their origins, aspirations, pet peeves, obsessions, and cleaning tips.

Embedded in these contemporary narratives are traces of the shift in domestic ideals from generation to generation, into the new millennium. We've come a long way from the idealized, smiling, be-aproned housewife of the 1950s, rebellion and the birth of feminism in the explosive '60s and freewheeling '70s, the rise of divorce and the single- and working-parent household, inflation and recession in the '80s and '90s. The Collyer brothers and Bouvier Beales, were they alive today, would likely be diagnosed with OCD and have their choice of Hoarders Anonymous or Serotonin Reuptake Inhibitors. And how many of our mothers, in their cleaning-frenzied heyday, might today have been in need of therapeutic intervention?

In this age of unprecedented time pressure, when space is at a premium, Container Stores are scattered around cities and shopping malls, and household cleansers are a potent chemical brew, we are faced with new dilemmas in dealing with dirt and clutter. As our stuff overflows our closets and attics into landfills and oceans, the ability to find creative solutions is imperative. Clutter has also gone cyber, as evidenced by the digital info-glut that besieges our minds and our hard drives. As an antidote to the time spent staring into monitors, housecleaning can be for some—myself included—a way of reconnecting to material, nonvirtual reality.

I owe the inspiration for this anthology to three sources, the first being that prime cleaner, my mother, from whose eagle eye a speck of dust has not a chance of escaping and who, I suspect, single-handedly keeps the paper-towel and plastic-storage-bag industry in business (thanks, Mom, for setting a clean example). Now in her eighth decade, my mom's eyes are still sharp, but her militant tendencies have relaxed.

The experience of growing up under the influence of a cleanliness-obsessed mother instilled in me some basic life lessons. Back in the days when divorce was a dirty word, single-parenting a rare phenomenon, and gender roles as well as salaries fixed and unfair, I witnessed firsthand my working mother's frustration at life's pressures being subjugated into vigorous cleaning rituals and saw that this activity seemed to calm and restore her. I learned early that order and cleanliness are essential life priorities that require vigilance. I also learned that styles of housekeeping reflect both psychological and cultural context, as exemplified by my thoroughly modern mom and my old-fashioned down-on-hands-and-knees floor-scrubbing but not overly meticulous grandmother.

Housekeeping also provided my first object lesson in social hierarchy and labor economics. Early in my childhood, when my parents separated, my mother took a full-time job and hired a housekeeper (then called a cleaning lady or, worse, cleaning girl). Marie came several times a week to our lower Manhattan apartment complex from her similar-but-not-equal Harlem housing project. In addition to cooking and cleaning, Marie bathed, fed, and walked me to school and taught me to tie my shoes and write my name. I learned that there were people you could pay to clean your house for you, who then had to go home and clean their own houses. A whole social macrocosm and psychological microcosm were revealed through the ongoing daily battle with dust, dirt, laundry, and disorder.

As a teenager in the 1960s, I perceived myself as an isolated victim of my mother's maniacal lust to eradicate dust. My rebellion was emblematic of an era, an age, a lifestyle (the Whole Earth Catalog vs. *House Beautiful*). Yet, when I moved into my own apartment at age nineteen, the very first thing I did was head to the local hardware store to buy my own mop and bucket and set out with determination to forge my own identity and cleaning style.

Which brings me to the second inspiration for this book: the creatively cluttered Manhattan apartment in which I have lived and worked and inhaled dust for over three decades. Over the years, my apartment has been alternately a haven of domestic solace, a creative retreat, and a dust-ridden workplace to which I gradually became allergic.

Finally, the idea for this anthology was inspired by the talented students in my nonfiction writing classes at The Writer's Voice of the Westside YMCA who responded to a writing prompt ("Write about your physical home environment") with insightful, revealing personal essays—several, included in these pages—that explored not only clutter, aesthetics, housekeeping styles, and cleaning habits but also family relationships. A spark was lit as I realized the universality and scope of the topic. Shortly afterward, when a friend invited me to see Sarah Ruhl's remarkable play, "The Clean House," the profound implications of the two sisters' different approaches to cleaning (one cleans, the other doesn't) brought chills of affirmation.

Since then, the concept has seemed to surface everywhere: in noteworthy books like *A Perfect Mess: The Hidden Benefits of Disorder*; in the email tips on personal organization that arrive weekly in my inbox, and in enticing tidbits that come my way by way of friends and Internet. (Thoreau, it seems, took time off from Walden Pond to visit his mother and brought along his laundry for her to wash.) Frequently evoked in literature, the topic of dirt, cleaning, and clutter can also be found in the classics (there's a special place in Dante's *Inferno* reserved for Hoarders and Wasters) and across disciplines. Anthropologist Mary Douglas's definition of dirt as "matter out of place"—an idea so seminal it's known to anthropologists simply as MOOP—points to the subjective nature of our ideas of cleanliness and order, underscoring what we surely already know: One person's order can be another person's chaos.

Then there are the anecdotes that pour forth whenever I mention this book. I've heard compulsive clutterbugs recoil in horror at the idea of dusting because "dust is only dangerous if it's stirred up." A retired psychiatrist friend confessed that although he knows he should discard the boxes of client records stored in his basement to spare his wife and children the task should something happen to him, he just can't bring himself to. *Why?* he wondered, then realized: The files not only contain intimate details of lives and psyches entrusted to him in confidence, they also represent his own professional life— his "best self."*

The greatest pleasure of editing this collection has been reading these essays. Amidst the dust and grime, there are some surprising moments—ranging from erotic (Mimi Schwartz finds consummate pleasure in waxing her floors) to familial (Joyce Maynard takes a break from cleaning up after her children to appreciate the glitter in her floorboards) to spiritual (Katy Brennan encounters Buddha in the closet, and Nancy Peacock ecstatically cleans other people's toilets). On the darker side, Mira Bartók excerpts tips on housecleaning and life from her homeless mother's journals, and Alissa Quart wistfully recalls a more authentic, dirtier New York City. In a comic mode, Richard Goodman imagines Thoreau's alternate profession in "The Walden Pond Cleaning Service." There's even a real-life postscript: Patty Dann and Michael Hill, whose poignant essays explore cleaning, loss, and

---

* Because I can't include everyone's stories in these pages, I invite readers to post your own housecleaning stories on our blog (http://dirt2009.blogspot.com) or email them to dirt. anthology@gmail.com.

catharsis after the death of a spouse, were recently remarried—to each other (no thanks to this anthology, but still, happy news).

Dirt, and how we deal with it, is a subject that goes far deeper than appearances. Identity and relationship are at the heart of these essays. Thought provoking, insightful, and deeply human, they present an honest look into a dusty yet sharply reflective mirror in which we can observe, empathize, laugh at, question, and recognize ourselves.

I invite you to set down your mops and buckets, put your feet up, and enjoy.

I. FAMILY DIRT

"Cleaning your house while your kids
are still growing is like shoveling the
walk before it stops snowing."

—Phyllis Diller

My Dirty Little Secret

Sally Koslow

*T*his morning my husband announced he'd had a dream in which
I starred. I was certain it was a lush sexual fantasy with me in
the role usually played by Angelina Jolie. Whoo-hoo! But, no. This
was a nightmare, he said, in which I had deeply disappointed him.
Had I neglected our children? Gained two hundred pounds? Run
away to Rome with Gabriel Byrne, a predictable yet understandable
choice? Unless it was the latter, I decided I did not especially want to
hear his download of nocturnal anxiety—what good can come from
such a conversation? But I had no choice.

In Dreamland, he'd walked into our kitchen and caught me
washing the dishes with the sponge relegated to wiping up grunge.
This cleaning device is, in his mind, apparently one molecule short
of the Ebola virus, despite the fact that we sterilize it daily via the
microwave's highest temperature. Dream-Me vehemently denied my
odious housekeeping. Dream-Him waved the foul object in my face.
"You're lying. I have evidence—the bad sponge has suds on it" were
his last words before he woke in a cold sweat.

Dr. Freud, is this sponge just a sponge? Or does it reveal the most obvious dirty secret within my marriage, that my husband believes—apparently, 24/7—that he is better than I, or at least the better housekeeper?

Consider further testimony. I am married to a man who after reading *The New York Times* will leave it not only out of order but with sections crumpled and opened to whatever page has last caught his fancy—never, for the record, page one. When he receives junk mail, he *reads* it, after which the torn envelope and its contents are strewn about, creating multiple heaps of rubbish where once there was a conveniently disposable piece. The man rarely feels the need to shut the door to a closet, even after he's forgotten to hang his coat in it. Carbon footprints be damned, he rarely turns off the light or television in a room he has exited, often for the rest of the day. In the morning, yesterday's socks greet me like dead hamsters. I choose not to discuss boxer shorts.

On the other hand, there's me. After reading the *Times*, I reorder its sections, which I daintily fold to prepare the newspaper for future users. I toss junk mail, unopened, into the recycling bin. I close cupboards. Closets, too, which I long ago discovered are handy storage nooks for recently worn clothes, which live on hangers. My undies land either in the bathroom hamper or in a lingerie bag—the flowery one for light-colored items, black mesh for darks. Obviously, I deserve to be canonized, yet my husband not only gives me no credit for these saintly acts, he persists in believing he is the superior housekeeper.

We have a long history, my husband and I. We met in college, when my culinary skills were embryonic. The trouble began the day he requested a sandwich. Innocently, I opened a can, scooped tuna into a bowl, plopped in a spoonful of mayo, blended, spread the tangy mixture on toast, and called it lunch.

He gagged. "Why didn't you drain the oil?"

You were supposed to drain the oil? Really?

We were off to the races. If I bug him to pick up after himself, he brushes me off like dandruff. But when my housekeeping isn't up to his and Martha Stewart's freakishly high standards, he reacts to my efforts with one glower short of a glare and has been known to, say, wrest a vacuum cleaner from my hands to complete the task at hand his way. The right way.

Glass-half-full people might say our differences balance one another. I love to live in my own personal Anthropologie store, with bag and baggage artfully arranged—alphabetized, let's say, or sorted by color (behold my closet, a rainbow of shirts, jackets, and pants), while the big guy's all about knowing the scientific way to poach an egg. The trouble is our differences don't complement; my husband often walks around pissed because not only does he see the glass as half-empty, he usually feels it's not washed as well as it might be.

Even when we more or less agree, our yin and yang go bang, bang, bang. Neither one of us can leave the house without making the bed. But my bed-making is, in his opinion, substandard. My corners wouldn't pass muster in a hospital, a barracks, or the Adirondack boys' camp he attended all summer long starting at age five. (You read that right; sadly, Child Welfare no longer gives a damn.) I'm not half-bad at laundry: I get the obvious principles, having learned from the unfortunate experience of turning my son's new white Armani shirt to pale pink—sorry, honey—but my folding isn't justified by a T-square. I've attempted ironing. There's something Zen-like about converting wrinkles into smooth planes, but try as I might, I do not iron as well as my husband, a man who, when he finally picks up his clothes from the heap in our bedroom, can press them as well as the tailor at Barney's.

The fact (and I hate to admit it) is that I like a home that looks fluffed and accessorized—candles lit, cocktail napkins at the ready—but I'm essentially an unskilled, undocumented worker, a neat freak who's only read the CliffsNotes. My husband, on the other hand (calloused from scrubbing) is able to overlook mess but, regarding the basics, has a self-taught PhD.

I trace my inadequacy to home economics, required in seventh and eighth grade. Because of some sort of celestial tomfoolery, I happened to have been raised in a midwestern town: Fargo, North Dakota. In my day, girls there popped out of the womb knowing how to darn and de-ice, to hem and to hoe. Yet clearly I sprang from a different gene pool; my pie crust was dry, my dirndl skirt lopsided, and my home ec grades all Cs. I never got past Rice Krispie treats.

Then it dawned on me: This is not the worst thing. When I grow up, I will simply relocate to New York City, where people think there are two choices for meals—restaurants and take-out—and it's a point of honor not to know how to operate a DustBuster. The rare woman in Manhattan who wants a hand-sewn dirndl finds some fraulein to whip it up. But I hadn't counted on marrying a guy who, while raised by a mother with live-in "help"—a laundress, even— and a father who didn't know a nail from a nine-iron, nonetheless mystically learned to reattach his missing buttons. And he's not even a girly-man. My spouse can split a log and flip a mattress. No, I hadn't counted on his strange competence, or that his feminine side expressed through mops and Murphy's Oil Soap would be more highly evolved than my own.

Regardless of how little attention I paid to the dowdy lessons of home ec, I slowly discovered there is cachet in a woman baking light-as-air biscuits, coaxing near-lifeless orchids into a second bloom, and knowing how to make a wood floor gleam. That I have fallen short in every one of these categories is a source of private humiliation but one I can bear. What gets me is public censure. Just last week Mr. Clean cast a jaundiced eye on the manner in which I was pouring champagne and removed the bubbly from my hand squarely in front of guests. A bolder woman might have whacked the bottle over his head. I simply sunk into myself and wondered how I could be so truly inept.

That is, until he had that dream, which caused my own epiphany. I suddenly realized that I will *never* get it right, and this recognition has offered tremendous liberation. After years of feeling inferior because my husband chops an onion faster and better than I ever will, it has finally occurred to me that I should simply let him knock himself out. I will watch from the sidelines, setting a pretty table and arranging bookshelves while he scours away like Cinderella.

Our son and his girlfriend recently moved in together. My motherly advice was for him to think long and hard about the daily minutiae of living, because deal-breaking habits take root faster than bamboo. You start with "Darling, did you rinse those dishes before you put them in the dishwasher?" and before you know it you're at "Moron, double-bag the stinking garbage before it leaks."

In relationships, the way we approach housekeeping becomes a metaphor, a power struggle, and a curse. Unless a couple is serviced by Windex-toting elves, someone always does it wrong. One of the partners has to back off. In my marriage, I've designated that person as me.

I've also decided I'm not that worried about our son. If he has paid attention to his fatherly role model, he already knows how to concoct a poultice to remove red wine stains from marble countertops. At least by one parent, the kid's been raised right.

No Elves in the Night

Joyce Maynard

I spent the winter I was pregnant with my first child cleaning the house. This was probably the only time in my twenty-three years of life on earth that I'd been interested in housework, and in the thirty years since, I don't think I've ever again summoned anything close to that level of interest. It wasn't really cleanliness that consumed me at the time, even then. It was order. The appearance of order, anyway. As defined by a tidy house, every object in its place.

So like a mother cat, a dog, a penguin, I was readying the nest for the family to come. All that long, pregnant winter I pushed my vacuum cleaner and dusted, folded, and refolded the same ten thrift-shop sleeper suits, the same little stack of cloth diapers, rearranging the baby powder, smoothing the sheets on the crib. A photograph of me a few weeks before my due date (a picture I made my husband take) showed me standing proudly next to our open freezer, which I'd stocked with a couple dozen frozen meals I was hoarding for the weeks after the birth. I barely let him eat anything I cooked in those days, I was so obsessed with stocking up for the future. I wanted things to be perfect once the baby came. As if a clean house and a full freezer could ensure those things.

Then our daughter was born and life got messy fast. With Audrey in my arms most of the day, Audrey at my breast, I moved through the house one-armed. Brushing my hair and getting dressed became as much maintenance as I could pull off, most days, as dust accumulated on the furniture and a mountain of laundry grew on the bedroom floor.

Nobody could have explained to me the kind of havoc a seven-pound infant could create in a household, and I never fully understood how it happened. But the diaper pail overflowed, the dishes from one meal lay buried at the bottom of the sink, under the dishes from the next, and when space ran out there, they teetered on the counter.

When she was a little over six months old, I left our daughter for the first time with a babysitter. But my child care story was different from most. I stayed home; my daughter was the one who went out, to Mary's house, three mornings a week. And though I wanted to write stories—a book even, was the dream—I remember how I spent that first three hours of solitude: cleaning.

Maybe this was the moment that revealed to me a central truth of parenthood that has continued to present itself in the thirty years since that long-ago summer. It's untidy. Not just in the literal sense—not just because of all the diapers and gear, the damp spots on the bed, the car seats and blocks and misplaced sippy cups and spilled juice and Cheerios between the sofa cushions—but because of how the fact of having and caring for children, and loving them as one does, messes with your mind. It is as if someone had opened a down comforter directly over my head and turned on the fan, leaving a million feathers to blow around the room before settling on every surface. Most particularly, my brain.

What I longed for most in those days was a clear head and concentration. I had this new person in my life, whom I loved more than I knew possible, but getting her had cost me dearly. It seemed that when I'd gained a daughter, I'd lost myself. I'd sit at the kitchen table, mornings after I'd dropped Audrey off at Mary's, and stare at the blank paper in the typewriter, with no thoughts but of her. The only thing coming out of me—by midmorning, or sooner, if I let an image of her come to mind—was milk, literally seeping through my blouse. And so I'd do the one thing I could that seemed, in tangible terms, to address the problem: the laundry.

For me, the act of cleaning house came to represent my endless pursuit of control, in a life where virtually none existed. We were broke. My career life seemed hopeless. (Barely more than a year earlier, I'd been a reporter in New York City, wearing my smart black suit, carrying my notebook, filing stories on deadline. Now, if I wasn't taking care of my daughter, I was folding sleeper suits or pureeing fruit.)

But the heart of the problem was this: My marriage was in trouble. And what we argued about, often, was housework.

Better, maybe, if it had been something like differing spiritual goals, or attitudes about sex or politics or the meaning of life that provided the source of our arguments, instead of something so foolishly insignificant as cleaning the sink. But housework and laundry (and the question of who took care of them) became one of the central points of friction between my husband and me. I thought he should do more. If he loved me the way I wished, he would want me to have time and space for something besides laundry and cleaning, I said. But he—a more naturally tidy person—couldn't understand where all the messes came from in the first place.

I wanted our home, and the meals I served in it, to be an artwork, an expression of love for my family—though at the time, if you'd looked at our home as in indication of our lives, it would have served as the physical manifestation of chaos. No doubt it didn't help that the house we lived in was a two-hundred-year-old farmhouse where heat came from a woodstove (a never-ending source of ashes) and that—lacking cupboards—our dishes were stored on bookshelves.

Nothing in this kitchen could be called efficient: The refrigerator was relegated to the pantry. A marble set on the floor would roll away and disappear.

At the very moment in recent history when women my age were off pursuing high-powered careers and reclaiming selfhood, I had chosen the domestic life, but with perpetual frustration and ambivalence. I wanted wonderful smells in our house: of roast chicken and homemade soup on the stove, pie in the oven. But on rare trips to New York City, I dropped in at the offices of *The New York Times* (the first few years, anyway; after that, never) to show off my baby and, afterward, wept for my abandoned career, my lost promise, my brain gone soft with scrubbing.

It was humiliating—pathetic, even—how much I thought about things like cleaning products and dust prevention, how the object of my dreams had gone from the sublime to the appliance section. Charter subscriber to *Ms.* magazine, I now longed for an orderly kitchen the way some women of my generation yearned for a corner office. Not just the tidy and beautiful house of course, but the life it represented. I wanted to bake pies (flour on the floor, blueberry juice dripping on the bottom of the oven). I wanted lilacs on the table, and craft projects, and homemade spaghetti sauce.

"It isn't fair that you go play basketball Saturday mornings and I do laundry," I told my husband. "You have all this free time."

"Let's be honest, Joyce," he said. "You wouldn't know what to do with free time if you had some."

He was probably right. When he'd take our daughter on a long bike ride, I'd drift through the rooms of our messy house, never able to stick with one project more than a few minutes, before getting waylaid and launching into another. When he came home—exercised and invigorated—he'd ask if I'd had a productive day.

"I polished the silverware," I said. "I canned our tomatoes." So there were fifteen quarts of homemade spaghetti sauce on the pantry shelf. And more dishes to wash.

"I thought you were going to write," he said.

"I couldn't think of anything," I told him. But one thing about housework that's different from the first sentence of a novel: Words may be hard to locate. Mess never is.

Audrey spent a lot of her life on the floor in those days, learning to crawl. While I'd be cooking, she was down at my feet, opening cupboards, taking out pots and pans. By the time I'd get the casserole in the oven, or the cake, every plastic dish and metal pan we owned would be out on the floor. I picked them up, mostly, but after a while, living this way, you begin to understand something about living in a house with young children: that it's a little pointless tidying up messes that will only happen all over again, a minute later.

Another baby came, and another after. I got better at certain things: I hired a friend to build me a little cabin where I would go to relocate my concentration and work in the morning, after taking the children to daycare and school. I managed to write books and articles. (About my children often, since they were the main characters in my life at that point. If a wave is about to knock you over, the best thing to do is dive into it rather than resist.)

It's not accurate, though, to suggest that I found my creative expression by escaping the responsibilities of the domestic life. Gritting my teeth sometimes, I embraced them. The truth is—books and articles, columns and essays notwithstanding—nothing I undertook or accomplished in those years I spent, home with young children, provided the satisfaction and creative possibility that raising our children and making a home for us all did. Our house was like a big art studio, and I wanted to fill it with projects and possibilities—markers and paints, boxes of collage supplies and pipe cleaners and old wooden spools and cardboard boxes and glitter and dress-up clothes and puppets and books, pots to bang on, egg cartons with seeds starting in them, avocado seeds on toothpicks in the windowsill, ripped-up newspaper for papier-mâché, and discarded wheels from the dump, and science experiments, and clay, and fabric, and ribbon, and glue. Given a choice between tidiness and fun, fun tended to win out.

But our marriage was unraveling, and with dismaying frequency it was the topics of our kitchen sink, the bathroom floor, the dust, and laundry, and the refrigerator bin that served as the battleground. When I was upset I reorganized the pantry. Or baked a dozen pies, leaving a trail of flour and apple peelings. I vacillated wildly between joyful abandon and manic scrubbing. There were days when I let it all go for a while. And days when I exploded and stormed around the house with a giant garbage bag, throwing in toys and socks, unfinished art projects, abandoned yogurt containers and (one terrible Christmas day) crumpled-up wrapping paper and even the gifts that came in it.

"No allowances for anyone this week," I told them when things got bad.

"I am not the maid in this family," I announced.

"There are no elves who come in the night to put things away."

But in a way, there was an elf. She was me. Sometimes, in the night, I'd tiptoe into our children's rooms and sit on the floor with plastic bins all around me, sorting tiny toy pieces. Green LEGOs in one bin. Blue in another. Ninja turtles. Barbie clothes. My Little Ponies. G.I. Joes.

"Come to bed," my husband sighed.

I'm cleaning. (Silent message: And you're not.)

I had to get our house under control. I had to get our life under control. I got the two confused on a regular basis.

When Audrey was around eight, one of her friends gave her, for her birthday, a doll called Crystal Barbie. Crystal Barbie was a regular

Barbie except for one crucial and irresistible detail: She had tiny little see-through shoes, like Cinderella slippers. Small as the nail on your pinkie but, to an eight-year-old Barbie lover, wonderful.

I knew my daughter well enough—and knew birthday parties with many eight-year-old girls in attendance, and knew our messy house, and knew most of all the importance of those shoes to Audrey—that the minute she opened the box I told her, "Let's put the shoes in a safe place." But all the girls at the party wanted to see, naturally. So there was a lot of passing Crystal Barbie around, with those shoes the main attraction.

Then the party was over, and I was (as usual) cleaning. Audrey was gathering up her presents and the cards and bits of ribbon that had decorated the packages. Suddenly, from one room over, I heard a sound like a scream. One of Crystal Barbie's shoes was gone. My daughter was heartbroken.

I spent the next three hours tearing our house apart, searching for that shoe. Somewhere around hour number two and a quarter, even Audrey urged me to stop, but by then I was a woman consumed with her mission. For a few hours at least, that afternoon, that shoe, and my inability to locate it seemed to signify everything that was wrong with our messy, messy house, my frustration at the books I wasn't writing, the evenings I wasn't spending in calm quiet, romantic times with my husband, the life I wanted and didn't have.

The marriage ended, eventually. My children and I moved to another house—where the struggles I once waged with their father over things like clearing away one's dishes and carrying out the trash no longer carried the same heat or tension. One thing I did, early on, after we moved to that house: I took more money than I had any business spending and put it toward a total kitchen renovation. There would still be bits of piecrust on the floor, but this one was covered in linoleum tile, not uneven pine boards. Easier to mop.

More important, though, I was a happier woman. Our house was hardly orderly. But the fact that it wasn't no longer seemed like such a big problem. For one whole season, Audrey kept a bucket of glitter next to our front door. Every morning, as she headed out the door to school, she'd toss a handful of glitter in the air, walking through it as she headed out the door, leaving faint, barely discernible flecks of gold in her hair and on her clothes, her eyelashes even. And our floor. No point in vacuuming. And anyway, I liked it.

When they were teenagers, we moved again—all the way across the country, this time to California. My daughter was heading off to college by now. My sons had grown into young men who cleaned up after themselves mostly and did their own laundry. Now it was Charlie and Willy who lectured me about leaving carrot peelings and coffee grounds in the sink, and sweeping up dirt only as far as the corner of a room, with the broom propped up over the pile.

Still, my children made their presence known in the house by the sheer volume of the space they took up. So there were CD cases strewn around, and bongo drums and art supplies and skateboards and bottles of Snapple, and drawings, and homework, not to mention— because they were outgoing boys—the possessions of their friends, and, eventually, of the girlfriends.

If there is one image that summons those years for me, more than any other, it is the sight of big sneakers scattered in the front hall by the door, sometimes more than a dozen of them. The old me had knelt on the floor to line up my children's Matchbox vehicles like cars in a parking lot, but the passage of time and maybe my own greater peace of mind had taken away much of my old, futile obsession with cleaning up. Somewhere along the line, I had ceased to need the appearance of order in our home—maybe because, at a deeper level, we'd located it at last, in a way that had nothing to do with whether or not the crisper drawer had been cleaned out lately.

When you're unhappy, those things can take on a great significance, and when life feels good, a little mess isn't such a threatening thing. The sight of all those sneakers in the front hall always made me happy. It meant the people who wore them could not be far away.

Then they were gone—first one child, then the other, then the last. At first they left their stuff in their rooms, but after a while they took what mattered to their dormitory rooms and apartments. I boxed up the rest, gave stuff away, sold the drum set, turned their bedrooms into a rental space for a tidy bachelor. Upstairs, too, the kitchen was clean at last, most of the time. No point baking pies just for myself.

For a while then, I felt as though a major limb had been cut from my body, but seven years since the departure of the last one, I've grown accustomed finally to life in an orderly house. The strangely tidy rooms, the washing machine idle for as long as a week at a time, the refrigerator almost empty.

They come home a few times a year now, seldom for more than a few days. Only it's not their home anymore, is what I have come to recognize. They have their own places. When my adult children speak of home now, they mean the apartment in Prospect Heights, the apartment in L.A., the cabin in New Hampshire, where they live their own lives. (What does it mean, I wonder, that the most recent musical composition by the older of my two sons—currently in play on YouTube—is a song that features the refrain "Why do we make the bed, just to mess it up again?")

There is no returning to the country I used to live in—the Valentinemaking supplies spilling out over the dining-room table, the half-completed papier-mâché dinosaurs and Halloween costumes and sticker collections and rock collections and baseball cards and glitter glue. All those socks lying around, no two of which ever seemed to make a pair.

For a while, I actually thought I missed their mess. But really, I understood, I just miss the ones who made it, the life we knew once—the happy clutter of days gone by when all of us were younger and glitter shone between the cracks in my floorboards.

I Don't Know What to Do with You

Lisa Selin Davis

*T*he house, when I arrived that summer, had fully succumbed to
my stepmother's preferred color palate, the walls and furniture
all awash in a womby shade of pink she doggedly referred to as dusty
rose. Everything else was cranberry—there was no such thing as
maroon at 28 George Street.

I was fifteen, freshly sprung from tenth grade in a western
Massachusetts college town; I lived there with my mom during the
school year in a working-class suburban subdivision, in a crummy
little mustard-colored ranch house that embarrassed me to no end.
My father, on the other hand, still inhabited the 1871 Italianate brick
house in upstate New York that I'd lived in as an infant, which he
and my mother had purchased for $13,000 in 1972. She told me
many years later that leaving the house was so much harder than
leaving my father, that its modest, elegant architecture always held
more potential than their marriage.

In all those years since we'd left, repairs and improvements had
been meager—some wallpaper torn down here, a floor refinished

there when a little cash was handy. But now, as I prepared to summer there once again, I encountered the most dramatic changes yet: The bedroom and living room had been outfitted with new custom cream-colored shelves and the bathroom renewed with flowered peach tiles (a diversion from dusty rose, at least). My stepmother had finished grad school and was now an official social worker—low paid but affording a tiny home improvement fund. I could see where she was going with this aesthetic, aiming to make the pages of *Country Homes Beautiful Garden Today*, or some such publication.

With the ameliorated house came a revised code of conduct. The previous summer I had discovered activities such as shoplifting, smoking pot, and standing in the center of the street screaming the word "abusive" at the top of my lungs in reference to my parents' treatment of me, and so my stepmother had sent me a contract before I came this year—a list, on dusty-rose stationery, of rules I was to obey. I must help either clean up or prepare every meal; attend family days at least once a week; pick up any of my items left orphaned around the house; hold down the full-time job they had selected for me, wearing a hard hat and shitkickers and digging footbridges in the state park for minimum wage—as if they were taking cues from *Flashdance* and preparing me to be both a nice Jewish girl and a JD all at once. I turned the letter over to look for my father's handwriting, to see which rules had been his design. Nothing.

My own summer plans had included certain rites of passage: Get the red-headed kid from three blocks over to have sex with me, so I could overcome this whole virgin thing; inhale speed through a $10 bill; drive around in the back of Rachel's Volvo with the Grateful Dead blasting, my feet, in beaded anklets, dangling out the window. Housework was nowhere on my list. My friends (the kinds most parents refer to as "bad influences") all lived on the east side, like me, in dilapidated Victorians perched on the narrow grid of streets; it was a city designed for disobedience. We could cut through a neighbor's yard and arrive at one another's homes without circumnavigating a block and risking surveillance.

My little sister was seven at this time, busy singing in musicals and looking adorable, but she excelled at her chores—she was a terrific sheet folder and already, at that tender age, agreeable and accommodating and demurring and other-centered. She was not me. My older brother, having finished his first year of college and purchased a car and a four-by-five camera, was excused from all housework, that he might realize his full artistic potential by zooming around the Adirondacks exposing his silver gelatin film. My father was largely exempt from chores in August, when he played music seven days a week to pay the mortgage. My little brother was two, dismissed, of course, from housework, but we didn't seem to be teaching him how to corral his LEGOs into their plastic carrying case. I could see the gendered expectations, the hopes for each of us laid out on either side of the chore list: Men were in one column (slobby artists with a wide berth) and women (housekeepers) on the other.

And so the arguing began. I came home muddy and exhausted from my job with the other almost-juveys too late to help bake the tofu, or whatever we were to sup on, and was relegated to clean up duty. How I longed for a dishwasher, something to help me scrape those hardened soy bits off the dusty-rose imitation Fiesta ware, purchased for twenty-five cents from a garage sale, like so many of our other goods. I had no talent for housework, it turned out, and this, perhaps even more than the scowl I wore like an accessory, seemed to disappoint them.

One night, a note appeared on my pillow in my stepmother's bubbly all-caps handwriting. "Lis—there are sticky bits on the plates. Please redo dishes." It was midnight, and I was stoned, lips blurry and red from making out with the redhead. I decided to let it slide, give the dishes a wash at the crack of dawn before I went to my ditch-digging job. And wouldn't you know, at 6:30 the next day, I forgot.

Notes appeared more frequently, gently admonishing reminders that I had left laundry wet and begging for mildew in the washing machine; I hadn't swept when I had kitchen duty; and no, I had not properly scraped the dishes. My most egregious errors occurred in the bathroom, where my curly hairs collected in the drain, damp piles of my discarded towels colonizing the floor—all of this was chronicled on paper and delivered to my door. I was often not there to receive the messages, out, instead, flirting with ignoring my curfew.

The house continued to slowly transform all summer. The sparkly linoleum in my old bedroom, which my sister had occupied for years, resurfaced with gleaming pine floors. The old forget-me-not wallpaper disappeared under a layer of eggshell cranberry paint. The more the house as I remembered it from my early childhood was erased, the less obedient I became. The less obedient, the more these notes came. The more they came, the more they prompted new notes, with more stinging errors: I had missed family day. I hadn't performed my babysitting duties. I had failed to thank my stepmother properly for the outing she'd planned, snacking on stinky cheese in a park in the Adirondacks, when all my friends were jumping off the Hadley-Lucerne bridge into the Sacandaga River below, the more notes came. My father's signature was never on them. Only hers.

And so the tenor of the notes continued to evolve, listing punishments, restrictions as time went on—no going out on Friday until I cleaned my room or did a better job wiping down the counters or retrieved my towel from the bathroom floor. Maybe they were all reasonable things. I'd probably want my own kid to live up to such minor expectations. But they seemed outlandish to me, mostly because they were unmitigated by my father. I looked at the two of them: Would I rather be an other-centered, picnic-planning, clean-freak social worker or a mildly stoned, emotionally checked-out musician? Would I rather be a free-range artist like my brother, or Cinderella-in-training like my baby sis?

So I broke the code, finally disregarding every last thing my stepmother had carefully meted out in the contract. One night, overcome by the pile of notes and my father's Switzerland status during my fights with my stepmother, I found myself out there in the street again screaming the word "abusive," waving the notes around, forcing a family conference of sorts—a concentrated, serious version of family day.

It was just me and my father on the back porch, which was all sanded and waiting for its delicious drink of glossy paint—probably the only time I spent alone with him all summer. I wanted to ask him what he thought, if he cared about the unwrung-out sponge or the clothes left to wrinkle in the dryer, but I didn't—I knew on some level I was asking him to betray her, and I knew whom he would choose. So instead I growled and stomped, griped about the tremendous injustice of housework.

Rather than continue to reprimand me, my father slumped down on the back porch and proceeded to cry. He said, mumbling into the prayer-positioned hands leaning against his mouth and nose, "I don't know what to do with you."

This was, I think, a missed opportunity. Had I been able to tolerate his shaking shoulders long enough to understand their meaning—he cared enough to muster this level of distress—I might not have fled. I might have stuck around that afternoon, that summer, and for the ten rocky years that followed, ten years in which contact was sporadic, dramatic, and always painful. I might have known that the reinvention of the first place I called home did not preclude my station in it. I suppose I might have felt loved enough to suspend my screaming-in-the-street pastime, felt insulated against the power of those reproving housekeeping notes. In some way the notes were about ensuring my place in the house, positioning me to participate and remain part of the clan, even if I rejected what they offered.

But he cried, and I straightened my shoulders and hardened up inside. I figuratively wiped away his tears with a precision I'd never brought to the kitchen counters and headed upstairs to shower.

It was a long shower, and hot—those were a no-no, too, what with the water bill—and afterward I wrapped one dusty-rose towel around my body. I wrapped a smaller towel around my hair, patted it dry, and left the towel there, returning to my room with the intention of slipping into my stepmother's old paisley Indian cotton tent dress—she gave me that and the bottle of patchouli she'd retired. I didn't notice it then, but she would have given me anything she had in exchange for my doing my part.

But not five minutes later a flash of pink was waving in my doorway, a terrycloth flag of antisurrender: the towel I'd used to dry my hair, which I must have left in a slump on the bathroom floor. She didn't write a note this time. She issued a command I'd heard at least twice before in my teenage years: "Get out of my house." I was still wrapped in the towel.

Besides the eruption of tears and the demand for an explanation, I muttered one logical claim: "You can't kick me out because it's not your house—it's mine."

This, of course, was the real problem, the architectural white elephant. Everything cleansed and polished, made pretty and proper and new in that house left me further dismissed from it. But the house really was my stepmother's now, the deed transferred to her name, her dusty-rose towels and peach tiles and pine floors and cranberry walls. And it was she who had the authority to tell me, again, "Get out."

So I did. I walked, mewling like an injured cat to my father, imploring him to exercise veto powers, to no effect. "Are you going to let her do this?" I asked him, or, more accurately, I screamed. He had shut the valve off, too, or disguised it in a cloud of smoke. So, clad in that dusty-rose towel and my muddy shitkickers, I left the house, trudging through the across-the-street neighbor's yard, behind her rusty aboveground pool, through the driveway to my friend Rachel's house, where I knocked on the door and she opened it to find me naked inside that terrycloth cloud, sobbing.

My friend couldn't help it. She fell over laughing—what kind of perverse stork would deliver such a package? But then she saw my face all puffed and red—practically cranberry—and invited me in, invited me to stay. I did, for the rest of the summer, casting off from Rachel's porch on my beloved 12-speed Fuji, my hardhat clipped to the rack on the back. I never did return myself or that towel to the house.

Funny, what happened in the years that followed. I never got good at chores. You can still tell when I've washed the glasses because a diaphanous glaze of dried soap clings to them. I make the bed every day, but it's rumpled, looks curiously like a body might still be slumbering inside. I am not fastidious, but I'm incredibly inflexible. I cannot stand to have dishes in the sink or the bed unmade, papers strewn across the floor. I'm livid when vacationing with friends who neither help prepare nor clean up a meal. I've long made up with my family, surrendered all sense of authority over the house, developed a tolerance for cranberry (though not dusty rose or peach). But I can't stand, especially, to have towels crumpled in a ball, anywhere, and I've been known to leave roommates gently admonishing notes over the years about such matters. The towels must always be hung, neatly, on the back of the door.

Family Heirloom

Rebecca Walker

When I was growing up, my mother taught me three things about keeping house: The front door and interior entryway must always be well lighted and inviting. The bed should be made no more than thirty minutes after rising. The dishes must be washed or put in the dishwasher immediately after each meal. By example, she also taught me that clothes and other items should never be strewn about, and one's personal space was a reflection of one's mind. It should be orderly, beautiful, and open to being rearranged.

As a young adult, I pressed these essentials into service as a foundation for living, my own coda for domestic harmony. Nothing interfered with my rituals of moving methodically from bed to closet and from desk to sofa straightening, positioning, and stepping back to admire my work.

A few months before I gave birth to my son, now three, I had an inkling that what I considered a simple habit of fastidiousness might be something more. To begin with, my baby shower yielded several items for which I could find no suitable place. I agonized for weeks about a Diaper Genie, only to conclude with horror that the only place for it was outside my front door.

A co-sleeper also presented a challenge. Because my bedroom was small, the bassinet had to sit flush against my bed, complicating the making of the bed. I was unable to adequately smooth the duvet, essentially giving the effect of an unmade bed all day long, which made my skin crawl every time I caught a glimpse of it from the hallway.

As my son grew older, the chaos spread. No matter how many brightly colored baskets or smart wooden block boxes I bought, there seemed no way to keep his room, or the rest of house, tidy. I found myself constantly picking up crayons, cars, and stuffed animals at the first hint he might be done playing. I soon grew frustrated by this state of affairs.

I brought my concerns to a dear friend, who promptly told me my complaints were nothing new. "You've always had a bit of OCD," he said breezily. "Don't you remember your apartment in college? We couldn't get a piece of pizza without everything being in its proper place." He continued, "It's just who you are. As for the impact on your son, perhaps you should see a psychiatrist."

My partner, whom I felt should be equally concerned with the increasing lack of order and the possibility our child would grow up to live a messy, uncouth existence, shook his head in futility when I raised the subject.

"I have given up talking to you about this," he said one morning, channeling his inner Dr. Freud as I begged his counsel on what I called the "LEGO situation." "Your urge to control the environment in which we live is irrational," he said in his most professorial tone. "It is either a coping mechanism from childhood that serves you and hampers others, or it is a function of your creativity that serves you and hampers others. Either way, the outcome is the same."

This gave me pause. Then, as if in a trance, I reordered the towels on the bathroom shelf by color, size, and degree of sumptuousness.

But my partner had struck a chord. My son, after all, is not a little adult. At three years old, he might be capable of putting his toys away, but not while still playing with them. My desire for order could not be good for his creativity either, as the latter depended on experimentation, openness, and, alas, some degree of mess.

When I looked at the roots of compulsion lurking beneath my fierce adherence to my mother's rules for proper living, I had a revelation. Somewhere along the way, I had started connecting the orderliness of my home with survival. I truly believed that if my living space wasn't perfectly tidy, everything—not just my house but my life—would fall apart.

At my beloved Sigmund's advice, I looked back in time and searched for clues as to why I felt this way. My mother's family was poor. The shack my mother lived in as a child had no running water, cracks between the floorboards, and tin sheeting for a roof. My father's family was working class with constant financial struggles.

I imagined what it was like for my grandparents to have so little control over their environments. Their worlds were unstable—sharecroppers like my mother's parents could be evicted without as much as a week's notice. They must have grasped at whatever rituals they could—planting prized hydrangeas, keeping clothes and linens sparkling clean and freshly ironed, displaying fresh fruit in simple bowls on the kitchen table—to ease a pervasive feeling of powerlessness.

My mother's rules for keeping house were more than a casual set of directives. They were a survival kit. This is the way to stay sane in insane times, each set of parents indicated to their children. Your house must be your sanctuary. It must suggest a sparkling future. Room must be made for your ship to come in.

Unlike my grandparents, I don't have to worry about sudden eviction or the wind howling through cracks in the walls. But the world is no less troubled, and humanity no less precarious now than when my grandparents were alive. The difference, of course, is that I have a great deal more control over where I live and what I do, when I move, and how.

This raises important questions. If my irrational relationship with clutter is a living survival kit, an heirloom passed from generation to generation, can I afford to let it go? Then again, if it's an outdated coping mechanism that makes everyone around me crazy, can I afford not to?

One day not long ago, my son burst into tears after I put his train set away before he had finished playing with it. I sat on the floor with him, looking from his sad, red face to the box of neatly arranged train track. I was mortified and vowed to do better. And right then, on the spot, I made a commitment to put the happiness of my family first.

Now, when the floor of my office is littered with wooden blocks and bright yellow school buses, I make an effort to step over them rather than toss them into a bin. I try to allow anything at all to happen in my son's room over the course of a day, but things still must be put away at bedtime.

But I also heed the patterns of the past. Every few days I move through our house the way my mother did when I was a child. I straighten stacks, reposition pillows, and put fresh flowers on my desk. I bring everything that is out of place back into alignment. My son watches closely, and I know I am passing on the family tradition.

Yesterday morning he woke up full of energy. "Mommy, wake up!" he yelled. "We have to make my bed!" I laughed and pulled him over for a hug. I was elated. My sweet boy wanted to bring order to chaos. He wanted, instinctively, to smooth the ruffled covers before he started the day.

His great-grandparents would be proud.

Country Living
Brian Gerber

*I*t is a perfect country day—the blue sky sparkles like sapphire, birds chirp and swoop and dip in the cool stream, and the grass shines with the fresh green of early spring.

I am sitting on the front porch, reading a book. Heidi, our dog, is sitting in an identical chair next to me. It is John's chair, but he's not there. I look up from time to time, staring at the lawn and the stream across the road. I can feel my face grimacing. Instead of the sounds of birds and the rushing waters of the stream, all I hear is *bzzzt,* the buzzing of a motor.

"John," I yell. The buzzing continues. I stand up and yell louder, "*John!*"

John is across the road, oblivious to my calls, concentrating on trimming (he calls it whacking) the weeds along the road. He has already whacked the banks along the stream, at the bases of various trees and bushes, next to the barn and the stone walls, and under the hammock. He does this with the focus of a surgeon. He walks, and then his arm shoots out, *bzzzt, BZZZT.* A stalk falls as if cut off at the knees.

Every weekend he goes to war. Squadrons of weeds fall before him. Purple loosestrife, a supposedly unstoppable invader, is whacked into submission.

John's brother had obsessive compulsive disorder so intensely that it drove him to suicide. John has managed to channel this obsessiveness into positive things, like weed whacking. We also have a very clean house. No thanks to me, either. But there is a limit to what I can take of the noise.

I walk off the porch and up to John. I plant myself in front of him, and he finally stops, lifting a plastic face guard.

"John, that's enough. You don't have to trim under the guardrail next to the road."

"Just a few minutes more," he says. "Let me finish the guardrail."

"Okay," I say. "But not in front of the forest. Enough is enough."

He once trimmed the roadside weeds in front of a forest. A maniacal look of self-satisfaction came over his face when I pointed out that everyone else would have left nature alone there.

I walk back to the porch, thinking how I came up here for peace and quiet, and all I hear is the weed whacker and the vacuum cleaner.

When we were both working we would arrive at the house at about 8:00 PM, go out to dinner, and then he would start vacuuming. One night, he was still doing it at midnight.

"John, dammit," I shouted down from the bedroom. "I worked all week and drove two hours to get us up here. I'm tired. The dirt can wait."

He seeks out every little dust mote as if it were an enemy. Spider webs disappear.

"You're supposed to keep the spiders," I say. "They catch other bugs."

He ignores me. I get a bit of satisfaction at finding dust in a place he's missed. Sometimes I even clean it myself.

John comes up to the porch, Heidi jumps off the chair, and he sits. I am too irritated at this point to relax.

"The Caldwells dropped by and said how nice the place looks," he says.

The grounds are groomed as if TRESemmé did landscaping. John trims the bushes, mows the lawn more often than I do (he gets antsier sooner about the length of the grass), sprays the weeds between the flagstones with Roundup, pulls weeds from most of the gardens, and sweeps the patio.

This may sound as if I do nothing except sit on the porch with the dog and get aggravated at John. We have divided up a lot of the responsibilities actually. I just don't have his zeal for neatness.

I willingly give him credit whenever we are complimented, but there are times when the noise and the time spent drive me crazy. He is content to work all day on the grounds; I'd like us to go to other places. Our friends hike, bike ride, go shopping in nearby towns, visit art galleries. We stay home a lot.

At times, when the noise has gotten too much, I have taken the dog for a walk, or gotten on my bicycle, or driven to a nearby town. But I feel like I am fleeing rather than doing it willingly.

We have come together more as the years have gone on. He does whack less, and the late-night vacuuming is only a memory. When he does vacuum, he's conscious of where I am in the house and does it on the opposite side.

And I've become more content to stay around the house, reading or doing small projects. I've even found that weeding the flower garden, a job I never had the patience or enthusiasm for, can be satisfying, declaring my own wars on Queen Anne's lace, red sorrel, and stray grass.

And then, I wait for him to finish so we can sit together on the porch and talk and read, and look at how lovely the property is.

Ba'lebusteh

Mindy Greenstein

I hate making my bed, a Sisyphean task if ever there was one. You wake up in a messy bed, fold the sheets and the duvet just so, fluff the pillow just so, only to pull out the sheets at bedtime, pull at them in your sleep throughout the night, and find yourself once again folding and fluffing in the morning. The only thing I hate more is doing the laundry. It's relentless. Unless you're naked, you're already creating tomorrow's laundry even while you're shoving today's into the washing machine. And the decisions! Oy! The blue tank top that will have to go into the cold water with other colors, my son's cotton khakis that are supposed to be washed in cold water but maybe should go into the warm wash because of the caked-on mud stains from when he slid into third base, the white gym socks that will need hot water, and the bleach that the package says never to use but that you use anyway if you want to actually clean them. And even though I know how to sew, I refuse to sew my husband's buttons when they pop off his shirts. After all, any idiot can thread a needle—why does it have to be the wife? My father was right. "Mindaleh," he used to say, "you'll never be a *ba'lebusteh*."

Technically, my father was wrong, since a *ba'lebusteh* is the "mistress of the house," which, with a husband, two sons, a dog, and a mortgage, I certainly am. But it really means something else, a throwback to a culture where womanhood was measured by the cleanliness of one's home. Think of it as the Yiddish version of Betty Crocker, with only an accidental resemblance to the word *ballbuster*. In my world growing up on Flatlands Avenue in Brooklyn, the highest praise a woman could earn was to be called a *ba'lebusteh*. The earliest sign of one was the presence of plastic slipcovers on the couches. But even more impressive was the woman who managed to keep the couches clean even without the slipcovers. My father would talk of such women with awe. "Ruchel is such a *ba'lebusteh*, you could eat from the floor," he would say, in part to reprove my mother, whose floor no one but the bugs would dare eat off. "Yeah, Dad?" I'd retort, "can you drink out of her toilet, too?"

My mother cleaned up irregularly, and my father never offered to help. He already had a job, and cleaning was hers by genetic design. The question of choice didn't come up much in those days. Dishes often piled up as she silently waited for someone else to chip in. But the cavalry never arrived. I could have helped more but didn't out of a mixture of laziness and principle—after all, no one was asking my brother Harry to help out. Why should only the girls do it? And so she was left on her own to do her woman's job. It wasn't as if she'd have gotten a great promotion for doing it well. I didn't mind the fact that she didn't set a good example; I felt it let me off the hook. No *ba'lebusteh*s in this home! I thought of it as the Eastern European version of burning your bra.

My bad attitude was cemented one day while I was eating in a kosher fast-food restaurant near Macy's. The bearded and yarmulke'd man in the next booth was complaining to his friend about his *shiduch*, or blind date, from the night before.

"She told me she doesn't even know how to cook a chicken!!! Can you imagine in this day and age, *a woman shouldn't know how to cook a chicken???!!!!"* His eyes glowed with an indignant fire while his friend sadly shook his head from side to side.

Fuck you, buddy, was all I could think. No, Daddy, I'll never become a *ba'lebusteh,* and I sure hope I never cook a chicken for a guy like that, or any guy for that matter. Let him cook one for me.

But it was more than feminist outrage. The life of a *ba'lebusteh* wasn't good enough for me. I was an intellectual. I would have More Important Things to do than take care of a home. I cared more about using who and whom correctly than finding the best way to get dirt out of the crown moldings. I would go to graduate school, get a PhD. What did I need to clean for?

It's not that I have no home skills. Even though I'm an Oscar Madison married to another Oscar Madison (would that make us *homomessuals?*), I'm still the one who cleans, because the mess gets to me sooner than it gets to Rob, and it never, ever gets to our kids. While Rob's finally learned that dirty socks are not to be left on a counter or kitchen table, that's as far as his education has gone. I once decided to teach him a lesson and hid all the socks and underwear he left on the floor, until he ran out and would learn to at least toss them in the hamper. But he never even noticed. When he ran out, he just picked up some more from the store on the way home from work, without ever mentioning it to me.

And nobody can beat me at packing a dishwasher. Even my mother-in-law trembles when daring to put a mug in the upper tray, knowing I'll eventually move it in line with some mental model of a more efficient use of space. "I know you're going to move it," she preempts. "I know you're going to move it." And I will, though I'll try to do it behind her back.

And there is one circumstance in which I can often be counted on to jump at the chance to do housework. Sitting at an almost blank and lonely looking computer screen, trying to put my thoughts together to write a paper or an essay—or even this essay—all I can do is look around my apartment and think, *What a damn mess. Who can work in a place like this?* I do pay someone to clean for me once a week, but I can never find anything after she's done, so I won't let her get near my piles of papers. My eleven-year-old son, Max, is out of underwear, six-year-old Isaac is out of the collared shirts he needs to comply with his school's dress code, and I'm out of the thick black socks I need to fit into my nubuck shoes that have already stretched out at least half a size. And come to think of it, those crown moldings really are looking a little skanky. This is, in fact, the only time I actually like doing housework—cleaning the piles on the floor to keep from dealing with the work piling up in my head.

I think of a time recently when I needed to get the name of a painter from my neighbor. All she did was walk over to her desk—with no piles on it—and pick the card out of a Rolodex under "p" for "painters"—no trying to remember which name she had filed it under, no rooting around for a card she knows she put somewhere in the pile on the northwest corner of the desk. She just walked over, picked out the card, pulled out a notepad from an easily found drawer, wrote down the number, and gave it to me. If the tables had been turned, it would have taken a half hour easily before I could have done the same for her. (Even now in the computer age, I'd have found different obstacles.) And I couldn't help thinking, *What a nice place to hang out.* The gleaming white kitchen counters were so pretty, and the uncluttered living room with the clean couches— even though they were light beige, with no plastic in sight—was so inviting. A *ba'lebusteh!* And a *shiksa*, yet. Who wouldn't want to stay there, instead of walking across the hall to World War III?

And I think of Ruchel. In fairness to my disapproving father, he didn't look down on housework the way I did; for him, making a home wasn't just a menial chore, it was an honorable vocation. It was more than keeping things clean. It was the creation of "yourness." A space that was special and yours, where you could find your things and sit on your chairs uncontaminated by last night's crumbs and eat your food that was prepared in the way you liked. It's what allowed you to own the space around you. There's something to be said for the ability to make order out of chaos. It is, after all, how we survive in the world. It's what writers do with ideas—make orderly arguments out of fragmentary thoughts; it's what scientists do with nature—find general principles to make sense of the world.

So, I've made my peace with the Ruchels of the world. I can appreciate them even though I'll never be one of them. In fact, sitting here at my computer screen, I just noticed those gym socks are really piling up. I think it's time to get the bleach.

Clean Fights

Patty Dann

The night my husband, Willem, died I stayed up weeping and ironing his shirts, in the room that had been his office, a room where we occasionally made love and the room where he finally died. As I sobbed, my tears fell, moistening the cloth. The funeral home had come for his body, and my four-year-old son, Jake, was finally asleep.

Ironing has always comforted me. As a young child I used to watch my mother sprinkle water from a Coke bottle with a special rubber stopper to dampen the clothes. As a treat she would let me iron handkerchiefs. A month before Willem's death, while he was having brain surgery, I fled home to do a load of laundry. I had been cleaning throughout his illness, and in many ways, although it did not save him, it is what allowed me to survive. I've often thought in the years since his death of opening a Mourners' Cleaning Service. I know I am not the only woman who cleans as she sobs in the night.

The long months when Willem was ill, cleaning was just about the only thing I could focus on, besides taking care of my son. Willem was from Holland, land of the clean people, and when he was well he cleaned as much as I do now. When Willem forgot the word for "paper clip," I knew he was sick. When I came home from teaching one night and there were dirty dishes still in the sink, I knew he was seriously ill.

Willem was an academic. He researched his dissertation so thoroughly we called him Dr. Footnote. He became an archivist and would bring order to collections of photographs of displaced people in camps after World War II. He was a Mennonite fascinated by Judaism. I was a Jew raised completely secular. He was forty, three years older than I. Neither of us had been married before. We fell in love immediately and wed a year later. Our marriage lasted a decade. He spent the last year and a half of it dying.

The day after Willem died I threw away his old slippers, preferring to remember him by his marathon running shoes. But when Jake saw the slippers now dripping in egg yolk in the garbage, he yanked them out and said, in all his four-year-old wisdom, "Don't throw away anything of Daddy's ever."

My son does the opposite of cleaning. He is a pack rat. When I take clothes out of the dryer, Jake's child pockets are full of dried-up ticket stubs and baseball cards. When I remember to check his pockets before I put them in the washing machine, I salvage coins and leaves and broken crayons. His room resembles his pockets. My son is a collector and an athlete, and he watches WWE wrestling on TV.

"Mom, there are three main kinds of wrestling: Raw, SmackDown, and ECW," my now-ten-year-old son explained patiently.

Last night I was in the kitchen, wiping an already clean counter, listening to NPR on the kitchen radio, as Jake was sprawled on the couch, watching his heroes.

"Each kind of wrestling has different wrestlers," continued Jake. "Raw has Umaga, Kane, and Triple H. SmackDown has the Great Kali (he's seven-two), Mark Henry, and Bobby Lashley. The ECW has Big Show (that's a man), Kurt Angle, and Sabu."

Last night I washed the dishes and listened to Mozart's Flute Concerto No. 2 in D Major, a piece my husband used to love. I do not have a dishwasher. I moved into my apartment twenty-five years ago, as a single woman, never knowing I would marry ten years later or that my marriage would telescope and I would be a widow there at forty-six. When my husband moved in we used to wash the dishes together, he with his Mennonite methodical style by my side. Actually, I washed and he dried. We had been given three kinds of kitchen towels from Dutch relatives for our marriage—one set for dishes, one set for silverware, and one set for pots and pans. Now I wash and dry dishes alone, trying to order my world and to soothe my messy soul.

At 9:15 PM last night I decided to make a bold move. I put down my sponge and left my station in the kitchen of eternal cleaning. I joined Jake on the couch and watched Friday-night wrestling with him. I had my first dose of watching frightening men crash chairs on one another's greased bodies, fighting and fighting, good over evil, not dying of cancer, fighting until they were exhausted.

I reached out for Jake's hand, and he let me hold it just for a moment before he pulled away. "Just because I see this stuff doesn't mean I'm going to do it," he said quietly, staring at the screen. "Somebody always wins. And just because you love classical music doesn't mean you do that either."

A woman raising a boy to be a man is not an uncommon occurrence in America today. Whether we're single mothers by choice and have never shared the task, or by death or divorce, and we're stumbling through life a bit stunned, it doesn't matter.

And then last night, at ten o'clock, when WWE wrestling was over, my son made an unexpected move. He got up from the couch. He went into the kitchen, grabbed the mop, filled a bucket of water, and began to mop the floor, mopping with frenzy, a fierce mopping to save his soul. We are wrestling. We are cleaning. We are doing the best we can.

II. DUST OF GENERATIONS

"But each day brings its petty dust our soon-choked souls to fill, and we forget because we must, and not because we will."

—Matthew Arnold

Windows

Kathleen Crisci

I'm sprawled on the daybed in my room of the tiny Bronx apartment I share with my mother. I'm chewing on an apple, enjoying the cool sweetness of it until, suddenly, the pieces get stuck in my throat and begin to taste like cardboard. My mother has just emerged before me, genielike, Windex and squeegee in hand, to wash the window in my room.

"Please don't, Ma," I say.

"Oh, come on. Look how filthy it is."

She pulls on the cord to make the venetian blind go all the way up. The noise it makes is like a deck of cards being shuffled, only much louder, and dusty light projects into the room. She throws open the window, allowing a *whoosh* of fresh air to enter, much needed because of the chain-smoking I do. She steps up on the inside sill and, in the same instant, propels her lithe frame onto the narrow outside ledge. She's now facing inward, but she's not looking at me, or even into the room; her focus is entirely fixed on the rain-streaked glass. Much as I would like to, I cannot avert my eyes or even move. I want to scream at her to come back in, but I say nothing. I don't want to distract her in any way from the task she's performing—one false step and she could plunge the four stories to the concrete pavement below. It has been a year since my father's death, and my number one fear is of being an orphan.

My mother is a bundle of raw energy as she aggressively attacks the minute flecks of grease that have proved too stubborn to disappear with the first wipe. I should be used to this by now—my mother has been standing on ledges washing windows ever since I can remember—but I'm not. It doesn't help, either, that every so often she sucks her breath in hard, as though she just averted a disaster, or that she stands on tiptoe to get to the upper corners of the windows; once, one of her slippers fell off, and she looked down and said, "Oh, crikey." I follow her every move hypnotically. I think that it's my watchfulness that keeps her on the ledge. If I take my eyes off her, she'll be a goner.

Time and time again I ask her why she risks her life to wash the windows.

"The windows are the eyes of a house," she says. "They make you see the world as either a dirty place or a clean place. And, if you keep your windows and curtains spotless, your house will seem tidy to those looking at it from the outside."

My mother made my bed until the day I left. Sometimes I'd get up to go to the bathroom in the morning—particularly if I had been out late drinking the night before—and I'd come back to find my bed made up for the day.

"Don't make my bed, Ma," I said over and over.

"I cannot live in a messy house," she said. "If you don't like it, move out."

So I did. When I was twenty-one I left home to live with my boyfriend David. We got an apartment together, a nice one-bedroom in the Bronx, in the days when rents were still reasonable. David was Chinese and had his own ideas about women and cleaning. I, on the other hand, knew nothing, since I had never been asked to actually help out around the house while growing up. So, for a while in our new apartment, we lived out of boxes. We didn't entirely unpack for close to a year. We never made the bed. Dishes piled up in the sink. I carved our initials in the dust and put hearts around them. Green mold attacked the uneaten food in the refrigerator until it became a guessing game as to which leftover a certain item actually had been.

"This place is a pigsty," David said one evening when the odors wafting to us when we opened the door to our apartment were getting too difficult to ignore.

"Didn't your mother teach you how to clean?" he continued.

"Didn't *yours?*" I countered. We both worked, and I went to graduate school two nights a week. Who wanted to be cleaning? And, if we were going to place any importance on the maintenance of our apartment, shouldn't we both have been responsible for it? Yet, with my mother as my role model, there was another part of me that believed that cleanliness was next to womanliness. So, instead of calmly discussing my point of view with David, we had a vast number of screaming fights, bordering on brawls, while I steadfastly resisted.

After many months of the same battle, David and I finally did reach a compromise and drew up a list of chores each of us would assume. It wasn't perfect, but it was a lot better than it had been. And once we started, we both tried our best to keep our home reasonably clean.

"How can you live like this?" my mother asked, when our apartment was neat enough to actually invite people.

"What?" I said. To me it was fine. I could see her staring at the windows with the bed sheets I had remembered to pull back for her visit.

"You need curtains," she said.

"Yeah, we're getting them soon," I lied.

"You have windows that are easy to clean," she said. "Do you want me to help you?"

"Out of the question," I firmly said, hoping to put an end to this particular turn in the conversation.

"Tell you what," she continued. "I'll buy you window treatments for your entire apartment as a housewarming gift. And I'll wash your windows for you."

"No, Ma. Stop it. I don't want curtains. I don't want clean windows. I *like* dirt on my windows—it helps keep out the sunlight. I'm actually thinking of painting my windows black."

"You're insane," my mother said calmly, rising to get her coat.

After David and I split up, I found a studio apartment on the ground floor of a Chelsea building, all I could afford in Manhattan in the early seventies. But I wasn't complaining—the apartment had a separate kitchen, tiny as it was, and a huge garden to which all five apartments in the back had access. My next-door neighbor, Rob, was the self-proclaimed gardener, and I loved to watch him, through the one window of my studio, busily putter around under the thirteen ailanthus trees we shared. Rob was good-looking, too, and I placed my desk in front of the window so I could watch him better. The desk was the only piece of furniture I owned besides the bed, and I did everything there. I ate, read, made shopping lists, wrote bills, listened to music, all sitting at that desk. It wasn't long before I realized how dirty the windows were and how that dirt interfered with my view of garden and gardener. So the next time I was in the supermarket, I bought a bottle of window cleaner. Standing on my desk, I squirted spray all over my window and wiped it dry with a paper towel. Then I ran out the back door, which had louvers, hopped up on the windowsill, and squirted some more. Finally, in a burst of inspiration and energy, I cleaned each glass slat in the door.

In a mixture of pride and satisfaction, I stepped back inside to admire my work. But, instead of the sparkly glass I had anticipated while I was wiping, what I got was a maze of hazy streaks. Determined to have clean windows, I repeated the process. Still those insufferable streaks.

"I'll bet you washed it in the sun," my mother said when I related my dismal failure to her. "You cannot wash windows in direct sunlight."

I purchased mahogany blinds, which framed the window and the door in an interesting way. Rob ended up moving, but his genius remained for a very long time, and I loved coming home to my back yard, which looked like a forest through my window, which I now kept permanently clean.

I met Javier and fell in love. We smoked dope in the garden and then came inside to gaze at the moon gleaming in through the trees in the summer, or boldly situated over drifts of snow in the winter. He bought me red and white mums, which looked dramatic on the windowsill in front of a snowbank. I put my Christmas tree outside, with dozens of lights, and watched them flicker through my lovely window, hoping a sparrow would fly into one of the branches. Then I had a baby, a daughter.

"Let's get married," I suggested one night as we sat in the living room/bedroom/nursery.

"Honey, we can't all live in this apartment together," he said as he affectionately scrunched the dog's ear. "First, I think we need to find an apartment that can accommodate all of us."

It wasn't easy to find a large living space in Manhattan unless you just happened to be acquainted with somebody who died in a rent-controlled apartment. Finally, someone mentioned Washington Heights, an area in the northernmost part of Manhattan where rents were still stabilized. We found an adequate one-bedroom in a quaint building—meaning moldings and cockroaches—that we could afford. We got married and moved in.

The apartment smelled of antiquity, but not in a good way. Doors didn't close because of layers of paint, the kitchen appliances were probably prewar, and the wood floors were dull, with years of ground-in dirt. The one feature this apartment had that was wonderful was its many windows, which let in copious amounts of sunlight. The building was situated on a hill. Our apartment faced east, and we had a spectacular view of what was left of Manhattan before it officially turned into the Bronx.

"The windows look fine," my husband said to me when he noticed that I'd gotten the ladder and the window cleaner.

"Fine?" I said. "Look at the streaks. Look at the dirt. I want to clean this before my mother comes tomorrow." It was three days before Christmas, and my mother was coming to spend the holidays with us. She would be sharing a room with her new grandchild.

"There's nothing awful about the windows," he said. "Besides, you didn't wash the windows when my mother came."

"You don't understand," I said. And he didn't. The last time my mother had been over, she made no negative comments, but I noticed the way she glanced at the windows and knew what she was thinking. Had she actually made a remark, I might have been able to respond in a way that brought closure to our age-old argument, but it was her silence that left me with no choice other than to make my windows spotless. Anyway, it wasn't difficult to wash windows in that apartment—the outsides could be collapsed in, so the entire window could be washed from the inside, and they were straightforward, not divided into those annoying small panes with many corners that meant extra work. When I finished washing them I framed them in white lace and hung ceramic pots of plants.

Nice windows," my mother said the next day, nodding her head in approval as she stepped over one pile of baby toys and another of magazine clutter.

I shot a proud glance at Javier.

"But you should pick up this junk," she said. Now I was annoyed. This was *baby* stuff, for God's sake. How could anyone with an infant keep a meticulous household? Still, I wanted us to have a good time together, so I kept my mouth shut.

"It could be dangerous to the baby," she clarified. She was saying I was a bad mother.

In the days preceding my mother's arrival, I had carefully shopped for her Christmas present. I wanted to get her something lovely that she would enjoy. Since it was my new family's first Christmas together, I hoped to make it a memorable occasion. I went from store to store until I found the unique gift I thought my mother would appreciate—bed sheets made of ultrasoft French flannel, and a pair of violet hand-embroidered Italian silk pajamas.

On Christmas morning we opened our presents next to the tree we had all decorated the night before. First we watched as Desiree tore open her presents from Santa. I watched in amazement as my daughter played with the wrappings, as if the paper and ribbon were the gifts, not what was contained inside. Life for a sixteen-month old is simple, I realized.

Then Javier and I exchanged presents with each other, as well as with my mother. My present to him was a bag, made of supple Italian leather, in which he could travel around town with all his necessities—camera, books, diapers, and whatever else he might need for himself or the baby, since he was with her as much as I was. He got me a gold locket in which he had placed a tiny picture of our daughter. Javier gave my mother our present while she handed hers to me.

Her present to us was a *DustBuster*. For a few seconds I was speechless, but I held it up for Javier to see.

"Cool," he said with enthusiasm I knew was fake. My mother must have noticed the expression on my face.

"You can even use it on the table," she said as she neatly un-wrapped her package. It seemed to take forever for her to open the box and look inside.

"Oh," she gasped. "This must have been so expensive." It had been.

"Nah," I said. "Not really. I bought it on sale." Half of a fortune is still a fortune.

I was busy scooping up papers and boxes the whole time presents were being opened. I didn't want a mess to build up and become out of control. At the end of our present exchange, I had a huge black garbage bag full of wrappings.

"Should I take that downstairs?" Javier suggested.

With the wrappings cleared out, our small living room was mainly trees and presents. It looked warm and cozy. Lived-in.

But when my mother was packing to return home, we couldn't locate her package. She had a bus to catch and had to leave.

"I'm sure it will turn up under something, Ma. And I'll send it to you."

"I can't imagine where it might be," my mother said. I knew what she was thinking. She couldn't imagine where it might be *in that mess*.

I searched and searched, but nothing turned up. No sheets, no silk pajamas—nothing!

"I think we threw your mother's present out," Javier said. "It must have gone out with the trash."

At first, I refused to believe that. Frantically I repeated the search, this time looking in closets and other areas, like under the bed, where I knew it couldn't possibly be. But then, when I thought it through, I realized my husband was right. In our haste to clean up on Christmas Day, we had to have put them into the big bag of garbage.

I couldn't let my mother know that. So I returned to the boutique where I had originally made my purchase. They had more of the sheets, but they were all out of the silk pajamas in violet. All they had left was blue.

"I'll take them," I said, hoping my mother wouldn't notice. Her eyes weren't as good anymore as they used to be. I made a package of both items, brought it to the post office, and mailed it.

Three days later the phone rang. It was my mother.

"Thanks so much, honey," she said. "It's funny, though. I could swear the pajamas were purple." I felt bad—really bad—but what could I do?

"Nope," I said. "Blue."

I could practically hear her scratching her head.

One day the following summer, Javier and I took the baby to visit my mother for a weekend. I couldn't help but be impressed that, even with advancing age, her house still looked perfect, windows and all. But as I was rummaging around in a drawer, looking for something, I stumbled across the present I had given my mother for Christmas. The sheets were still in the cellophane wrapper, the grosgrain ribbon still taut around it. The pajamas were untouched, as well. My first impulse was to bring them to her and find out why she had never used them, after all the trouble I had gone through to get them. Then I remembered she didn't even know the extent of the trouble I had gone through.

After giving the matter even further thought, I decided not to say anything to her. After all, *I* hadn't used the DustBuster she had given *me*.

And I had no intention of doing so, either.

Dirty Work

Ann Hood

*H*appily, I watch a dust bunny dance across my living-room floor. "Hello, dust bunny," I say. I consider leaning over and scooping it up, but instead I keep knitting, enjoying the click of one bamboo needle against another, the feel of the soft yarn in my hand. There are plenty of dust bunnies in my house: under my bed, tucked cozily into corners, nestled on shelves. Eventually, I will mop the floors and dust the tops of everything. But right now I am knitting. Right now I am content with my yarn and my dusty, slightly messy house.

Everyone has housekeeping issues they cannot tolerate. For me, I never leave dirty dishes in the sink, and I close cupboard and closet doors. If walking barefoot across my kitchen floor leaves the bottoms of my feet black, I wash that floor. After I cook, I clean up thoroughly. Otherwise, I don't worry too much about housekeeping. In fits and bursts, I pull out rags and cleaning products and scrub everything in sight. This might happen four times a year, max.

When I was growing up, uber cleaning happened every Saturday. My mother worked full time, five days a week. On Saturdays, she rose early, plugged in the vacuum cleaner, and noisily went to work. Have you ever tried to sleep while someone vacuumed outside your door? It is impossible. To this day, the sound of a vacuum cleaner makes my jaws clench. I would slide under my covers with a pillow over my head to muffle the noise. But soon enough, the door flew open and the vacuuming continued all around me. Right behind my mother and her Hoover stood my father with clean sheets in his hands. His job was to change the bed linens. Every Saturday. No sooner did I roll out of bed then it was stripped, the mattress swept, and new sheets pulled taut across it. My father was a career navy man, and he could make a bed that, he liked to brag, a dime could bounce off.

Downstairs was no better. Instead of getting greeted with the smell of frying bacon or warm cinnamon rolls, I was met by the chemical aromas of Lemon Pledge and bleach. Toilets had already been scrubbed, sinks had been Cometed, and furniture had been polished. It wasn't even 9:00 AM yet. Worse, by the time my mother appeared in the kitchen, I was expected to be doing my own chores.

I had two cleaning jobs. The first was to clean all the baseboard radiators in the house. I sprayed them with some chemical cleaning solution, then wiped it off with paper towels. Along the top, the front, the sides, and inside the unit. My second, and more hated, job was to dust tchotchkes. Our staircase had a ledge that ran upward its full length, and on that ledge my mother kept a variety of orange glass dishes of various shapes, all of them with abstract curled and scalloped edges that loved dust. Beside these stood the wooden statues my father had brought home from Haiti, women in native costumes with fruit baskets on their heads. More nooks and crannies. More dust. Then came the glass bunch of grapes with its purple balls and green leaves, perfect hiding places for dust.

Every Saturday, still in my pajamas, I sat on those steps and wondered not only how so much dust could return in just a week but why anyone would want these ridiculous things in the first place. Their main purpose seemed to be to collect dust. I never even noticed them, except when I dusted them. The native women were already, even in the mid-1960s, an embarrassment. And the orange glass dishes with their oddly modern Danish looked out of place in our Ethan Allen colonial-decorated house. As to the glass grapes, who knows? Another anomaly, another form of torture for me. I hated every purple orb, every serrated glass leaf. I vowed on that stairway that I would never line a shelf in my own home with anything that required dusting.

Once a month, our Saturday cleaning ritual became even more intense. I am sure that you know people who decorate their homes for the various seasons and holidays. This usually involves hanging a windsock with an Easter bunny on the front door or stringing some whimsical skeleton lights at Halloween. But to my mother this was a weekend-long event that required changing all the curtains, the lamps, the rugs, and every tabletop accessory.

Let's say I woke up to the roar of a vacuum cleaner on a Saturday morning in mid-February. Downstairs, when I went to bed the night before, everything was red: red curtains, red tablecloth, red throw rugs. There were heart-shaped pillows, photographs in heart-shaped frames, heart magnets on the refrigerator door. Heart lights lined the edges of cupboards and counters. Cupid lurked around every corner. Even the bathroom had red votive candles in holders decorated with hearts, a red shower curtain and bath mat and fuzzy toilet seat cover.

But once Valentine's Day passed, my world turned green. Dishtowels that had pictures of conversation hearts now had shamrocks. My cereal bowl had ERIN GO BRAGH written across it, and leprechauns grinned down at me everywhere I looked.

"We're not even Irish," I grumbled.

My father was too busy hanging green curtains to even hear me, and my mother was too busy packing all the red stuff into plastic bins to pay any attention to me.

Next it would be yellow and Easter bunnies, carrot-shaped plates and wooden chicks hiding in daffodils. Then Mother's Day pink and summer blue; patriotic flags and Uncle Sams; by September fall arrived at our house, everything burnt orange and gold, then Halloween and on and on, a never-ending variety of color schemes and holiday cutouts.

During those weekends, I dusted the tchotchkes and stayed out of the way. My father was always on emergency errands, off to find fish-shaped shower-curtain hooks or magenta throw rugs. My mother, a pre–Martha Stewart Martha Stewart, hemmed and taped, arranged and built. She had visions, my mother, of her house magazine perfect, decked out in seasonal glory. Even the forks we ate with matched whatever image my mother created. Surely we were the only family in our small New England mill town that ate their spaghetti with fiesta-striped silverware for Cinco de Mayo or hung nautical paraphernalia for the America's Cup races.

When I had my first grownup apartment on Bleecker Street in New York City, my parents arrived for a weekend visit that fall with a suspiciously odd-shaped bag.

"This will make your apartment more homey," my mother said. She reached into the bag and pulled out a ceramic scarecrow, papier-mâché pumpkins, and apple-cider-scented candles in various sizes.

I looked around the tiny room, wondering where I could fit this stuff, but my father was already hanging a string of lights shaped like witches above my one window.

The table/desk was slowly filling with more surprises from my mother's shopping bag: mugs decorated with jack-o'-lanterns, spider-web dishtowels, a large bowl shaped like candy corn.

"I don't think I'll be getting any trick-or-treaters," I said as my mother filled the bowl with miniature candy bars. "I live on the sixth floor," I added.

But it didn't matter what I said. I was twelve years old again, on a Saturday morning, making the house thematic. After they left, my boyfriend looked around the apartment, horrified. "What is all this stuff?" he said. He'd grown up in Berkeley, California, surrounded by avocado plants and macramé. He didn't understand the world according to my family.

"It makes it more homey," I said uncertainly. "Doesn't it?"

"No," he said. Then he wiped a thin layer of dust from my ceramic scarecrow. "It just makes everything dusty."

That was enough for me. I grabbed a box and put all of the Halloween tchotchkes inside. At first, I felt guilty. After all, my parents had lugged all this stuff almost two hundred miles. And I knew the joy my mother got from choosing these things. She loved shopping for her holiday decorations. Still, by the time I laid the witch lights on top of the pile, I no longer felt guilty; I felt liberated. My mother loved to vacuum, and she loved to decorate. Thanks to her, perhaps, I didn't like either.

Don't get me wrong. My parents were not at all controlling types. They gave me freedom to choose what I wore, what I read, whom I dated. They always let me voice my own opinions and to disagree with them. But in matters of housekeeping, my mother could not hold back. She didn't like that I let my cats walk on my tabletops. She sniffed and peered and shuddered at my piles of books and papers. And she loudly and often commented on my style, or lack of style, in everything concerning my various homes.

"You need curtains," she might say, shaking her head.

Or: "I would buy you a bedroom set, you know. A three-piece matching one."

Or: "A nice cornucopia would put this place in the Thanksgiving mood."

But I held firm. Sure, I decorated my Christmas trees and hung a wreath on my front door. Sometimes on Halloween I might even toss a skeleton in the front window. But mostly I keep my dusty house holiday neutral, my piles of stuff in their crooked piles and the Swiffer my mother gave me in the closet.

Still, life has a funny way of surprising you. One day I sat at my mother's kitchen table and watched as she unloaded bags of Valentine decorations she'd bought at the dollar store. A pair of dishtowels decorated with conversation hearts caught my eye.

"Cute," I said, smiling at the messages there: I Love You. Call Me. Honey Pie.

My mother brightened. "Take one," she said. "We'll share. One for me, one for you."

I can't say if it was her excitement or the cuteness of that silly dishtowel, or maybe a combination of both, but I did take that dishtowel. I hung it on my oven door, and I swear that every time I saw it, I smiled. Around Easter, my mother shyly held up two dishtowels for my inspection. I admit it's hard to pass on a gift of a happy yellow dishtowel with a floppy-eared rabbit that says: Hoppy Easter. Or a red one with a roly-poly snowman grinning out from it. This is our truce, the place where we meet, my mother and I. The two-for-the-price-of-one holiday-theme dishtowels make both of us grin. She thinks I'm coming over to her side; I know a dishtowel is decoration enough for me.

I know something larger and more important, too.

Last Saturday my mother babysat my kids so I could get some work done. When I went to pick them up at her house, I was met by a confusing sight: leprechauns and Easter bunnies mingled on the stove on salt and pepper shakers and paper napkins. Shamrocks glittered on cupboard doors, but baby chicks peeked out of ceramic eggs on countertops.

My mother is seventy-six years old, and thoughts of dementia or even a stroke did pass through my mind as I raced into the kitchen. She was sitting at the table, smoking a cigarette and playing poker on a hand-held machine.

"What's going on?" I said.

She didn't look up. "What do you mean?"

"You've got St. Patrick's Day and Easter decorations up."

My mother took a long drag off her cigarette. "Tell me about it," she said. "These March Easters drive me crazy. There's not even a week between the two this year." She shook her head.

Relieved, I squeezed her hand. "It looks good," I said.

Annabelle, my three-year-old, came into the kitchen wielding a dustcloth. My mother had pinned a KISS ME, I'M IRISH button on her shirt. I could have reminded my mother that not only aren't we Irish, but Annabelle is adopted from China. But I didn't.

"Phew!" Annabelle said. "That was a lot of dusting."

Then my fourteen-year-old son, Sam, entered carrying a stepladder. "Easter-egg lights are up," he announced.

"Good," my mother said. "Now all of you get out of here so I can enjoy my house."

We headed for the door, but not before she handed me two dishtowels, a green and white one covered in shamrocks, and a lavender one covered in Easter eggs. I paused a moment, taking in the hodgepodge of holidays, the smell of Lemon Pledge, the satisfied smile on my mother's face in the glow of Easter lights. It made me happy, this tableau of my childhood. It meant home to me, and love.

I held my children's hands and went toward my other home—the dusty one I had created on my own.

The Beauty of Help
Kyoko Mori

My mother, Takako, loved to surround herself with beauty. She embroidered tapestries with flowers, birds, butterflies, and musical notes floating over enchanted forests. For my tenth birthday, she baked a cake and decorated it like a rose garden with a fountain in the middle, and I entertained my friends in the black velvet dress she'd sewn. An afternoon tea with her was an occasion: Earl Grey with a lemon slice, a cut-glass jar of honey and a wooden dipping spoon, and, carefully arranged on each plate, the sugar cookies she'd baked, a pink Fuji apple with just enough skin left on for color, a strawberry sliced open into a fan. She was a dedicated homemaker, but I have no memory of her vacuuming, mopping, or dusting. In the 1960s in Japan, even well-to-do women cleaned their own houses. Tidying up after her husband and children was every wife's responsibility. Takako must have done these chores while we were gone.

My stepmother, who came to live with my father soon after I turned twelve, did nothing else. Every morning she'd start in the spare bedroom upstairs and work her way down to the kitchen. On her knees with a rag clenched in her bony fingers, she squinted at the floor, complaining about the strands of hair (always mine) she found stuck between the boards. She was a witch who believed herself to be Cinderella. If I offered to help, she got angry. Even the way I held the broom, she said, was wrong. "If you don't know how to clean the house by now," she hissed, "it's too late. Your mother should have taught you a long time ago."

While my mother had worn sweaters and slacks around the house, Michiko favored clingy shirts and tight pants in colors like lime green and mustard yellow. Her hair cut in the pixie style, her eyes smeared with mascara, she didn't look like anyone's mother, but our father, Hiroshi, told my younger brother and me to call her *Okasan* (Mother). Because she arrived at our house two months after my mother's death, I knew she had been my father's girlfriend.

As far back as I could remember, Hiroshi had worked late, traveled often, and played golf and rugby on weekends. On the nights Takako waited up for him, he called from noisy bars to say he was leaving on another business trip (at one in the morning). While he was with one girlfriend, others telephoned our house looking for him. From their voices and local accents, I could tell there were several. When Takako started crying every night, insisting that her whole life was one big mistake, or later when she killed herself, of course I blamed him.

Once he was married to Michiko, Hiroshi resumed staying out with his other girlfriends. Every evening after our supper without him, Michiko scrubbed and scoured the kitchen in a fury. My brother, Jumpei, did his homework at the table to keep her company. She didn't expect him to help with the dishes or learn to sweep the floor—he was a boy. She brought him juice and cookies and sat with him to drink her tea and smoke her cigarettes when her chores were finished. From my room upstairs, I could hear them talking and laughing. By the time I left home to attend college in Illinois,

Jumpei remembered nothing about Takako. Michiko had wiped his memory clean.

I've seen Hiroshi and Michiko only four times in the last thirty years I've lived in the States. The first time, in the late 1980s in New York, Michiko couldn't stop talking about the disposable paper underwear she'd packed for her trip.

"I can toss the used ones in the garbage, so everything in my suitcase stays clean," she said. "Whatever you do, don't be like the American women who let their laundry pile up for a whole week. At the very least, you should hand-wash your panties every night before going to bed."

I only did my laundry once every two weeks—underwear, socks, towels, and sheets all thrown into one big pile, but I didn't say. The kung pao chicken they ordered in China Town was spicier than the version back home. Michiko mopped her face with her balled-up napkin while my father unbuttoned his shirt and fanned his chest with the menu. Hiroshi worried, loudly, that the $700 he had in cash, in his pocket, might not be enough for an afternoon of shopping. I took them back to the Sheraton in a cab, helped him cash additional traveler's checks at the front desk, and went to stay with a friend. Though they were in New York for a week with a tour group, I flew back to my home in Wisconsin the next morning.

Michiko's enthusiasm for the throwaway underwear reminded me of the first night we'd spent under the same roof in 1969, when she sat in her see-through baby doll nightgown, rubbing cream into her arms and legs. Scattered on the white towel under her, the dead skin resembled the wormy gray droppings a rubber eraser makes over pencil marks. Michiko had wished for a new skin, I understood twenty years later, to overcome her shame. In the lobby of the Sheraton, the other wives from the group tour—arranged by my father's alma mater—were standing around in their beige or navy blue travel suits. Michiko stuck out in her white pants and pale pink T-shirt with a picture of a cartoon teddy bear. Her hair was dyed brown with one gray streak left in the front and combed back like an absurd feather.

My stepmother had met my father while working as a maid at a bed-and-breakfast. Maybe Hiroshi was attracted to her in the first place because she was the kind of person who talked about underwear in public. She must have struck him as a free spirit, utterly unlike my mother, who had grown up in a genteel, old-fashioned family. Takako would have been mortified to see her husband unbutton his shirt to fan himself with a restaurant menu. She believed that talking about money was rude. With Michiko, Hiroshi could open his shirt down to his belly button and brag about all the cash in his pocket. Still, Michiko must have squirmed when she first met our neighbors, his business friends, or the mothers of my classmates at the private junior high school I attended. As a businessman who made a lot of money, Hiroshi was allowed to be loud and obnoxious, but a woman who had married into "a good family" was expected to be quiet and refined. Michiko kept the house spotless because cleaning was her only perfect accomplishment. I might have felt sorry for her if she hadn't been so mean, if she hadn't insisted that my mother had taught me all the wrong things.

"Maybe she planned for you to marry someone who'll let you hire a maid," Michiko scoffed, "but no respectable woman pays a stranger to clean up after her family. Your in-laws will be horrified. After all the money your father's spending on your education, you can't even sweep the floor the proper way. You'll embarrass our family when you marry. I wish I could teach you, but it's too late. Your mother should never have spoiled you the way she did."

Michiko pretended that housecleaning was an advanced skill, like playing the violin, that I was doomed never to learn.

I had actually spent most of my childhood sweeping and mopping the floor, though not at home. At the public elementary school I attended from the first to the sixth grade, we were divided into six teams—one for every day of the week (school was only closed on Sundays)—to clean our classroom. First, we moved the desks and the chairs to wash the floor; then we put them back in precise straight rows and dusted them with a rag. The boys sat around laughing and pretending to supervise while the girls did all the work. In my last year there, I got into a fight with the boys and ended up wiping the ringleader's face with a wet rag. No one defended me when I told our teacher, Mr. Kawamura, that I was angry at the boys for their lack of cooperation. Mr. Kawamura sent me home with a note saying I had to help the other cleaning teams every day for a month. Takako was outraged. Of course I was wrong to attack my classmate with a dirty rag, she wrote back, but the punishment would only be fair if the boys on my team had to share it with me. She didn't get a response, and I didn't stay after school for the extra cleaning duty. Nothing more was said by anyone, but I knew this was one of the reasons Takako arranged for me to attend a private all-girls school the following year. My new school was known for promoting bilingual education among women. No one made us clean our classrooms there.

In the 1980s and 1990s, when American educators started praising the Japanese public educational system ("The kids attend classes six days a week and even clean their own classrooms!"), I recalled the trouble I'd gotten into, along with the smell of floor polish, the spotless windows, the shiny mirrors and tiles in the bathrooms. Our daily cleaning teams only used water out of the tap. We didn't wash the windows or tackle the common areas like hallways and bathrooms. Though public, our elementary school was in Ashiya, a suburb where only rich people lived. Obviously, the school had a professional crew who did the real cleaning. The daily chore was an empty ceremony, another dress rehearsal for the "teamwork" that never happened.

Michiko didn't have to worry about my embarrassing our family. I had no intention of staying in Japan and marrying anyone even remotely like my father. When I did marry after graduate school in Wisconsin, my husband, Chuck, was as eager as I was to divide our household chores equally. He mowed the lawn in the summer, and I shoveled the snow in the winter. We each washed our own clothes and took turns with the sheets. Whoever cooked had to go grocery shopping, so the other person dealt with the dishes, the garbage, the weekly housecleaning.

"We could hire someone to clean," I suggested after a year because, every week, I'd beaten him to the cooking and shopping duty.

"No," Chuck said. "We're not such pigs that we can't clean up after ourselves. If you don't want to do it, I can put cleaning on my permanent list."

I couldn't believe how lucky I was to get the easier half week after week. Chuck and I had the same level of tolerance, so our house stayed moderately clean instead of dirty or antiseptic. But gradually I became puzzled, then bothered, by the way my husband refused to accept help unless the job required professional expertise, like rewiring the electricity or patching the roof. Everything else, from cleaning the house to changing the motor oil, was a chore he insisted "people should do for themselves."

The two of us had met in Milwaukee, where we were students; then we moved to Green Bay, his hometown, for my job as an English professor at a small liberal-arts college. Chuck taught first and second grades at an elementary school. He was one of the few people from his high school to get a college degree. His childhood friends held factory jobs, and their wives cleaned houses or worked as nannies for the doctors, lawyers, college professors, and business managers who'd moved to Green Bay from somewhere else. The few college-educated professionals from town—like Chuck—did not hire others to perform simple everyday tasks. They believed it was elitist and embarrassing not to be self-sufficient just because you earned a salary instead of hourly wages.

Chuck thought all rich people and most PhDs were evil. He didn't want to get to know my friends at the college. When we divorced eleven years later, I was admitting that I, too, was a college professor who'd grown up in a well-to-do family. I couldn't live up to the do-it-yourself pride of a small town where everyone believed in hard work.

I don't clean the one-bedroom apartment I bought in a co-op building two years ago when I moved to Washington, D.C. Mariza, my cleaning lady, brings her vacuum cleaner and mop because I no longer own any serious equipment. Every other Tuesday, I hand her the envelope with the money and walk down to a café while my two Siamese cats dive under the covers to hide. When I return two hours later, the bed is remade, the cats are sniffing the floor and looking miffed, and the place is clean as it would never be if I'd spent all day on my hands and knees. Mariza angles my framed photographs and knickknacks just so, making the dresser top resemble a photograph in a home-decorating magazine. In a day or two, the cats would jump up there and knock down the whole arrangement, but that's their job: keeping the cleanliness in check, allowing me to live in the ever-shifting balance between tidiness and clutter. A perfectly clean house is a pleasure only because it is temporary.

Between Mariza's visits, I pick up after myself (and Ernest and Algernon, the cats) with a whisk broom, a hand-vac, and a sticky rolling pet-hair remover. I don't throw my clothes on the floor or leave the dishes in the sink. My apartment is never so messy that I'm embarrassed to open the door, but I'm relieved when the pristine aura, post-Mariza, wears off a little. A home should look comfortably lived in. I didn't leave my stepmother's angry spotless house to live in a prison of cleanliness.

To maintain the optimal two-week cycle of clean and not-so-clean, I pay Mariza to perform a "menial" task. Out east in our nation's capital, the guilt of this privilege is more complicated than in the heartland. Had I hired a cleaning lady in Green Bay, she would have looked and sounded like any of my neighbors: white, high-school educated, a firm believer in the traditional "family values." A Green Bay cleaning lady would have wondered why I didn't have children or vacuum my own floor. She would have found it odd that I, a foreigner, worked as an English professor and made enough money to hire her. Though she would have kept these thoughts politely to herself, I would have been a little afraid of her. Back there, *I* was the minority. In my neighborhood in D.C., the property owners are mostly white or Asian, and the people we hire to take care of our houses and gardens are from Central or South America. Mariza is no exception: she's Brazilian. I can say that I respect the job she does and consider it "professional" rather than "menial," but using a different adjective doesn't erase the gap between us or the guilt I feel about it.

I used to believe that guilt was a harmful emotion because it didn't motivate us to do the right thing. Instead of improving our conduct, we kept taking advantage of other people and letting ourselves off the hook by saying we felt guilty. I still think this may be true more often than not, but I also know that some situations are too complicated for us to understand what "doing the right thing" and "taking advantage of other people" even mean. If I cleaned my own apartment, it wouldn't improve my life or Mariza's in any way, and yet if I didn't feel guilty about it, I would be taking something for granted that I shouldn't. An immaculate conscience is as impossible as a spotless house. It's naive or even arrogant to assume we can ever attain total psychological cleanliness.

People who do everything for themselves often feel virtuous in an angry way. The other day, my neighbor Andrea lost her patience when an older woman in our building telephoned her about a shattered ceiling lamp over our front stairway. Andrea is our co-op president. Residents are supposed to contact her when they find broken glass in our common area.

"Why are you calling me?" Andrea yelled at Emilia all the same. "Why don't you go and clean it up instead of bothering me about it?"

"But I didn't break the lamp," Emilia protested. "The fixture must have come down on its own. There's broken glass all over the steps."

Though it was late at night and she was tired, Andrea swept and threw out the glass, mopped the steps, and complained about it for days.

"I don't think Emilia was saying *you* had to clean it," I had to point out when she told me, still outraged about how our neighbor had failed to "step up to the plate." If Andrea had been out of town, Emilia would have called me: I'm the co-op secretary. Only, I don't consider it my job to remove broken glass unless it's in my apartment threatening my own or the cats' safety. If I'd gotten Emilia's phone call, I would have put up a sign (DANGER. BROKEN GLASS. USE THE BACK STAIRWAY.) and notified our managing company, who would have sent a handyman to deal with the mess in the morning. Then I could have thanked our neighbor for alerting us, instead of yelling at her. I'd rather be a lackadaisical but pleasant co-op secretary instead of a hardworking and angry one. It's kinder to lower my expectations for everyone, including myself.

I'm sure my mother didn't sweep and scrub every day. Our house was neither so dirty nor so pristine that I noticed and remembered it. Besides, she was too busy doing other things. Before she started crying every day, Takako loved having her neighbors over for needlework. I often came home from school and found a dozen women seated around our kitchen table with their cups of tea. Everyone was talking and laughing. My mother might have been the only one who really liked embroidery.

"Your mother made such beautiful things for your house," the women reminisced years later when I visited Japan. "She was very artistic. But it was her company we came for. She made us so happy. As soon as she walked into any room, everything looked brighter."

My mother's friends wished she had confided in them. Takako believed that my father's affairs were her fault, and—like most other women in Japan in the 1960s—she was too ashamed to discuss her marriage problems with her friends or to see a professional counselor. If she could have been easier on herself, if she could have asked for help, she would have gone on living and spreading her happiness. Of course she wouldn't have minded my not cleaning my apartment, or getting divorced, or leaving the country of my childhood. She had raised me to do what she couldn't.

Clutter

Karen Salyer McElmurray

At ten o'clock each Sunday morning, I call my mother. "What do you know!" she always says, as if she hasn't heard my voice in months. "I didn't expect to hear from you!"

And then we discuss the usual. How hard it is to keep up a home by herself. How she watches television, the good, old shows like *Andy* and *I Love Lucy*, but only at night, since she has so many responsibilities during the days. How she needs to wash her hair before she could possibly go anywhere, and she may not go this week to the appointment with the foot doctor. Her feet, she tells me the last few Sundays, are really hurting her. I can see those feet—the thick layers of calluses, the spidery veins—as they walk her living room, kitchen, bedrooms—back through the four rooms of her house.

My mother has lived in Eastern Kentucky, first with her parents, and then by herself, for the last forty years. She has had one job, at a Cato Women's Apparel store in downtown Prestonsburg. She has never had a boyfriend, unless you count the would-be gentleman caller who drove her home from work twice and asked her to a movie, an invitation she declined. She once lived with her mother, also named Pearlie, until she passed away at age ninety-seven. My mother cared for her father, Leroy, until he passed away, also in his late nineties. And she has cared for the house itself as if it were a lover.

The four rooms. The green and white linoleum peeling back from the edges of the floor. The kitchen shelves filled with knickknacks—little china animals with rosy cheeks and welcoming paws. The bedroom with its tidily made bed and its photographs of me, at age six, and her, at age twenty-seven, walking down some snow-covered sidewalk, having her picture taken by my father, who loved her, then. And, throughout the house, the reign of neatness. The preponderance of shine. Torn linoleum gleaming with kitchen wax. Leaking pipes in the scoured bathroom sink. The walls polished by hand.

And yet, in the last few years, I've seen the way the rule of clean is slipping. My mother is short, all five foot one of her, and the tops of things have begun to go unnoticed. The china cabinet's dusty on the far reaches of its shelves. The light fixtures aren't as pristine as usual. And her accumulation of paperwork by the telephone has grown and grown. Her notes to self. *Call dentist. Call Karen. Buy vacuum cleaner bags.* Of late, since the onset of early dementia, my mother's notes to self are overwhelming—stacks of them here, scratched-out versions of them there. She has four phone numbers for me in that pile of notes, some numbers dating back ten years. I wonder, when I talk with her some Sunday mornings, whether she'll begin writing down the most elemental of things. *Now is daytime. This is night.*

It's nights I remember most vividly from my childhood. Nights and their sounds of voices and prayers. Around six o'clock I would be stationed in the recliner in the living room with the television, but I could still hear their voices out in the garage, where they'd be for a while after my father came home from work. I knew the garage routine exactly, having long experienced it myself after school. Some days my mother would have my father take a shower out there, before he could come in the house. Other days, he'd merely be subjected to the routine of tape and sock feet and waiting. He'd have to remove his shoes, stand on a piece of paper (never newsprint, since it shed ink), and turn slowly, clockwise, while my mother inspected his work clothes for stray lint, hair, fuzz. Once the clothes were debris-free, she'd have him stand still, remove his clothes—a decidedly unsensual ritual—and hand them to her one by one for folding, carrying indoors. Their conversation, during this divestment, was usually softer, and over the sound of the television, I could make out individual words. *Late. No call. Just what I'd expect.* On the days when a shower was necessary, the words became more distinct. *I know what you're up to. Who do you think I am, anyway?*

In my memory, what we were up to, the three of us, was being a family. As I watched the six o'clock news, my father, clad in his jockey shorts, paper bags taped to his feet, would be walked through the living room, clean enough now for his house clothes. After he was dressed, I'd have to move to the next seat, a folding art table from when I was little, and the two of us would watch *Star Trek* while my mother made our supper. The mess and splatter of hamburger patties. The shiny gristles of store-bought beef stew, eaten on white bread, to keep our plates clean. And on other days, the fatty edges of ham. The watery cheese from macaroni in a can. And every evening, a prayer for us from my father. *Thank you, Lord, for our bountiful blessings.*

While she washed the supper things, my father stood in the kitchen with her, listening to the details of her day. The sweeping up. The dusting. The endless cycle of dust's absence. He recited the details of his own day as my mother screened these details for the suspiciousness of person or place, the oddness of this incident or that. And when she was finished with the dishwater and the sink was immaculate, she held out her hands to both of us. I remember the misshapen little fingers, ones she'd smashed somewhere, in a window screen at night maybe, when she was a little girl. I remember the white, soaked skin and the cracks and crevices, the rough, wet patches where her hands hurt from all that she did, for us. I didn't know why for years, after dinner, my mother put on white gloves, ones with little pearl buttons, to wear to bed at night. Gloves laden with lotions to heal her wounded hands.

Even now, I question the recitation of the details of these evenings. The reason I must take them out again, these memories, these tastes and scents and moments of my childhood. Why did I need to rehearse these memories of my child-self, bathed and dressed and left to sit and listen? I want to see, as my father says he does, how we were happy enough, just as happy as any other family in any other house. But in my own memory, we are a Hopper painting. My mother sits upright on the only end of the sofa where anyone was allowed. My father is in the recliner. The white streetlight from our subdivision spills across us, washing us clean.

A couple of Sunday mornings ago, I called my uncle's wife, Mae, before I called my mother. I wanted to check in, see how the doctor's visits were going, see if the new medication for the dementia was doing any good. I'd called the doctor's office myself just a few days before, telling them how my mother has started to confuse time and place. And I'd told them about what I believed about the years before, the obsessions, the compulsions about cleanliness. Couldn't they give her something for OCD and dementia? Yes, the nurse said. And they phoned in the prescription.

But now, talking to Mae, I feel both sad and frustrated. My mother's confusion has deepened. She's checking the thermostat a hundred times a day. *Hot. Cold. Hot.* She's down to eating almost nothing. Chocolate chip cookies for breakfast. Sandwich cookies for lunch. Animal crackers for dinner and in between. And she's also started seeing things. A polyester pillow on a living-room chair has one cloth square that, she is sure, is a little girl, crying. It's not a resemblance to a little girl but the girl herself whom my mother speaks to, just as she does to the other little girls, the ones who come and go in the rooms of her house. But the other night, Mae tells me, was the worst.

My mother, sometime in the night, heard what she thought were voices in the yard outside her bedroom window. *Boys, out in the yard.* She saw the rustle of the fiberglass drapery. Heard the rumble and whir of the furnace reigniting. Watched the window glass grow thinner and thinner. Saw hands reaching inside to get her, her and all those little girls. As I talked with Mae, I could see her, my small mother grown shorter with age, fighting those boys with all she's worth, kicking them with her thick-skinned feet.

"I really gave them a good one."

That's what she told Mae and my uncle the next day, when they tried to figure out why the curtains were ripped from the rods, the bed's frame in the floor.

"She's got us so nervous," Mae said, "we don't know if we're coming or going."

And yet, when I suggest to Mae and to my uncle that they might consider some different remedies—a doctor's hard look at her history of OCD as well as at her dementia—I'm stymied.

"She don't need that stuff for depression," they say. "That's just, well, Pearlie Lee."

Right up to the time I ran away from home when I was sixteen, I hated my mother. I mean the kind of block-you-out anger that fuels the sixteen-year-old spirit. By day, I sat in a recliner in the living room and went outside only when she allowed me to go to the confines of a small patio.

"Can't you do anything but make a mess?" she'd ask.

She dressed me, combed me, and bathed me until I was nearly fourteen years old. But at fourteen, fifteen, I was taller than she, so tall that, before my parents divorced, I believed I could tower over her, defeat her once and for all. Once my mother moved away, I found all the freedom I could have wanted and more. Pink Floyd and Black Sabbath led me down roads I'd never seen. At sixteen, I became a runaway and junkie devotee on the streets of Columbia, Missouri. I gave birth to a child I surrendered for adoption.

In my now-favorite essay, "Memory and Imagination," Patricia Hampl talks about memory's power. "Memory possesses authority," she says, "for the fearful self in a world where it is necessary to have authority in order to Question Authority." At sixteen, I wanted the tape of my life to skip whole tracks, pause. I wanted to erase the dominion my mother had held over my life. And so I didn't see her for over five years, and after even today, I still sometimes find myself putting her photographs on the mantle away into the locked china cabinet, where I can't see them. For this half century called my life, I have teetered on the edge of both remembering her as deeply as I can and remembering her so that I could wipe the slate clean and start over again, motherless and in possession of my own life. I have written a memoir about her and about myself. And, on some Sunday mornings, I delay. I make coffee and sit and watch the news. I forget that ten o'clock call to Eastern Kentucky and my mother's sad voice.

On the one hand, there's dementia. *An acquired loss of cognitive function that may affect language, attention, memory, personality, and abstract reasoning.* And on the other, there is obsessive compulsive disorder. *A disorder in which individuals are plagued by persistent, recurring thoughts (obsessions) that reflect exaggerated anxiety or fears.* Would it not be a kindness, then, for my mother to forget? Imagine one such day in her life. The luxuriousness of forgotten dusty tables. The unscrubbed bathtub. One day a few years ago, when I visited my mother, she showed me a leather purse she keeps in a drawer in the bedroom. In it are newspaper clippings, parts of letters, photographs, greeting cards. Some are from me. Some show my father, back when the two of them were young and happy. What solace to forget these lost times, these disorderly connections to the past?

And then there's that white light I recall from my childhood. The fine white light over us, that family at night in its living room, in its rituals of day-to-day. Suppose for a minute that this is the way that it all could work. A clean canvas, our minds, our hearts. At ten o'clock some Sunday morning I could call her, my mother. Or she could call me. We could reach out across the distance with our voices, with one uncluttered hour. Forgiveness? Not quite that. But the day could be like this: as swept clean as the tunnel of light after our deaths or before our births. We could forget, for a little while. *Karen,* she'd say. *Is that you?*

Dust

Markie Robson-Scott

*T*hese are some of the things I fly across the Atlantic to do: change the vacuum-cleaner bags, wash the sofa covers, replace the lightbulbs, and add salt to the dishwasher. Other people who live in my London house—the house/dog sitter, or my sons when they're there in their college vacations—could do these things, but they don't.

This double life, half in a new New York apartment, half in an old north London house—has been going on for almost four years, because of my husband's job in New York. I go back to London often to see sons, dog, house, garden, and my mother in a nursing home, all given new poignancy by my absences. At first, I resented finding things not up to scratch. How could they allow tea stains in the kitchen sink? Why did my husband's nephew, our first house sitter, leave his fifty ties—he was a stockbroker—draped over the banisters? What was the brown gunk in the fabric-softener drawer of the washing machine? Why did no one clean the lint filter in the tumble dryer? I emailed instructions that everyone ignored. Then the nephew got married, bought a house of his own, and moved out. A new house sitter, a friend who wanted to move from west to north London to be nearer her job, was waiting in the wings.

I expected things to get better. After all, she was a friend, an artist. And she did have lovely old tins, a big improvement on the nephew's melamine trays and plastic boxes that I'd put out of sight whenever I came home. But other things were worse. The lavatory, for example. Hadn't she heard of Harpic (Britain's Lysol)? And the kettle was full of limescale. London suffers terribly from limescale and hard water. You have to ladle salt into the dishwasher to soften it, shower heads get clogged, shampoo doesn't lather the way it does in New York. One has to be constantly vigilant, a fact that my friend didn't seem to appreciate because she hadn't been using the Brita water-filter jug to fill the kettle from.

"I've never used a jug. I didn't have room in the kitchen in my old flat," she said sniffily, which I felt was beside the point.

She didn't see things. I left some spiky blue flowers in a jug in the sitting room, and when I came back two months later they were still there, sitting in fetid water. She didn't change lightbulbs. The Miele vacuum-cleaner bag was stuffed full. The sofa covers were muddy from Rusty the Cairn terrier's habit of wiping himself on them when wet. The recycling baskets weren't organized in the rigid way that I liked—she threw screwed-up pieces of paper in with the cans and bottles, and she mixed cooked food with raw in the compost bin, which I was sure would attract rats.

Every time I came back, I had an orgy of housecleaning before I went to bed. It was always around 11:00 PM by the time I walked in the door, but that was five hours ahead of New York, so I wasn't tired. My friend was in bed, my sons were out. First I went out into the dark garden and inhaled the wet lawn and the bamboo, mixed with the sharp smell of foxes' pee. Then I bleached the sink, including the metal sink filter. Then I removed the greeny-blue sofa covers and shoved them in the washing machine. I pulled the pink IKEA rug straight in front of the hearth so that it touched the marble surround. I cut off the bits of sea-grass matting that had unraveled even further since I'd been away. I changed lightbulbs. In the bathroom, I scrubbed limescale off the tiles with a toothbrush and polished the slate shelf beside the bath with linseed oil and white spirit, which prevented soap stains. I changed my sheets, using the Egyptian cotton ones I kept hidden in a storage bag under my bed, knowing that various people, i.e., sons and girlfriends, had been sleeping in it. I also brought American home improvements with me: an over-door hook for the kitchen cupboard from Bed Bath & Beyond, sponges and cloths that were far superior to the British varieties, Glad Press'N Seal, and Murphy's Oil Soap spray.

In spite of the low standards that prevailed in the house, it was much easier to keep clean than our apartment in New York. American dust was different. It was impossible to win the fight—every day, it returned in the same sinister thin gray layer over our new, dark furniture. Where did it come from? The windows were mainly closed, so through the air-conditioning units, I supposed, even when they weren't turned on. We lived downtown, near the West Side Highway, so perhaps the dust was connected to the traffic, or to the construction of all the new buildings, or to Ground Zero. I bought a Swiffer duster and antistatic cloths, but nothing worked. In London dust came into a house more slowly, creating little everyday impact. Suddenly you'd see that a white windowsill was littered with hard black specks, you'd get rid of it, and it wouldn't reappear for weeks, even months. Our scratched, stained old tables never looked dusty at all.

Somehow, the house sitter and I remained friends. We had different approaches—mine obsessively anal, hers not obsessive enough. But I stopped minding because cleaning the London house had a new dimension now I was away from it so much. It wasn't just part of everyday life anymore but something important to be savored. And it gave me control, which seemed, in general, to be slipping away.

"Why don't you leave it till after breakfast?" said my friend as I unpacked the dishwasher before making a cup of tea in the morning.

"No, I can't," I said, my head in the cupboard, reorganizing the bowls.

After my cup of tea and a walk with the dog, I got into the rental car and drove down the hill to the nursing home. I visited my mother almost every day while I was in London. What excuse did I have not to, when I was in New York so much of the time? I signed in with the time: 11:30. I always tried to stay a full half hour. I pushed open the door to the second floor, the dementia floor, which was kept locked on the inside. Not that my mother would ever try to go anywhere. She couldn't move unaided.

She reached out to take my hand and said what she always said nowadays, "Cold hands."

They'd painted her nails pink, and her long gray hair was piled on top of her head, done up with a scrunchie. This grooming, along with the dementia, had turned her into another person, unlike the dirty, difficult woman clinging to her character in the last years in her flat in central London. The mess there had driven me mad for years—the moth-eaten clothes and carpets, the smell of urine as she became incontinent, the dishes put away dirty in the cupboards. Finally, in the nursing home, she was clean.

Before the dementia took hold, each time she went into the hospital for stomach problems or falls I would dash round to the flat, racing against time before she was released, calling the carpet cleaner, spraying moth killer, washing the floors and tidying her chests of drawers, where clothes were balled up and secured with rubber bands. This balling-up, my therapist told me, was typical senile behavior, but at first I'd found it difficult to grasp that my mother could fit into that category. It just seemed an extension of the way she'd always been—everything under control on the surface, muddle underneath. In the cupboards of my childhood, you'd unlock a door and piles of nameless stuff would bulge out, covered tightly with old sheets. My adult cupboards were models of decorum, with clothes folded as if in a shop.

Now, after a year of nursing-home bills, I had to clear the flat, redecorate, and rent it out to ease the financial load. The stained carpet was going to be ripped out and replaced with oak boards. The bathroom, with its disability aids, was to be retiled and remodeled. Sacrilegiously, I would chuck out my mother's beloved trolley, along with most of the other furniture, deemed not up to scratch by the realtor. Walls would be repainted. Waiting for me to finish the clear-out was Robbie the builder, who was in charge of a team of Polish and Croatian men. He came by to inspect my progress, and sometimes, feeling I was lagging behind, he helped, holding up a thick plastic builders' rubble bag for me to drop things into.

"This bathmat must be about fifty years old," I said as I emptied a bathroom cabinet.

"My dad gave me a suit from the fifties," said Robbie. "I wear it when I go to the races—lovely it is."

I discovered that she kept clothes under the mattress of the spare bed with the collapsed springs. I washed the many, many little pottery bowls and jugs, put most of them in my mother's peeling, non-wheelie suitcases, and gave them, with the clothes, to the temporary charity shop around the corner, where a guy with an earring and stained teeth was happy to take anything, even old electrical goods banned by other charity shops. He made a window display out of the stuff I gave him.

Every day or so, guilty but determined, I took more of the good things back to my house: the dark pink china set that matched the dragon's-blood red on the back of my shelves, the leaf-shaped unglazed Wedgwood china plates, the blue rearing horse, many paintings, and finally, my father's huge, well-made old desk. First I had to empty it, which took days. There were his passports from the 1920s, driving licenses, tiny old diaries, and tons of letters, as well as notebooks, in one of which my mother had described a nightmare about snakes

I'd had when I was six. There were my old school reports and all the letters I'd ever written to my parents.

But the desk was nothing compared with the musty, splitting cardboard boxes under the stairs, full of older letters that were black with dust, possibly coal dust, antique in itself. Some letters, sealing-waxed, dated from the 1700s; some were from my father at boarding school in 1911 to his father. Others—hundreds—were from his friends in the thirties. There were bills from the County of London Electricity Supply in the twenties, receipts for linen laundering when he was at Oxford, cards from Berlin tea dances. It was a fascinating archive, but it was also a lesson in OCD, for which I discovered later my father had spent years in analysis. The dust stuck to my fingers and under my nails. It was history come to life, my parents' history, part of my genes.

I transferred the letters into other boxes—an old red hat box and a trunk my mother had used when she went as a student from south Wales to Vienna in the thirties—and took them home to my dining room, with their dust. They stayed there for a year; then I started bringing batches of them over to New York, to read and collate at my white IKEA desk. The dust from the thirties letters covered the desk, joining the new, downtown dust, until you couldn't tell one from the other.

A Clean Well-Cluttered Place

Lisa Solod Warren

66 "*I* guess this is why parents have more than one child," my sister said to me as we carried yet another large green plastic garbage bag full of old magazines and newspapers outside and tossed it on the back deck.

"Yes," I answered. "I can't imagine doing this alone."

We were at my mother's house in Providence cleaning it out and preparing to "stage" it for an open house that had been scheduled for three days hence, to take advantage of the spring market and beauty of her garden. Her nearly hundred-year-old cottage, quaint but in dire need of updating, sat in one of the city's best neighborhoods so we were not particularly worried about the house not selling (buy the worst house in the best neighborhood, the adage goes); but we were supremely worried that there was no way on earth we would possibly be ready for the open house.

Before her diagnosis with Alzheimer's, my mother had lived in that house for twenty-six years—she bought it soon after her divorce from my father—and she had the paper to prove it: every *Brown*

Alumni Monthly, every Sunday *New York Times Magazine* and book review, every *Cape Cod Life* and *Rhode Island Monthly, Newsweek, New Yorker* she ever received had been stashed away on some bookcase, in some basket, on some closet shelf. She also had financial records dating back to her divorce as many years ago, insurance policies for things she no longer owned, and warranties for items we could not find. And that did not include two four-drawer file cabinets filled with copious manila envelopes containing hundreds and hundreds of torn-out articles and labeled "Things to read some day."

My mother had also collected numerous objets d'art from her travels around the world; she had huge numbers of photographs from her many travels around the globe. A monk in Tibet, his orange robes brilliant against the beige sand background; multicolored laundry hanging on a line at the beach; windblown repair tarps on a Cape Cod bridge; fruit and vegetables in the south of France; Rio's Christ the Redeemer, his face crisscrossed by telephone lines. There is something completely honest in the photos: as in Goya's paintings, the ugly becomes truth. She was a wonderful photographer and in another time, perhaps, could have been a professional. She also had boxes and boxes of her own writings and journals, all sadly unpublished, along with hundreds of books and scavenged leftovers from her own mother's house—silver, glass, silly tchotchkes she would have never displayed (they weren't her style) squirreled away in cabinets and closets. She still owned, it seemed to my sister and me, every item of clothing she had worn for the past quarter century. And that was just the beginning.

Some years ago, my two sisters and I had proposed that our mother begin her own weeding out, that she prepare to move into someplace more suitable for an older woman, a home without narrow stairs to the second floor and even more hazardous ones to the basement laundry, a home with central air and a roof that someone else would see to, where someone else would take care of snow removal and gutter replacements, weeding and mowing: a home, in

ter years. She listened to our arguments and then
d.

e were, my sister and I, trying to assess the last many
other's life: what to keep, what to throw away, what
ave, what to give away, what held meaning, what did
owing took forever as each letter uncovered demanded
st a cursory glance, some of them screaming out to be
ach piece of paper called up a memory of our mother,
is like then, what she is like now. My sister and I culled
otographs of ourselves tiny and helpless, dressed in
esses, posing on vacations we can barely remember. We
thank-you notes from our children, and even the menus
and bills from the caterers of our weddings decades ago.

How could either of us be sure which statuette, which small
painting, which tea cup, had real meaning for our mother and which
did not—when my mother herself could not even remember where she
collected half of her possessions? How could we be confident about
what to save and what to toss, what to keep for our own children and
what would merely be another burden? We could not. Were my sister
not there to hold my hand and I to hold hers, both of us would have
quickly fallen apart. Our middle sister had gone through the house a
couple of weeks earlier: editing books, choosing things she wanted,
and she phoned daily to provide much-needed support and love. But
all of us found it painful and troubling to decide for someone else
what to keep and what to add to the quickly growing mound of black
plastic garbage bags. Our mother would want some of her things
with her in her new place, a small apartment in an assisted living
complex twenty miles away; but that space made her tiny house look
huge—there was simply no way that even a third of what she had
gathered would fit. And truth was, most of it was junk.

I had had no idea my mother was such a pack rat. She hid it
well. On my many visits to her house, it seemed a little "overstuffed"
but still clean and lovingly decorated. I explored neither the closets

nor the basements with any care; I did not rummage through the shelves and baskets and filing cabinets; I had no real idea of the enormity of her collections. The surface order of her house merely served to mirror the surface order of her life: For years her mental health had been deteriorating, a condition my sisters and I put down to her growing intake of alcohol. She seemed to function at least fairly well; she rose, put on her clothes and makeup, tended to her daily duties (although we were never sure exactly what they were after she retired). But when we finally got her into rehab, the doctor's prognosis was dire: Her brain was shrinking for sure; Alzheimer's, in who knew what stage, had gotten hold of her. Decisions had to be made quickly—she simply could not go home again, she could not live alone. In the pile of papers were unpaid bills, charges for things she did not own, as far as we could tell, and reams and reams of letters from charities, some of which she had obviously donated to more than once, more than twice. Her finances, despite her brother-in-law's efforts to try to oversee them, were chaotic.

Growing up, I thought my mother was a great cook and a wonderful housekeeper. Part of this was wishful thinking, as there was little evidence of any other motherly traits, but part of it was as true as I knew it. Yet age and distance change things, just as they cause the house you grew up in to shrink when you return to it as an adult. I now know my mother was only a better than average cook who happened to serve "exotic" things for the South of the late fifties and sixties: her own homemade red sauce, sautéed liver, spinach, rump roasts marinated in wine. She made cheesecakes from scratch. We had salami and eggs for Sunday-night supper and sometimes stopped at the deli on our way home from Sunday school in Knoxville, fifty miles from home, to buy bagels and lox. In August we would have suppers of nothing but sweet corn and fresh tomatoes from the garden she had for several years. But she quickly slipped into routines, too:

Friday night was boiled chicken for Shabbat, and meatloaf was served at least once a week. Her repertoire might have been interesting the first several dozen times, but it grew repetitive once we realized what night it was and what we were going to be served.

Her housekeeping was another story. The house was picture perfect, neat as a pin, and clean as the proverbial whistle. But that was due to a series of housekeepers: Edie, who came every day, smoked Pall Malls and was picked up by her husband, Willard, in his huge black Cadillac (but only after she changed into black stilettos and a slash of red lipstick); Sylvia, who came twice a week and sullenly and indifferently spent hours ironing in front of the soaps; and, finally, Lucinda, who showed up three times a week and thought the world of my fragile mother but insisted that we three girls were insolent, mouthy, and disrespectful. Edie, Sylvia, and Lucinda were all black and all wore uniforms, something I didn't even think about until I was older. This was the South before and right after civil rights, but not much changed either way.

My mother sent all her cotton sheets out to be laundered and pressed. The ironing, washing, and heavy cleaning were done by the housekeepers, and my mother turned the dishwashing over to my father after dinner (he stood at the sink with a dish towel around his waist, dropping ashes from his ever-present cigarette into the sink) until we three girls were old enough to take over.

So the fact was that my mother was no housekeeper at all. What she did was dictate standards that the rest of us had to follow.

As we grew older her distaste for clutter became obsessive. She would gather anything she found lying around the house: books, papers, shoes, whatever we three girls had dropped, and put it in paper bags, which she would then store in a back closet. When we asked her where such-and-such a thing was, my mother would offer it back to us, for a price. Each item was a nickel. Our clothes suffered the same fate. They would be washed and folded by the housekeeper, but if we did not take them, within a day of their laundering, out of the large wicker basket where they had been placed, in they would go to paper bags, until, with no clean underwear left, we had no choice but to ransom them back.

Finally, despairing of the cleanliness of our bedrooms, she took to closing the doors at all times and instructing the housekeeper that our bedrooms were off limits. The rest of the house was cleaned and tidied; our rooms were left to rot. Luckily for me, I inherited my mother's penchant for neatness and began my own campaign against clutter and dirt and learned housekeeping skills that would stand me in good stead. My middle sister was slower to learn; my youngest sister remains, well, a slob, God love her.

But as my mother's unchecked manic depression worsened, and as she began to drink more heavily, the house suffered. Stacks of the Sunday *New York Times*, which mother read throughout the week, gathered on the fireplace hearth. She no longer had the desire nor the energy to gather our errant books, shoes, papers, or articles of clothing and put them in the bags, although right before I left for college I found a paper bag, hidden away in the back of the closet, which held two pairs of earrings, a ring, and a pair of socks I had long given up finding.

After her breakdown my first year out of college, my mother finally got her life back on track and bought the small dollhouse on Providence's East Side, furnishing it with castoffs from her marital residence and never, ever changing their arrangement in more than a quarter century. She got a job and then retired from it. She traveled the world. She read and wrote and collected and horded, and none of us had any idea just how much stuff could fit into one tiny house. But her decorating skills, coupled with her ability, like a magician's, to make you look at one hand while the other does the trick, kept us from realizing how serious her own mental health issues had become and how serious the clutter gathering around her had grown.

I have two children, a boy and a girl born five years apart, and I wonder, will they be close enough, friends enough to be able to make decisions about my care together? Will they be able to do what my sisters and I did for my mother? Should they *have* to? Is it not possible for me to make things easier on them now that I am fully aware of the emotional cost of doing someone else's life-cleaning?

I like to think that I have pared my life down to the essentials, but one look at my shoe collection puts that to rest. I feel proud of my lack of clutter, but, on the other hand, I have a huge box of old letters from friends and lovers that I simply cannot bear to toss, and a carton holding ten years of journals. I have baskets and pottery collected from my own travels, and far, far too many books, even as I continually pack up boxes for the library, Goodwill, the battered women's shelter. As one friend said wisely, "Our things are important to *us*, but to everyone else, it's just stuff."

I recently moved house and, with a new husband, downsized from thirty-four hundred square feet to half that. I have let go of a lot of the detritus of my own life: old papers, files of taxes, warranties, purchases, even old writing. Books, clothes, furnishings that no longer make sense have been given away. Two years earlier my ex-husband and I split up the marital assets of twenty years. But still, still, I have too much stuff cluttering my house, my head, my mind. As much as I toss, new stuff enters at will, it seems. I hate clutter in my environment, even as I can put up with a little dirt; I hate the way it takes over and begins to own you. I have seen the way people become immobilized at the amount of their stuff, not even up to going through the piles of papers on the kitchen counter. I think that happened to my mother. Only she knew the extent of her hoarding, the numbers of her file drawers, the amount of papers in the baskets, the piles of clothing in her closets. She kept it all hidden so that the facade looked pretty good, just as she kept her own deterioration hidden for far too long, until the job of keeping up appearances became too much for her.

I am grateful I had my sisters to help sort through the messiness of her house and her life. At the least we laughed and wept together as we hefted the literal and emotional garbage bags together. I would like to hope I leave my children with a lighter burden to bear and the good sense not to agonize over what to keep and what to discard.

In the best of all possible worlds, our collection of stuff should reflect the purposefulness of our lives. Each thing we add to our homes should be something we treasure. Once, my mother's home was like that: Our childhood home was filled with art and sculpture and books. But as the years wore on, and as her mind unraveled, she lived, unchecked by others, and the clutter around her grew too large for her, or us, to handle.

III. DOWN & DIRTY

"There is no need to do any housework at all.
After the first four years the
dirt doesn't get any worse."

—Quentin Crisp, *The Naked Civil Servant*

Dirty Nostalgia

Alissa Quart

$\mathcal{J}$ust recalling New York before it was gilded, when it was still in its age of detritus, when antiambition was a popular pose, fills me with dirty nostalgia.

As a child, I rode around the city on subway cars encased by graffiti, filth and dust so thick you could write your name in it. This was thirty years ago when adults lived in slovenly rooms connected by thin hallways, apartments that were strung together like beaded necklaces encrusted in dirt. Manhattan parents, including mine, made the living room their bedroom, making do with little money, as dust accrued in every corner of their small homes.

Back then I liked our giant industrial vacuum cleaner but only as a toy: my whale. I was Jonah. I rode around on the vacuum, which was exciting and menacing—it could swallow my belongings and me in one gulp. Even then, I preferred my own dirt to cleaning: I threw my things on the floor in a semicircle around my bed. I felt that by surrounding my bed with refuse, it became the safest place in the house. My father sometimes picked up my mess or screamed but he didn't care that much about it. He thought neatness was bourgeois. He saved his compulsions for the broken glass covering the sidewalks—he sometimes picked it up with his bare hands, which was civic but terrifying.

As a child I would visit the many filthy curiosity stores that abounded, where ancient women sold mid-century silk dresses and chipped mother of pearl lockets, piled so densely you couldn't see in or out of their windows. Back then, the city's blocks served as ad hoc bathrooms for thousands of the newly deinstitutionalized population: though unpleasant, it was fascinating to children. When I went home at night, there were rust stains on the tub where I took my bath.

A few years later, I was still attracted to the dirty. I went to see Lou Reed when I was thirteen at the old Ritz on 11th Street. I walked home singing "Street Hassle" with my Greek American friend from Astoria—he was fourteen, with a receding hairline. Even then I felt born too late, too long after Lou's *Transformer* phase—*"You hit me with a flower, you do it every hour."* It was after the late New York School poets had died or left the city in search of local arts funding.

Any style of hopelessness was more hopeful to me than a 12-Step Program.

Then, the term "urban blight" didn't only mean Detroit. It also meant New York, and a band whose T-shirts the kids of the city wore proudly. I pushed through fighting tenants to get into tenements and to visit friends. I slept in beds with girls I had just met—one of these young women put cigarettes out on her arm in front of me, like she did at clubs for attention. There were neighborhoods that were dangerous, that you had to walk through with your shoulders squared, Washington Heights but also much of Brooklyn. I walked through said districts with a macho swagger, at night. Sometimes I'd be smoking, in a red blouse with a zipper and gold sequins.

I found my first apartment in the East Village, not far from where I had grown up. I went to the same dinged-up dive bars my father had drank in before I was born. I subsisted on lightly defrosted pierogis. I lived in an apartment where there was a hole in the center of the floor of my kitchen and smoke from the bar below filtered up through the break in the boards. I and people like me believed that there was moral superiority to chaos, to having cockroaches skimming across your floors and lianas of weeds poking through, of having your hair knotted, as mine was, as if a swarm of bees had lived in it. New York was not quite a careful place then: There was even independent publishing. There were many more used book stores and many more dusty older men in aged wool gloves who collected things and had dropped out of college and spent their days in the library even though they weren't even crazy. New Yorkers did not trust clean people, although some were corralled on the Upper East Side.

My aim then was to write prose poetry so encoded, so intellectually rarified and emotionally private, that no one would ever understand it. I went to incense-filled, dank apartments, where I tried not to fall in love. I usually succeeded. The only shiny places I had ever seen were the buildings of the fancy college I attended and the apartments of the art celebrities whom the young people I knew worked for: I illicitly slept in the bed of an eighties art star—with his assistant—and in the bed of a famed mid-century writer with his.

One never gets so close to the famous as when one is young enough to know all the assistants.

Then, I wore Salvation Army coats, especially when I was asking other people to save me. Antique books told me how to play parlor games in raised gold letters. Real books told me how to live and also that I should read all day instead of getting a job. Under the clutter, there was a telephone, for talking my friends through their crack-ups. This was a time in Manhattan when people not only admitted to having crackups but boasted about them.

Around home, my first apartment, I had created an assemblage culled from the streets outside—streets where you could still find gold shoes in any garbage can in the snow. The cases of hundreds of CDs scattered, some with the plastic broken. My giant teacups, inevitably missing handles.

It was cracked—all of it—and I loved it.

You could say that these feelings were merely a coefficient of youth. You could say we are cyclically averse to cities we live in, and that their luxury and our repugnance to their luxury operate like sine curves. Throughout the last century, people have commented on the awfulness of a New Slick New York City. Henry James, who was born on the same block I was, called it a "terrible town" in 1904. He denounced it for having turned into "a vast crude democracy of trade," one that betrayed the New York City of his own childhood.

In 1969, the artist Donald Judd left New York City for the West, although not for good, calling the city "glib" and "narrow."

But I am sure that it is more than my nostalgia for my own youth that makes New York of that time seem happily shine-free and low-gloss when compared to today. A street would boast a succession of fire-eaters, male dancers on tiny bicycles—I rode a miniature purple bicycle, too—literary pornographers who lived off people they met at Narcotics Anonymous, people whose medical bills were being paid for by all of their friends.

If I was emotionally honest, which I wasn't then, I would say I was avoiding both the past and the future. I was in a state of panic rapture, the flight side of fight-or-flight. My flight was an escape from conventional structures but those structures that had never held, protected, or sustained me and meant less than nothing to me. In my twenties, I was in a constant state of "Just say no" to illusions about social status and propriety. I replaced them with my own new fantasias of purity and freedom that were only possible through the truth of mess. I saw women—all people, really—as dragged down by repetition and minutiae. Drudgery of any kind was bad for you. It was part of being put-together. I hated that.

I did try, briefly, to romanticize the feminine arts. I talked about the power of cleaning with my in-recovery yogi roommate—she wore velvet body suits and scrubbed the floors with mint natural cleaner, both at the East Village yoga center and at our shared home. Cleaning was *ahimsa,* or nonviolent practice, she told me, yogically, long before the yoga center became a palace of sorts, with a large cleaning staff. I read Marilynne Robinson's novel *Housekeeping,* where chores were the glue of solidarity between destitute, dedicated women and girls: they started smoldery fires to boil water for tea and soup and whacked the woodpiles with brooms, always together. I tried emulating their domestic skills. I even tried to start knitting like all the girls that year did, those who were dropping stitches in quasi-homey circles. But the idea of women finding their strength through housekeeping just didn't work for me. I took no joy in picking up a stitch. I had never shared a jolly chore with my mother or cousin when I was growing up. By the time I was an adult, it was too late.

Keeping clean in New York on the edge of a new millennium meant something else. It was all there for the perceiving in the later 1990s, the dot-com heyday. Cleaning up was no longer the woof and warp linking woman to woman. It was neither ablution nor meditation. The city was expanding into a giant, globalized, technocratic prom queen. Suddenly, there were people calculating their lives as if they were characters on *Sex and the City.* They stripped the gold paint on their walls, repainting them sage and eggshell. Hair was double processed.

I remained a creature of the old untidy New York.

I am not alone in my dirty nostalgia for a city and a way of being that has gone. I was reminded of this a few years ago by a Luc Sante essay on New York City of the 1980s. He wrote of its "potsherds and tumuli" and being entranced by decay and eager for more of it.

In the late 1990s and early 2000s, I should have seen the end of dirty New York on the horizon. Once bars were still full of American

Spirit smoke, killing us: in the days before the New Gilded Age, dive bars were honorable. No longer. The new, omnipresent lounge bars arrived into a flush city. They were a dark, overpriced harbinger of the New York to come.

In these venues, I met men who were fastidious and elegant with very well-cut hair. I was attracted to this type—my opposite. They all wore more scent than I did and tended to themselves and their homes like the oligarchs of ancient Rome. I resented and envied them for this.

Through them, I saw there were new expectations of self in the tidy, carefully appointed New York—of "stepping it up," of "turning up the wattage," of "taking control of your life." By then, the term "selling out" had been retired, its paradoxes collapsing. With this useful reproach gone, the new New York inflated: Luminous ATMs proliferated as did their music, a steady buzz of receipts being printed out in thousands of franchises and boutiques. The city was slouching toward perfection.

Now, the women who best survived New York performed their femininity without glitches. They were part of couples that once went to suburbs when they had children. In the new New York, they stayed here, expanding—anodyne, luxurious—through the dining tables with the extra leaves, the designer shoe closets, the kitchen islands, and the extra bedrooms for the nannies. I watched this all, on the edges of the cleanup.

I missed the vanished analog city. I held on to it so hard I became belated. I was now in my thirties and I was told that it was time to grow up. I would talk about the time I was a teenager or a young person with friends and they would be aghast by how fresh and present these memories seemed. "That was a long time ago," these childhood friends would say, with some relief. "I was so different, then. We are old, now."

Perhaps I was getting old but I wasn't growing up, no matter how many times I told myself to. I had enough maturity to survive, though, and I survived, ironically, by publishing. Because I had published one book and then another, people wrote things about me and in one newspaper, I was described as slim, wearing gold sandals, and having ink stains on my handbag. I had thought a pen-dirtied handbag was cool, of course, like self-deprecation and androgyny. I realized then that these things no longer functioned as smoke signals of authenticity.

I bought a new handbag. It was of a piece with the new Manhattan, a place where strangers' smiles were suddenly freakishly bright, like bone china.

In the last few years, I have forced myself to neaten a little, not out of desire, but adaptation. I buy the ecological-esque Seventh Generation dish liquid but mostly for the brand name's happy sociology.

When I met my husband, he was a Mr. Clean. He had immaculate files and ordered reporting notebooks, going back to the early 1980s. He also had a large, spare apartment, the sort of home where everything has its place and its folder, as ordered as a terrarium. True, it was a little short on color and life, but I reasoned that this was all for the good—it meant my presence would be necessary.

My husband-to-be was surprised at first that I did not like to clean. When we first got together, he was disturbed that I left a fort around my bed of yesterday's clothes. To me, it was like a diorama of when New York's streets and buildings looked Martian and charred.

He still nags me daily to pick up my boots, to comb my hair, and to send thank-you emails. And under his tutelage, I have learned to save my receipts, throw away my junk mail, cook complicated dinners, and brush my hair until it shines. Today, I like to think that he accepts me as I am.

In my middle thirties, I have outlived my unclean New York, and yet I am still here, like a self-appointed living ghost. It's a little like being a very old person who has outlived her friends. I still create a nest of cast-off things in our apartment, my protection from the rest of New York and also the world, which I know to be equally disordered. And in my mind's eye, I recall a bohemian ruddy palace of spilled shiraz; of manuscripts accidentally crisped in an oven; of butch tree houses; of emotional dachas; of squats; of a palladium of the thwarted yet thoughtful.

Maybe one day I—and far more of us—will live like that again.

A Portrait of Ten Bathrooms

Sonya Huber

The bathroom is never the deal breaker in an apartment decision. You survey the sunlight glinting across the golden wood floors and marvel at the open space of a bedroom—so much cleaner, simpler, and more hopeful than your complicated life. You pull the drawers of the kitchen cabinets, run your fingers along the countertop, printed with a fifties pattern that reminds you of your grandmother. The door swings shut with a solid smack, the street noise is tolerable, the rent is more than you wanted to pay, but the bus line is nearby. The bathroom is . . . well, it's the bathroom. You peeked in briefly before you signed the lease, made sure there was a toilet and nothing dead in the bathtub. It's a room the size of a closet with a few faucets. How bad or how good could it possibly be?

I never look at the bathrooms when I find a new home, but they are what I remember. In house shares and walk-up apartments, I cleaned the bathroom to cash in on double-chore karma points. As a habitual slob, I needed an easy project; white ceramic tile was my cleaning worksheet, an even surface covered with dirt. Haul out the industrial-strength Comet, a sponge, toilet cleaner, a bottle of

Windex, and a roll of paper towels. One hour later, at least one small corner of the universe will look different.

I moved in and out of ten apartments in ten years: eighteen roommates in Minnesota, Massachusetts, Ohio, and Illinois. I signed leases glad to be the fifth housemate, the one you'd never see, the one whose name would get penciled in on the chore wheel above the crossed-out name of a woman who'd just left for California. I cleaned the bathroom for temporary siblings, wiped away the intimate soil and straightened the toothbrushes, borrowed the herbal shampoo and breathed the steamy air from the showers of people whose last names I never knew and whose first names I forgot.

I don't know whether the inch-high mushroom growing from the bathroom baseboard was a tenant before we sent our first rent checks to the town's notorious slumlord. My college friends and I were too drunk on the freedom of an actual door with keys, our first grown-up apartment, an independent address with a mailbox, to notice how crappy that place was, how the unventilated attic apartment trapped heat like a steam bath in the Minnesota summer.

The bathroom wasn't crawling with mold or fungus. There was just this one white-capped mushroom with a stem about the thickness of a pencil that curved like a fish hook out into the air and then up toward the skylight, in its own steamy ecosystem a bit behind the door. One housemate screamed in laughter and called us into the bathroom. We crouched down to examine our botanical oddity. We were outdoorsy women, so the mushroom didn't seem disgusting. If anything, it was a testament to a tough strain of fungus that could travel to the second floor of a building, take root through a layer of paint, and suck nutrients from a slowly rotting strip of planed wood. I think we left it there to grow for as long as it could.

By my second rental, I was well versed in chore negotiation and what it could get me. A woman in Minneapolis invited me to rent a room in her house. I won a cut in rent by helping with housecleaning and caring for her eight-year-old son and her Huskie. I vacuumed the clouds of dog hair that filled the apartment and collected like ghosts of blackberry bushes at the baseboards. I liked to clean the bathroom in this house because it was pink and black, with a small high window in the shower where our shampoos and soaps perched on the sill like a row of flowers. I always forgot to vacuum the bathroom, though, and puffs of dog hair, coated in shower moisture and trapping dust and dirt, congealed behind the door like gentle, rolling hills of black fuzz.

Crisp and glowing in memory: I stood in that shower and turned my right shoulder away from the stream of hot water, then twisted my body to see the wrinkled plastic wrap taped over the fresh lizard tattoo on my back. Droplets of Saran Wrap caught light from the window and sparkled. A few days later I peeled back the bandage to see the red-pricked skin and the lines of fresh ink. Reborn, amphibian, in a quiet place that life had never predicted I would go.

Scrubbing Bubbles, a bathroom cleanser in an aerosol can with a blue plastic cap, foamed out of the nozzle, thick like shaving cream. In the 1970s there was a cartoony TV commercial of the animated bubbles with scrub-brush feet. They had eyes with thick eyebrows but no mouths. I was scared of them as a kid; I thought they were hiding in the drain and would sneak out to drag me with them into the pipes.

My parents set up a chart for my brother, sister, and me to claim chores for money. The bathroom had a high price attached, so I always took it, getting the cleaning done as quickly as possible. Maybe this cemented my economist cleaning approach: maximum gain for minimum effort. I have a normal fear of toxic chemicals, yet this leaves at the bathroom door. I will gladly sprinkle a bathtub with turquoise-powdered germ killer and scour away, never mind rubber gloves or proper ventilation, as if the chemical molecules have brains and eyes and know to attack only the germs.

It's one thing to clean up after family, the soil that germinated my seed. Having been born messily from someone else's body, and having stolen half-eaten pizza from a sister's plate and engaged in spit fights with my brother all confirmed our physical and organic links; we were swimming in each other's genes and germs. But how strange to clean up after a stranger, or even someone I disliked.

It was vaguely satisfying to blast the white basin with Scrubbing Bubbles and remove, even temporarily, the skin cells of a nasty housemate in my next rental. The triple-decker house in Somerville, Massachusetts, looked comfortable and casual on my housemate "interview," stocked with short-haired women, houseplants, and worn paperbacks. But the fresh smell of Pine-Sol should have been my warning. One housemate liked to mop the kitchen floor every day; she had been raised in a convent. I might not have blamed her if she had not hated me so much, had not lectured me about the health of my kitten or the proper ordering of spices in the pantry. To spite the chore wheel that hung on the refrigerator, I put off my cleaning duties until Sunday night, the cleaning deadline. Yet even here, the bathroom served as solace. After another break-up, I stood in the shower, which smelled nicely of cedar, holding a round cake of lilac organic soap. I laughed for the first time in days at my ridiculous life—once again saved, naked in the water, once again with a windowed shower where my skin caught the light—and saw how funny it was to be able to remake myself for another day, as if clean meant ready, meant together.

The shotgun apartment on Pine Street in Cambridge, Massachusetts, saved me from clean. The whole building left something to be desired, with its drafty windows and the mud pit of a front yard. A crack dealer set up every day on the corner, as casual as a hot dog stand. But the rent was cheap. My new housemate and I shared and bonded over a disdain for extensive cleaning, as if we would embrace the world in its gritty glory rather than spend the day on our hands and knees.

The bathroom was alive and should have been condemned. Lit by a bare hanging bulb, the high ceiling glistened with an evil consciousness. It was splotchy and black, a mold that grew in patches between the curls and springs of paint rippling off the plaster like pencil shavings. It seemed that an effort to clean the ceiling would have destroyed the surface tension holding the plaster in place. We used scented soaps and shower gels to cover the dank stink of mold. The bathroom felt palatial and indulgent because it had my first claw-foot tub. I turned on the hot water and lay down in this porcelain tureen, playing spa. The steam obscured the moldy sky above. I reached around the side of the tub for a letter that had arrived from a friend, and my wet fingers moistened the paper and released a rivulet of pale ink down the page into the water. I was old-fashioned, Virginia Woolf in an ancient tub, soaking in words. We had a $2 inflatable bath pillow, and there were bubbles in this heaven of hot water. A votive candle on the toilet tank cast orange flashes and shadows onto the walls, making the surface of the water look like a silvery lake at night. This, I thought, this is the life I have been looking for. The common forms of bathroom denial have nothing on this final, redemptive bathroom coping skill. Any bathroom, with the lights turned off, a candle lit, and a hot steaming bath poured, becomes an oasis, a Calgon commercial.

The loss of a lease led me to Broadway Avenue in Boston, where I shared a slanted, parallelogram house. Fire shot from the outlets. The rooms were ringed with char marks. Perhaps because the house seemed to whisper "Carpe diem"—seize the day, for tomorrow your roof may cave in—a few of my five housemates seized moments and more. The living room in this Dr. Seuss house hosted at least two orgies complete with body glitter. I steered clear but knew glitter-spackled bodies had rinsed themselves of massage oil in the bathroom at the top of the stairs, in the simple, plain beige bathtub with the brown stick-on flowers.

The women in that house were all breaking up and making clean sweeps into new lives. We painted the floor a Mexican blue-indigo, luxurious and bold. I, too, was mid-breakup, trying to resist the centrifugal pull of a destructive relationship. In the tipping point in my tipping house, I leaned into the mirror one morning to trace black eyeliner above my eyelids, slip hoop earrings into my earlobes. I stood back to see whether I looked ready for work. The mirror cut my heart; it showed skin blotchy from crying, eyes too hopeful and earnest despite themselves. My toothbrush stood surrounded by strangers' brushes in a cup on the sink, lonely and sad in that crowd. Something caught in my throat—the randomness of this anonymous moment. I was so loosely attached to the place where my cardboard boxes had come to rest.

I moved in and out of these apartments and houses throughout my twenties, and I flattened my cardboard boxes after each move and stacked them in each basement. Leases ran out, rents shot up, jobs were offered, relationships were founded and then went up in flames, and buildings were slated for renovation or demolition. My tattered cardboard boxes with the permanent marker tags for their contents—KITCHEN, BOOKS, RANDOM CRAP—were always there to catch me. In that falling-down Dr. Seuss house on Broadway, a housemate's cat peed on my long-lived boxes, and I almost couldn't throw them away. They were my constants, these cardboard hope chests layered with clear tape, their corners mashed in until they threatened to become spherical, their surfaces softened to a brown fuzz.

If the cardboard boxes were my roots, each bathroom of each new apartment was my future: There was new hope, a chance to stow my conditioner and shampoo in a crowded shower caddy, steal a bit of a roommate's fancy freesia shower gel, then wipe the steam from the mirror, and psych myself up for the day, or to take a blurry, satiated, post-sex shower, an alone-on-a-Friday-night-in-February bath.

After the Broadway house, I shared an apartment in Dorchester, Massachusetts, with a boyfriend. Our third housemate had gray teeth and had stolen thousands of dollars while working a register at a convenience store. But he was nice, with a shy smile. I crossed my fingers for him when he had a job interview. I washed his coffee cups and winced forgivingly at the stench of cigarette smoke from his bedroom. I scrubbed the bathtub, another claw-foot in a peach-painted room with curling linoleum, but I don't remember ever relaxing there in a hot bath.

Eventually we had to go into his room for something, maybe a key in an emergency, and we saw glossy towers, neat stacks of pornography, his only substantial furniture. Then we learned about a few things that were too scandalous and disturbing for cohabitation, and he left along with his magazines in cardboard boxes. Then my relationship with the boyfriend ended, and my boxes left with me.

In that narrow, steamy bathroom painted peach, I know I breathed in invisible flecks of his shaving; his whiskers and skin flakes must have landed on my toothbrush, on my soap. How can I say I am not in some small way a piece of him?

After a brief stint on friends' couches, I found a second house share in a rehabbed Victorian with an immaculate paint job. The white-tiled bathroom gleamed as in a commercial. I should have been more honest during the roommate interview—"Sure, I'm clean," I said. I should have noticed the overly careful slipcover on the sofa, the doily on the coffee table.

Once again, too clean. I spent my time elsewhere, made edgy by the constant straightening, the wiping after every breath and move. My two housemates and I communicated through notes we left on the telephone table beneath the stained-glass window.

"Sonya—When you do your dishes, please rinse/empty out food particles from the sink and drain. It's disgusting finding them later. Also, please recycle cardboard and plastic items, and please also change the toilet paper roll when it is empty. Thank you." I still have this note eight years later, and the fact that I found and still find this so hilarious probably reveals too much about my qualities as a roommate and person.

I moved on, rented apartments with bathrooms; I fell into love's speeding vehicles and then fell off their tailgates onto the gravel. Two years later, I found myself brushing my teeth every morning in a little bathroom in Columbus, Ohio. It seemed that someone had taken a full can of lilac paint and swung it against the bathroom walls. The woman who'd lived in the duplex had broken up with her girlfriend and then wanted to make herself feel better with a color that would cut through the gray, wet gloom of an Ohio winter. This was the story passed on through two other tenants to me. She painted big round lilac spots on the wall. She painted the toilet seat and the rusted pipes under the sink. She painted the gray venetian blinds, brushing right over the dust and the strings that held the blinds in place. She painted the windowsill and the baseboard. She painted the sides of the old medicine cabinet, creating lilac moonscapes over craters of rust. The sloppy, smudged paint on the blinds was more a reminder of impermanence than a Zen retreat.

I added a blue shower curtain with orange plastic rings because I wasn't going to make too much of an investment in changing the decor; this was just someplace I was passing through. Yet I remember moments there—the raw yet hopeful wound of the house—more than I remember almost any other moments in any day that year.

Another boyfriend and another move-in; we played house in an apartment on Como Avenue where the shower wall was soft to the touch. The bathroom seemed to belie our hopes for adult lives. The stall had been fitted with one of those tub-surround kits that promise to hermetically cover bathroom rot, but the glue was not stuck to a solid substance. Beneath this faded layer of plastic was something mushy and alive. Black mold crept around the edges, and each time I cleaned the shower, I told myself it was just shower grime and soap scum. During a shower, the steam billowed up to the painted ceiling above the bathtub, cloaking the surface in heat and moisture, creating a hothouse environment perfect for a strange species of brown fungus that formed circles on the ceiling. If we didn't wipe the circles every week or so, they developed into pointed stalactites that hung downward, each sporting a glistening drop of water at the tip.

I leaned in one morning—hands shaking—to apply a black line of liquid eyeliner above my lids. I slicked on shimmering gold lipstick, puckered and vamped in the dusty mirror, and left. When I came back that afternoon, I was married. The wedding is a blur, but that moment, twisting my lipsticked lips wryly in a mirror that held so many faces, is clear and solitary, the true hope in getting married, putting on a different face. I tried to clean the lovely green and black marbled tiles in that old house, and when the tiles came loose I set them in a careful pile on the floor next to the toilet. Every stacked tile said someday someone will repair this. Every bathroom hopes to be reborn.

Keeping It on the O/C

Thaddeus Rutkowski

I am obsessive/compulsive in many ways, and my housekeeping behavior is one of the ways. "Housekeeping" might not be the right word; I mean house tidying or house ordering.

I can't leave our Lower East Side apartment without going through a mental checklist that involves windows, appliances, faucets, lights, locks, and personal possessions. An unlatched window could admit a burglar—our windows are two stories above street level, one opens onto a fire escape, and one is within stretching distance of the metal ladder. A leaking valve on the stove could fill the apartment with gas—a time bomb waiting for a spark. A slowly running faucet may fill a stopped sink and flood the apartment below, and the storefront below that. An unattended electrical device could somehow destroy the place. The toaster oven might overheat, and the radiant elements may ignite a nearby box of tissues or roll of paper towels. A lit light-bulb, if it is stronger than the recommended wattage—100 watts instead of 60, say—may cause voltage to pool in the wiring and ignite the insulation in the ceiling. A computer visible through a window may incite a passing criminal to make the leap onto the fire ladder.

If my wife and daughter are leaving with me, they have to wait while I physically complete my checklist. I have to latch, unplug, tighten, switch off, and conceal. The two of them may be outside the front door of the building, ringing the buzzer to get my attention, but I will ignore them so I can put things in order. The refrigerator always presents a problem. Are the doors to the freezer and cooler sealed? Will the vibrations of passing traffic ease the doors open and shake loose breakable containers, sending them to the floor where they will burst?

Such a thing has happened. Once, I answered a knock on our apartment door and faced a man who lived below. "There's white liquid dripping from our ceiling," he said.

A search for the source of the white liquid led to an overturned carton of milk.

Should I unplug the giant appliance or leave it plugged in? Will a disconnected refrigerator flood the place with meltwater? Will a connected refrigerator rumble amok while we are out?

On the outside of the door, I have to use two keys repeatedly. The door locks require only one key turn. But I have to turn each of the two keys ten times, for a total of twenty turns, to make sure I've thrown the tumblers. Then I twist the doorknob to the right three times and repeat this process three times to make sure the locks are tight. Next, I bang on the door with my hand to make sure it will not swing open. Then I twist the knob a few more times. If my wife or daughter rings the buzzer while I'm outside the apartment door, I ignore it. Going in to answer the intercom would mean repeating the lock-locking and knob-turning. As I walk away from the door, I look at the seam between the door itself and the frame. I don't want to see any large cracks that mean it isn't shut.

My wife and daughter, as far as I know, are not obsessive/compulsive, unless an inability to discard things (on my wife's part) is O/C. Crates of my wife's papers, from all stages of her life, fill our shared bedroom.

Actually, I can't discard things, either. I have stacks of books signed by authors who are my friends, who will never be famous but whose signatures are somehow meaningful to me. These stacks are so precarious I knock them over frequently, then pile the volumes on ledges again. I don't want to cart these books away. I'd be embarrassed to have a stranger pick one up in a used-book store and read the affectionate inscription.

Our seven-year-old daughter is too young to have a pattern of housekeeping behavior. She likes the idea of washing dishes, for example, but doesn't know how. She'll stand on a chair at the sink and let the water run over a dish, but she won't scrub the ceramic. She'll take a broom to a rug, but she lacks the strength to work the sand out of the fabric. She'll push a wet mop over the kitchen floor, but she'll get more water on the floor than she'll pick up with the sponge head—and the floor will hold a large puddle.

She is good, however, at picking up wooden blocks with me. "Put the big ones on the top," she says as we stack the shapes in a box. "I don't want to have to dig for them."

My wife is good at cleaning certain areas. Her specialty is the kitchen countertop and all things on it. She sponges the dish drainer and the coffeemaker, as well as the Formica. Then she moves on to the stovetop, where she removes the metal grills to get at the grooves around the gas burners. When she is finished, it is my turn to attack the floor. Clean kitchen surfaces make it easier to spot nocturnal insect pests.

The tank holding our daughter's pet turtle is my wife's responsibility. I won't go near the cloudy water—replacing it with clean water is beyond me. But my wife empties, scrubs, and refills the tank without hesitation. She admits she's closer to the turtle emotionally than our daughter is or I am. All I'm good for is carrying the tank to a faucet and watching the untanked red-eared slider while the cleaning is going on.

I credit my wife with getting at the bathroom tiles. I can apply grout, but I don't clean grout. The idea of scraping at the dirt between tiles with my fingernail or a toothbrush reminds me of what a Norwegian houseboy might do while his mistress prepares for her bath. I'm not at all Norwegian, but I suppose I could play the role when I'm in the mood. Yes, my spouse could call me Mr. Clean while I work on the mold in my apron and nothing else. I would not stop until I was told.

How do we live together? Well, we accept each other's cleaning shortcomings. Our standards for neatness are low. A swept rug constitutes a clean living room. Never mind the stacks of child's games, videocassettes, and ancient newspapers that fill a window and block the sun. And never mind the mysterious dust-covered objects—finger rings, hair fasteners, plastic parts of larger constructions—that occupy the spaces between the furniture bottoms and the floor.

Some places are just too gross to clean, and the idea of going to those places makes me squeamish. The floor below the refrigerator is one such area. I'll clean there only for a special occasion—to prepare for the visit of a close friend or relative. I went there recently. I embraced the refrigerator with a bear hug and walked it out from its niche in a slow dance. I took a broom to the oily dust on the exposed linoleum tiles. By sweeping, I collected magnetic alphabet letters, a spatula, uncooked pasta, and the dried carcass of a small rodent—a grim reminder of one of my previous poisoning efforts.

I couldn't keep quiet about my grizzly discovery. "I found a dead mouse," I announced to my family.

My wife recognized it first. "It looks like it's been dead a long time," she said.

Our daughter couldn't make it out—it had changed so much from its living form. Then she said, "It has no skin."

Actually, it had only skin; it had no flesh, no meat, no juice.

The good news was, along with the garbage, I found a dollar coin that our daughter had lost. The coin had been kicked under the refrigerator. I returned it to her, and she put it in her bunny-shaped wallet. "I have $54," she said. "If we had $15 million, we could buy a mansion."

The mansion, I hoped, would include a cleaning staff.

After I'd mopped the floor and replaced the refrigerator, I was proud of my achievement. "Doesn't that look good?" I asked, pointing to the four-inch strip of rodent-free linoleum between the refrigerator and the wall. I said it more than once, but my wife and daughter weren't interested in re-inspecting my work.

I didn't get under the stove on that occasion. I don't know when I will, and Lord knows what I'll find when I finally do.

It might be easier to tackle the wall above the toaster oven. Our daughter, from her seat at our eating table, noticed the area recently and asked, "What's wrong with the wall?"

What was wrong was that it had grown greasy fur, which not only stuck to the paint but also framed a painting I'd made of an orange, a green pepper, and a wine bottle. The still life would definitely get brighter, sharper, when I got around to dusting it.

Adventures in Fluff

Teena Apeles

I have thick black hair. It's been many other warm hues over the years and varying lengths, but the point is, unless you live in a home with all dark furniture and dark floors, you're gonna see it—everywhere. My partner, Charles, on the other hand, has thin, light-brown hair, which miraculously never shows up anywhere. But our roommates more than make up for his weak contribution to the hair universe that seems to rule our single-story house in Los Angeles. We share our abode with a menagerie of animals, which included at its height a Pekin duck, a multicolored chow-chow, a white cat, a blue parakeet, two white-headed nun finches, and three tanks of fish—making quite a household of hair, feathers, fur, and (fish food) flakes to do battle with daily.

It's been a constant fascination of mine to visit people's homes in which not a trace of hair can be found. Because in my world, hair marks the spot. I've read that people lose an average of a hundred hairs a day. So add my daily hair loss to that of my animals' and that would be a good reason to hire someone to cope with the furry madness. I know that the majority of my friends who live an enviable speck-free existence don't have as many animals as we do, if any, and most of them do have a weekly or monthly cleaning person who helps out. Well, we've tried that. Or, rather, my sisters and parents have graciously hired folks as a present to us—knowing our plight—to try to alleviate the stress and lighten the burden of keeping our home tidy. (We don't have much disposable income after all.) On those few occasions, even the cleaning professionals have left our home completely exhausted—one young woman said, "I can't do it, it's just too much, so much pet hair. . . . " And they rarely came close to being as obsessive as I was over wiping down every surface, seeking out every wandering feather. Plus, I needed to do it for my own good. The truth is, cleaning gives me a sense of purpose at times when it doesn't seem like I have a role in this world. At home, there are always things to be dusted, sucked up, disposed of.

Until recently, the majority of our home was covered in carpet, ugly old turquoise carpet, to be exact. The room that we spend the most time in—like most people—is our (sunken) family room. This is the same place where all but two tanks of fish spend their time. Well, yes, Panduck lived outdoors most of the time, but when we hung all together, it was in this perfectly square room into which six different doorways (kitchen, two hallways, living room, guest bedroom, sliding door) emptied, along with whatever stuck to people's feet and our animals' paws or webbed feet on the way in. This was my greatest battlefield: tufts of dog fur, white cat hair strewn along the carpet with mine, colored fish flakes around one cabinet, and assorted feathers throughout (birds and ducks flap around like hyperactive children).

How does one begin to confront such a mess? We choose to be resourceful with what we have. While a vacuum would be a no-brainer, we've actually killed three traversing the hairy room, from old to new to borrowed. When that much hair gets in, belts break, engines smoke, brushes forget how to turn. Another one bites the dust or drowns in hair. I guess most people—those with disposable income—would invest in a Dyson (so many upper-middle-class people I know swear by it), but my freelance writer's salary combined with Charles's archaeologist salary leaves us little to splurge on such extravagances. That goes for hardwood floors as well. Other necessities come first. Like food.

We have taken some precautions over the years to explore ways to prevent such a hairy mess. Brushing our dog Pogi and cat Samantha often or dressing them in sweaters to contain their furriness. Buying elastic mesh to put around the birdcages to keep their feathers (and seeds) at bay. Me pulling my hair back daily. Being extra careful putting fish food in the tank. But such actions did little to decrease our cleaning workload. And Pogi and Sammy simply hated sporting an extra layer. They had enough on their own after all.

So I developed my own cleaning program. You know how there are activities you do when you're alone that you're too embarrassed to do in front of other people? That's me when it comes to my program. I am pretty anal. My dad is the same way actually, pacing around busying himself until every speck is gone. I used to make fun of him for it, but my pets often stare at me in horror as I zip around the house nitpicking in the same fashion. It's as if they're saying, "Stop the crazy woman." That's especially the case when I tackle the family room by doing the Teena shuffle.

Once a week, I put on my pair of blue Adidas running shoes—that never get used for running—to do my cleaning dance. I generally am dressed in workout clothes, because this is how I keep in shape. My typical soundtrack: a mix of NPR programs, indie rock, and R&B. I start at one corner of the room and map out an approximately two-by-two-foot square. Imagine a Dance Dance Revolution control pad, and you've got my typical square footage covered. And I move in the same direction that the arrows would be on the pad. To the right and back to center, to the left then center, forward and back to center as well. And just as the game orders the player in different directions and speeds on the pad, the ordering and beat of my steps during the Teena shuffle vary as well.

Most of the time I favor my right leg. In fact, it's probably the most toned for this reason. First there's the side step where I drag my right foot across the carpet, carrying whatever extra fuzz, hair, crumbs, what-have-you into a bunch in the center. Then left, then right, up and down. With each stroke of my trusty Adidas tread, I drag unwanted mess into the center. Once I finish a square, I move on to the next. For that one room, the whole process can take anywhere from a half hour to an hour depending on the workload. These piles of fluff accumulate around the room. I always feel a sense of accomplishment just looking at them. The turquoise carpet never looks so blue. Of course, there's also that moment of disgust thinking about all the crap my Adidas collected. Then, one by one, I go around the room, pick each mound up, and throw them into the trash. Then I bring the vacuum in for the final cleanup. (So far our fourth one, a purple Bissell, compliments of my dad, has survived because of this new cleaning program.)

Charles has his own on-all-fours method. He likes to attack things at eye level, which means getting down on his hands and knees and saying to the hair, fur, feathers, seed, and flakes, "You're in trouble." His weapon of choice—a steel pet brush. And whereas I tackle a square at a time, he likes to move across like a typewriter. Start at one end and brush, brush, brush all the way across until he reaches one wall. Then move over a couple feet and move back toward the other end. Charles brushes, I scrape. Pet brush vs. Adidas trainers. Which one dominates? As long as the job gets done, it doesn't matter, though Charles claims his program leaves no hair behind.

"Just look at my piles compared to yours," he likes to argue. He, too, finishes it off with the vacuum. Who looks the most ridiculous when tackling the carpeted rooms? It depends what each of us is wearing that day, I suppose. My family thinks we both look stupid.

We've thought about building a sculpture out of these mounds. I remember seeing an (arguably disgusting) art installation that a woman created out of used waxing strips. The artist collected a pretty obscene amount of hair, which probably represented the hair of 50 or so women, that filled a whole room. Could our fluff be museum worthy? I would have to say yes. What once was considered annoying or disposable can become treasured. And I'm not talking vinyl records or antiques. In our case, it became feathers.

Oftentimes, when I clean up after my animals—their food, their vomit, their fur, their waste—I reflect on what it would be like for me to clean up after a child, many of them. Having a menagerie is the stomping ground to prepare me for a life as a mother. Or cleaning up after any loved ones, say an aging parent. But such chores can drive a person crazy, me included. There are those moments when I can't believe how much time I spend caring for these animals, cleaning up their respective messes. That is, until they die. Many fish have passed over the years, as is to be expected. No more tanks operate in our home, and flaky food isn't on our grocery lists anymore. But the worst loss to date, was a couple of years ago when our beautiful and talkative white duck, Panduck, was killed in our back yard by a raccoon. Experiencing the death of a pet taken in such a manner, so unexpectedly, was really difficult for us.

I actually miss having to fill and rinse out his pool and food bowls every day. I miss having him flutter about the house leaving his feathers everywhere—feathers that sometimes ended up in the mouths of our other animals or on our clothes. Cleaning the house took on a whole new meaning after his death. Instead of sweeping and brushing up hair and whatnot indiscriminately, we searched out Panduck's feathers. With each remnant of him we found in the house, I built an altar with photos and placed his feathers in a special locket and keepsake box. I collected enough to even remind me of his smell. It's now been a couple of years since that dreadful event, and I still find random duck fuzz on a bookcase or in a corner during my cleaning expeditions, and now it actually makes me smile. I take that old Panduck feather and add it to his shelf.

I don't stockpile Sammy and Pogi's fur—yet—but each time my budgie Birdie or finches, Merlin and Ibon, leave large feathers in their cages or the feathers find their way beyond the mesh onto our floors, I start a collection that lines the shelf above our fireplace. Every piece counts.

This past fall, when Charles moved to Edinburgh for the year to pursue his master's degree, I moved temporarily into a studio apartment in Montreal and took just Sammy with me, but the adventures in fluff have continued. After living in a four-bedroom home for a decade, I was extremely excited about the prospect of cleaning up after just me and one other animal in a tiny space. Goodbye, turquoise carpet; hello, dull confetti linoleum floor. With a smaller space, I thought, my fuzzy headaches would subside. Not so. Now I clean daily.

As I type this, I spot in the far left-hand corner of my apartment the enemy. Tucked away underneath my bookcase is a ball of ivory carpet fuzz, Sammy hair, and, yes, long black hair tumbled up in them. It taunts me. I always thought it would be funny to have some high-powered fancy cams, like the ones they use to examine bugs and flowers, and have a number of them positioned throughout my apartment to capture the development of such balls. Obviously it has much to do with my and Sammy's movements throughout the day, pushing these things every which direction. Of course, my cleaning program has changed. No need for Adidas here. I have but a small shaggy carpet to deal with, and for some reason, with this type of carpet, the mounds collect on their own and then are blown around my itty-bitty studio.

Now I attack my furry hybrid friends with just my hands and throw them into the trash. I also have a tape roller and lint remover to take care of my and Samantha's hair on the furniture. "Jaws" (Shark wireless vacuum) eats up the rest of the dust and random cat litter left on the floor. Surprisingly, the little dust bunnies provide entertainment and fascination for Samantha and me. We are actually comforted by their appearance or go in search for them. It's like, "Oh, hey, I know you." And wrapped up in these little mounds are us . . . her fur, my hair, and that of our lowly rug. We should enjoy it while it lasts, because in a few months, the menagerie, Charles, and I will return to the house that fluff built.

Meanwhile, I'm amused to see the little balls dance across the floor and even more charmed by seeing visitors to our very humble abode leave with a piece of me and Samantha or our rug on them. It's funny. We touch people. Maybe when they go home, instead of thinking *Damn fuzz*, they'll think, *Isn't it nice to be close to our friends.*

Cleaning Up

Nancy Stiefel

W hen I was a child, our house was clean and orderly. My mother, who stayed at home, did this without resentment, and perhaps with some pride. She was not a martyr. One could argue that without an audience, martyrdom cannot exist, and we never saw my mother cursing and yanking the vacuum cleaner or muttering on her hands and knees, scrubbing. When my brother and I came home from school, the house was clean and we didn't give a thought to it. The housework was done beyond our view, but the downside of this was that we never learned to do it ourselves and so are bad at it. Children do learn at the knees of their caregivers. If a parent washes, sorts, irons, folds, and puts away clothes unnoticed, the child does not see how it is done and does not seek opportunities to proudly help. I taught myself these tasks as an adult, but it was a lonely business, with no pleasant memories to guide my hands to efficiency. And to this day, I cannot put the clean clothes away in a drawer. I cannot put things away. My father contributed to cleaning when he was at home. Orderliness pleased him. I remember opening his drawer in my parents' bedroom and admiring the contents: a pen and pencil and eraser; a penknife, ruler, money clip, comb, and nail clippers; a watch, keys (when he was home)—each calmly in its place. Drawers in my kitchen contain jumbles of disparate objects, some stuck together. Sometimes the drawers won't close or open without a struggle. There are no drawers in my bedroom because I cannot put things away. Clothes and books remain expectantly in piles, on chairs, on top of full boxes, testaments to failed attempts at cleaning up.

In my childhood kitchen, my father's domain when he cooked, each implement was kept clean and in its place, at the ready, cleaned right after use, and replaced in its special spot. "While it's in your hand, put it away," I hear his voice saying as I leave the mayonnaise jar in one place, drop the spoon somewhere else, and make the top of the jar vanish, to my father's contempt. He had a grasp of the graceful whole of an act, an arc of preparing a meal with pleasing efficiency that included using the precisely right knife for the job that he had precision-sharpened beforehand. I am embattled in the kitchen. Preparing a meal involves futile searching for the right implement, making do with an inferior substitute, casting it aside when I'm finished with it. The meal reflects the resentful carelessness with which I prepare it. Lately, though, I enjoy cleaning up, because the kitchen is a finite area responsive to concentrated work. The house is another story.

Order pleases me enormously, but it is a pleasure I do not wish to work to create, nor does any one else in my household. As a result, home is chaotic. I've named it "The Shambles." Important documents disappear for weeks, sometimes months. No sock has a mate; even shoes become separated from each other. Only the book I am currently reading is safe, because I leave it with my glasses next to my pillow, where I can find both the next day.

I blame my parents for my housekeeping failures. Since my mother did not call attention to housecleaning chores, did not complain or ask for help, or make us aware of her daily commitment to our ordered lives, I never understood that a neat and clean home requires constant, daily work. I passively wait for the miracle of neatness to occur, and it does not. I resent that after cleaning and polishing my kitchen, the same thing has to be repeated the very next time a meal is cooked. This is an outrage to humanity. It reminds me of how my four-year-old son resisted brushing his teeth. "I did it yesterday!" he would argue.

Perhaps I am waiting for a parent, an adult, to step in and take care of things. Or perhaps life for me must be confusion, with everything in sight: a kaleidoscope of piles constantly shifting and re-sorting themselves. My household matter is a living, breathing thing made up of many things that move, hide, and resurface before being covered up yet again. They possess a mischievous energy. Put them away and they are dead. Perhaps I unconsciously believe that if I put things away, my life will be over.

I fear that if I pare down my possessions to essentials and put each item away in its own place, the work of life will be finished. The frenzied search for the passport—it was in that drawer, with the takeout menus, for so long!—will not be necessary. If I don't see my things all around me, I won't have them, won't need them. The striving to gather, to collect, to search, and eventually find will fall away. There will be no required, annoying effort, no hope for progress. There will be only quiet neatness, clear surfaces, the peace that I yearn for each day and that each day eludes me.

Abhorring a Vacuum

Mindy Lewis

" *I* hesitate to say this, darling, but your apartment is frightening."
My neighbor, a retired piano teacher, speaks with motherly
concern. "Suppose you meet a nice man. How can you invite him
over?" She gestures at the piles of papers, paintings, and books that
dominate my living room/home office.

I know she means well, but I'm taken aback. I pride myself
on my sense of order and think of the clutter in my apartment as
charmingly eccentric evidence of the three-headed hydra of my
creative life: graphic designer, painter, writer. Paintings hang along
every inch of the walls (the best lateral storage). Stacks of books
represent a stratified archaeology of interests over the decades:
calligraphy, psychology, Buddhism, French symbolist poets, artistic
anatomy, landscape painting . . . all the way up to computer manuals.
My stuff is *who I am.*

Like my neighbor, I am one of a rare breed, destined for
extinction: a native New Yorker with a rent-stabilized Upper West
Side apartment in a classic prewar high rise. I consider my absurdly

low rent—a relic of a kinder era—my own little artist's subsidy. It's mine by inheritance: My mother's second husband grew up here with his parents, who remained here until sweet Sadie of the trembling ladle passed quietly away and dapper, dignified Sam moved to the King David seniors' residence, leaving the apartment to me and his hat and cane in the hall closet.

When I moved into this apartment in 1971, I had no idea I'd still be living here thirty-seven years later. From my home base, I've watched the neighbors' kids grow up, go off to college, get married, and come back to visit with their own kids in tow. I've witnessed familiar faces exit the building a final time, wheeled out to waiting ambulettes. Having spent my entire adult life in this building, I can't help but wonder if one day I will be carried out of here, too, though I imagine being hauled out by crane—if they can find me in the midst of this clutter.

My place wasn't always such a mess. In the early days, I worked hard to keep it pristine. In fact, when I moved in here—my very first apartment—at age nineteen, I arrived with next to nothing, just a small trunk filled with clothes, books, and treasured possessions (the trunk would double as living-room table, surrounded by throw pillows). Just beginning my adult life, I considered myself a pioneer and dedicated myself to shedding my mother's defining influence, taking pleasure in discovering—or inventing—my independent self.

Newly arrived, I registered each detail: the herringbone parquet oak floors with maple trim, picture moldings, cut-glass doorknobs, honeycomb-pattern hexagonal bathroom tiles edged in age-darkened grout. Wherever you looked, the place had character. It also had layers of grime. Evidently Sadie and Sam didn't see too well in their old age; the ancient stove and dishes were encrusted with remnants of Sadie's cooking (now nourishing the resident roach colony), and the colorful balloon-pattern linoleum didn't hide the crumbs, spills, and decades of dirt quite enough. The place smelled musty, dusty, *old*.

I double-locked the door, looked around, and felt the buzz of possibility. I would make this place my own, starting from scratch. I decided to get rid of the heavy, dark furniture; I'd sell what I could and give the rest away. I unfurled my Indian-print paisley bedspread over the indentations left in the sagging mattress by Sam and Sadie, headed out to Broadway to buy cleaning supplies, then came home and *attacked*. I spent my first two weeks stripping the place down, doing my best to make it light and airy.

At first I swept and dusted daily and mopped once a week, usually on Sundays, while listening to my beloved scratchy records of flute duets, Doc Watson, the Grateful Dead. My newfound domesticity felt poignant and piercing. "Home sings me of sweet things, my life there has its own wings," I'd sing along with Linda Ronstadt. As I worked, I pondered the great questions: What was my life's purpose? Did I have it in me to be an artist? How would I make a living? Would I ever find lasting love? With each swish of the mop, I'd vow to be strong, capable, independent, creative. All I needed was a true heart, elbow grease, and a do-it-yourself attitude.

My methods were primitive. I sloshed ammonia-laced water over the parquet floors, but instead of dissolving the dark, brittle layer of floor wax, it turned it a lurid green. In one of the kitchen cabinets, I found a chisel, hammer, sandpaper, and, under the sink, Sadie's scrub brush. Down on my hands and knees, I rubbed, scrubbed, and scraped the blackened wax, until I found it yielded more successfully to dry sanding. Inch by inch, using squares of sandpaper wrapped around a block of wood, I hand-sanded the floor, beginning in the corner of the bedroom, working my way toward the center. The logical solution—renting a sanding machine—was beyond my budget but also an insult to my romantic notions of self-invention. No machines for me! No fan, no air-conditioning, and, most emphatically, no vacuum cleaner!

I have always hated vacuum cleaners. For one thing, there's the sound: an impersonal whining drone that drowns out comfort and pleasure, screaming: *Nothing is permanent, there's nothing that can't get sucked up into my nozzle, and if you think you can escape you'd better get out of my way! If not, I'll swallow you and you'll disappear in an instant!* It's a sound of arbitrary, voracious hunger. A vacuum cleaner does not discriminate. Anything that crosses its path—coins, lost earrings, buttons, fallen paper clips, small living creatures, dust balls, crumbs, outdoor dirt, indoor dust, microscopic particles—is equally stripped of value.

Supposedly a timesaving tool, a vacuum puts humans to work. Dependent upon its user for locomotion, it lurches behind like a demented pet, blindly banging and crashing into furniture, walls, and shins, while its cord, an uncoiling snake, wraps and tangles and trips us up. When it eats something it can't digest, it chokes, screeches, whines, grinds, and wheezes a protracted, staccato, hair-raising aria of machine complaint.

I grew up with the sound of the vacuum. The appearance of the vacuum—wielded on weekdays by Marie, our part-time housekeeper, while my mother was at work—signaled an interval of empty time in the afternoon. For me, its roar was the sound of inescapable loneliness that in an instant cut off the sound of the human voice. I'd hum loudly while it was going and be startled at its cessation by the sudden reappearance of my voice. Marie hummed, too, her voice warm and melodious and comforting; between strokes of the vacuum I'd catch strains of bluesy gospel.

On Saturdays, in preparation for a dinner party, my mother would vacuum, too. Often she'd be irritated at having to clean on her day off, or annoyed at my brother and me for making a mess. I knew to stay out of the way. The drone of the vacuum provided a cushion of sound that both muffled and contained a queasy, unnamable anxiety. It hinted at a larger vacuum: a malaise, a paralysis of life force, a void into which everything familiar disappeared. An absent father, a dissatisfied mother, an unknown future—everything swirled into the vacuum's relentless roar.

Then it was over, the cord unplugged and recoiled, the air stunningly silent. Always, that sudden sense of difference, the living room made too perfect to feel at home in. The beige carpeting, its nap standing newly on end, posed a tempting challenge: I could surreptitiously draw in it with my toe, reversing the nap, then swoosh my socked foot over it to erase it, leaving in invisible writing the secret mark of my presence.

Over the years, I shared my apartment with a succession of roommates—seventeen in all—each of whom had their own cleaning (or noncleaning) style. One roommate dubbed me Olive Oyl, for the way I stood, arms crossed, foot tapping, as I struggled to find a way to ask her to clean up that didn't seem too controlling. Who was I kidding? I couldn't go to sleep with dishes in the sink, or without straightening the things on my dresser. I didn't have to look far to see the reflection of my mother.

My longest cohabitation, in my early twenties, was my first, indelible, live-in love affair. As a gift, my boyfriend's mother gave us a compact, portable General Electric vacuum cleaner in a fashionable sixties palette of orange and gray. A hand-me-down that had already afforded years of use, this machine was seemingly invincible (even after it stood on end for many years in my broom closet). During the three years my boyfriend lived with me, I vacuumed around him as he sprawled on the floor (the parquet temporarily covered by a rhya rug, another hand-me-down from his parents) in front of the TV. I enjoyed these domestic scenes and felt womanly and grown up (although once, as a statement, I deliberately left his socks out of the wash, which hurt his feelings).

After the relationship ended, the sight of the vacuum was painfully depressing, reminding me of the vacuum my life had become. I had dropped out of college, my relationship had failed; I couldn't get a grip, couldn't calm down. I was too upset and ashamed to see my friends. But I could clean. Washing dishes, scrubbing the tub, mopping, dusting, straightening, making the bed—I couldn't undo my mistakes, but these were things I could control.

Then, when everything was in its place, I'd walk. No destination, just whichever way the light was green, until the din and dust of the streets turned me back toward home. But the solace of arrival only lasted so long before my empty, orderly apartment again became a prison. I had a clean apartment, but I had no life.

Slowly, I healed. I left the GE in the broom closet and did my best to fill the void by focusing on work, art, and the care and feeding of a series of cats who ran hissing from the sound of the vacuum. When I finally gave it away, its motor still functional and bag intact (a quality machine), I felt a physical sense of relief.

My life fills with work, art, friends. I graduate from paste-up artist to graphic designer, continue painting, start writing. My apartment fills with stuff, which grows out from the walls in layers, the floor space gradually diminishing. A boyfriend wedges slats of wood atop the moldings high in the hallway, where I pile canvases, easels, rolls of canvas overhead (I imagine the headline: "Artist Crushed to Death in Hallway"). With so much stuff, vacuuming becomes more difficult; even digging the machine out of the packed closet is a time-consuming, frustrating effort.

Dust gathers. I ignore it. My sinuses rebel, making me miserable, and I tire of taking round after round of antibiotics. A long-overdue paint job—the first in twenty-three years—forces me to clean up . . . for a while. Afterward, boxes sit around unopened, onto which are piled papers, folders, books—and more dust. When I receive the advance for my first book, the first thing I do is buy appliances: a new air conditioner, an air purifier, a DustBuster.

DustBusters are a doable compromise. They're compact, easily portable, and don't make that hellish noise. They're small enough that I feel they're under my control, but cordless ones aren't powerful enough. A good solution, until, sooner or later, they ultimately gurgle, whine, and die. I've listened to a half dozen of their little motors bite the dust; they may be fine for cars but just can't stand up to my kind of dirt. Nor can I stand up to their demands; bending over was fine fifteen years ago, but now my lower back rebels.

I ogle state-of-the-art machines posed like sleek, alluring mermaids in hardware-store windows; extravagant, sultry models in citrus green and lipstick red, with names like Carina and Botticelli—a far cry from the clunky cylindrical Hoover my grandmother dragged behind her for decades.

Then I find the one made for me, on sale at Target. My silver Super Shark is slightly bigger than a 'Buster and more powerful than a cordless. Plant stems and leaves, paper clips: It all gets sucked up into the cup-shaped filter by a compact but capable motor hidden inside the handle. Beautifully designed—if not quite as "whisper silent" as the packaging promises. At first I use it often, but soon, reverting to my neglectful ways, I leave my new toy to gather dust.

So how do I clean? I wipe away the dust I can't ignore with whatever's nearby—a Kleenex, a sock, my hand. I blow on the tops of books. I gather tumbleweeds from the floor with my fingers, and when there are too many I enlist the help of my Super Shark to suck up the accruals along edges, in corners. I sweep on occasion with my nesting plastic broom-and-pan duo. I mop the floors maybe twice a year. There's too much stuff to mop around, and not enough time.

Gradually, I just stop *seeing*. The dust is ubiquitous; it's become part of the surface of things. The drips on the kitchen floor blend with the speckled linoleum I installed—was it eighteen years ago? Can it be that I've become like Sam and Sadie? I imagine with a shudder what this place would look like to strangers if I were to suddenly drop dead.

I know I need help, but I resist the idea of hiring someone. The thought of an outsider judging my familiar squalor fills me with shame. Besides, how can anyone possibly clean here, with all this stuff? And how can I trust a stranger to comprehend my sense of order? The piles of papers are my external memory. I know what's where: drafts-in-progress, graphics layouts, billing, travel plans, receipts to be filed, bills to be paid, essays to read, and the unclassifiable. I would have to spend hours cleaning up for the cleaner, and then, what would be the point?

A friend tells me about a Hungarian couple, Attila and Rita, who clean her apartment. They work as a team and use only green cleansers. There's something about their names . . . they sound just exotic enough, strong enough, old world enough to do this job. It would take a warrior, or a couple—Attila and his Hon—to clean this apartment.

On the appointed morning, Attila and Rita arrive at my door. They are younger than I expected, a pleasant, fresh-faced couple. Tall and open-faced, Attila does most of the talking; diminutive, inscrutable Rita breaks in occasionally to address him in Hungarian.

"What would you like us to do? Would you like us to do this room only?"

I tell them I'd like them to clean and mop all the floors, and dust wherever it's dusty.

"We have only two hours, and we can't do everything," says Attila. Rita's face is expressionless—or is that a frown?

"Oh, yes," I add. "Could you please vacuum the rug?" I've had the kilim for three years and have DustBusted it only twice.

"Do you have a vacuum cleaner?"

"Well, sort of. . . . " I escort them to the place in my bedroom where my Shark sits neglected on the floor. I'm afraid my quirky ways may be deemed unacceptable. Maybe they'll think this is too hard a job and decide not to do it.

"I know this machine. I can work with it," Attila answers, and I relax.

But the clock's ticking. Rita's already working on the bookshelves, lifting and replacing each framed photograph to dust beneath it. My presence no longer needed, I head off to the gym.

Two hours later, I'm excited to get home and experience my "new" apartment.

I walk in. The place is so . . . clean, smelling slightly of citrus. The floors appear less scuffed, without that familiar dull film. All the exposed surfaces have been dusted: bookshelves, tabletops, file cabinets. My desk is a marvel—I haven't seen so much of its bare surface in years. Everywhere I look, I sense Rita's hands have been there, while Attila has run the mop over every inch of exposed floor. I inspect each surface: tabletops, bookshelves, desk. Mostly, everything is where it should be, just more neatly arranged. And I know the vacuum has been at work: The kilim looks renewed, its earthy reds and greens just a shade brighter.

They've used half a roll of paper towels, two inches of Citrus Magic All Purpose Cleaner, and fourteen of sixteen Pledge Dust & Allergen Unscented Dry Cloths. Yet the place is gleaming. I don't know how they did it, and in only two hours. I'm excited about the possibilities. Next time, I think I'll ask them to do the kitchen and bathroom.

Meanwhile, if they can do it, why can't I? I pluck one of the remaining hypoallergenic wipes from the packet on the kitchen table and run it along at random, looking for places they missed: corner shelves, windowsills, kitchen blinds. Satisfaction! With each stroke I rediscover not only the pleasure I used to take in cleaning but also the energy and spirit of my younger self, long buried under the dust. When I'm done I scour the sink with Bon Ami and feel I am indeed a good friend, back in my own good graces.

Attila and Rita have left little trace of the dirt they've gathered. The sponges are all rinsed clean. The mop sits in the bucket, just outside the bathroom. The Shark is enthroned on a chair in my bedroom, hose dangling, its cord wrapped neatly around its little silver body, looking sleek and shiny. They've even cleaned the mighty mini Shark and restored it to a place of honor.

Seized by a sudden urge to tell my mother about my new apartment, I pick up the phone—it, too, is free of dust. Before I dial, I look around once more. There are still papers to sort, things to throw away. But for now the dust is under control.

The Mess at Midlife

Rand Richards Cooper

*T*en years ago I was asked to do a piece for a magazine series about writers and the rooms they work in. I wrote an essay called "The Holy Mess," in which I described the chronic chaos of my study. Actually, I didn't simply describe it but celebrated it, perceiving in the mayhem around me something like a writer's creative chaos.

The other day I dug this essay out and reread it—first with mounting incredulity, then annoyance. Who was this person who surveyed his personal chaos with such complacent serenity, waxing lyrical over "the sea of pens and magazines, festering coffee cups, accusatory bills, and chewed-up dog toys," over "books strewn and piled, propped open to the page where I finally tracked and cornered some vagrant, fugitive phrase"?

That mess was my mess, identifiably still the same. But the attitude was different—the voice, with all that lavish, rhapsodic metaphor. "A writer plants these things around him," I had written, "making a garden rich with stories, where—he hopes—his own imagination may be coaxed to flower." And further:

Housecleaning can be strangely redemptive, and for a writer even more so. The unconscious heaping things up for the conscious to order and shape: there's a dialectic to creativity, which means, you gotta be messy and then you gotta clean it up.

Come on, I thought as I read, give me a break! I found I disliked the person who had written those lines. In fact, I hated him. I hated his style, or something about it, anyway. But what?

The truth about style is that it arises from the entirety of one's circumstances, and from the self amid those circumstances. The person who wrote those lavish sentences a decade ago was someone with a lot of time on his hands. The sentences reek of leisure. That is what I hated—envied, really. The relaxation. The confidence. The ease.

And here's the difference in circumstances: Back then I was a thirty-nine-year-old writer with a live-in girlfriend. Now I am a forty-nine-year-old husband . . . with a two-year-old daughter.

I won't stop here to catalogue the joy, wonder, and hilarity Larkin has brought into my life. I'm focusing here on the challenges. By the time you're in your late forties, you've had decades to perfect your system, and an infant makes for a very large monkey wrench thrown in the works. I go through my days clanking, leaking, hissing: a writer with a blown gasket. I'm so badly in need of repair, I sometimes suspect people can hear me coming halfway down the street.

The main problem is time, time, time—the lack of it. Every day I'm overwhelmed by that always-behind feeling, that running-around-like-a-chicken feeling. Red alert! Red alert! Which crisis is bleeding too badly to ignore? What can I let wait? What is beyond saving? For an older first-time dad who takes care of a toddler half the day, life feels like a constant triage.

Okay, so I was never the most organized person to begin with. (I've been known to run about the house shouting, "Where are my car keys?" only to discover them *in my hand*.) And my office has always been a mess. But, as my previous essay attested, there used to be a method to that mess. Yes, things piled up, but I knew, more or less, what was in the piles. If I needed to find the car registration renewal I'd put aside a week before, or the article I'd torn out of the newspaper, I could hone in on it. And every few months I'd go on a massive organizing binge where I'd get to the bottom of everything, and start all over again.

But then came Larkin, and the holy mess became quite unholy. Those piles of stuff in my office: I go digging in them and I uncover all these dread surprises. Like three long-overdue bills shoved inside a magazine contained in a shopping bag buried beneath a sack of stocking-stuffers I got for Christmas. Ouch. Eventually you just start to avoid the piles. You don't know exactly what's in them, just that it's bad.

No more "creative dialectic." No more "garden for the flowering imagination." If I had to use a botanical metaphor, I'd say that chaos, like a man-eating plant, has burst forth from my office and enwrapped my entire house, my entire life. Ten years ago, I owned the mess. Now, to put it bluntly, the mess owns me.

The list of things I don't get done is awesome. For instance, fixing anything around the house. A year ago, a four-foot end section of rain gutter became partly detached from the roofline below a gable. It now tilted the wrong way, so that instead of draining, it filled with water during a storm, sending a cascade pounding down onto the garbage cans below. First I ignored it. Then . . . I moved the garbage cans. Finally I took a rope, leaned out an upstairs window, lassoed the end of the gutter, and pulled it up level—then closed the window on the rope to hold it.

And that's how it has stayed. For a whole year now, we've been living with a taut rope sticking out our landing window. Every time I see it, I wince. And there are dozens of winces like that in my life. The license plate on one of our cars is missing a screw and hanging askew. I finally got to the hardware store, but . . . I bought the wrong-size screws. Who knows when I'll go back for the right ones? The interior of the car, meanwhile, is a disaster. Nowadays, giving someone a ride means first taking handfuls of garbage from the front seat and throwing it in back, while they politely pretend not to notice.

Our house is nearly as bad. I don't know where anything is. Where's that new doorbell system I bought three weeks ago? Our current doorbell is so feeble, visitors often have to call from the porch with their cell phones. And they'd better keep them handy, because I made the mistake of putting the new doorbell down somewhere, and it disappeared into the maelstrom. It's probably in the "guest" room. I put that in quotation marks because in reality the guest room is our junk room, where two mornings a month we frantically stash the clutter from all the other rooms, so that our cleaning lady can do her job.

The system works fine, until we have an actual *guest*. This dreaded event occurred last week. One hour before our friend was due, I steeled myself and ventured into the room. There was an ugly situation on the ceiling, where for months the paint had been peeling away, right over the bed. I'd been meaning to scrape and repaint, but now all I had time to do was pick off the peeling flakes. First, though, I had to move the bed—covered with boxes and chairs and suitcases, stacks of unread newspapers, old toys of Larkin's, shopping bags full of Christmas tree ornaments we still hadn't put away, and on and on. Working like a maniac, I hurled stuff down into the basement, shoved stuff into the closet, and managed to remove the peeling paint before our guest arrived. The ceiling looked blotched and hideous. But at least paint flakes wouldn't fall down on our friend's face in the middle of the night.

Which was good, because I can't afford to lose any friends. At this point I'm lucky to have any left. Friendships need maintenance just like cars, and I haven't changed the spark plugs on most of mine for way too long. My "For Follow Up" email box bulges with 114 flagged items, some going back months. Three are from friends who sent stories written by their teenaged kids for me to read. Because it will take me an hour, I haven't done it. Another black mark on the neglect list.

And that's just the tip of the iceberg—no, the Iceland, the Antarctica—of my disaster. What about our paperwork calamity? I'm late with bills, with taxes. Bank statements pile up. Checkbooks go unbalanced. For months we've been driving one of our cars without the new registration sticker, because I can't find it in the mountain of stuff on (and around, and under, and behind) my desk. Does it really matter, since the license plate is going to fall off anyway, because I never got the damn *screws?*

I sometimes indulge a personal fantasy in which I possess the power to call time-out and stop the world for three days. In novels and movies, this is usually the chance to do something subversive, thrilling, or illicit, like stealing the *Mona Lisa* or repairing to a Mediterranean island with a supermodel for some *Swept Away*–like romance.

Me, I would clean my office.

Imagine it. For one weekend, time stops: The whole world ceases to move forward for seventy-two whole hours, except for me. And in that frozen, dreamlike interlude . . . I clean. I organize. I reduce the enormous, terrifying pile of papers and notes in my office to nothing. I ransack my file cabinets, tossing out old folders and installing new ones, creating whole new categories of reality; I even remove the tiny tabs of white paper out of the folder heads and relabel them! Oh, I can practically feel it, the little plastic doodads dislodging from the slots in the top of the file folders, opening to my prying fingertips . . . yielding to me . . . yielding . . . . From there, I bust out of my office and go rampaging through the rest of the house. I fix that hanging rain gutter. I empty out the garage. I'm bingeing on orderliness, drunk with it.

Twice a year, my wife and I visit the World's Most Amazing Children's Yard Sale, one town over from us, where for $50 we haul away more swag for our daughter than you'd believe. But the real reason I love going is the high I get from seeing how insanely well organized the sale is. The woman who runs it has her system *down*. Everything is in perfect order, with shoes up front, toys in the garage, and clothes on different racks, proceeding by age. Color-coded tags denote different sellers. When you make your purchase, the tags get filed in the right place, all the paperwork is sorted and totaled and accounted for and filed away. Exact change is always available, down to the penny. There are even *bags*.

I find it breathtaking to watch this organizational acumen in action. It makes me swoon with envy, in fact with something like lust.

What a sad state of affairs, when the bureaucratic becomes erotic, and getting organized is your abiding fantasy! In the past year I have coined words like "bureaurotica," meaning the indecent thrill you get from redoing your filing system, or "organizasm," meaning—well, you can piece it together. And I'm not the only one in this household who's afflicted. My wife, a teacher, spent her first six days of summer break cleaning out the basement. Every day she'd come up happier, rosier, her eyes full of joy and mischief. She actually seemed breathless.

"This is better than sex," she said.

Of course, as Freud understood, eros goes hand in hand with thanatos, and in midlife one's deep thrill at tackling the accumulating mess is surely bound up with the still deeper awareness of having less and less time to do so. At thirty-nine you're still close enough to your teen and college years to recall the struggles with your parents about your room, and thus to see the mess around you as a sign, even a form, of independence. At almost fifty, clutter has other, generally darker meanings, a literal and figurative bundle of the things you can't face, won't throw away, and haven't dealt with, all piled up in one huge mass of Don't Go There! This is why getting organized can be so frankly traumatic . . . or therapeutic.

Finally, though I don't want to sound morbid, clutter in midlife compels you to look further down the road. As people go, I'm pretty far along the pack-rat end of the spectrum, finding it hard to part with the bags stuffed with old letters, ticket stubs, grade-school sports medals, and on and on: all the ephemera that make up, and document, a life—my life. As you get older, and your parents become elderly and then die, you develop a sort of custodial, even curatorial, relationship to your past. You want to preserve it from oblivion.

And yet eventually, and competingly, you begin to want less clutter around you. I've seen this happen again and again with people moving from middle age toward early old age: a reversal of the pack-rat instinct, a paring-down in which simplicity does battle with sentimentality, and ultimately wins. When my mother approached the end of her life—not the last phase, but the next-to-last—she undertook a comprehensive regimen of trimming, tossing, and unloading. "Ditch it!" she'd exclaim, jettisoning this or that bit of memorabilia that she no longer wanted to be carrying around in her life. It was breathtaking, how unsentimental this winnowing was. She got everything down as close to a spartan simplicity as her basic love of life would allow. It wasn't the end of her life. But it was a way of preparing for it. Knowing that at her age, it wouldn't be all that long before she died, and not wanting to leave a mess behind her when she did. A final act of housekeeping.

Okay, well, I'm not there yet. I'm just turning fifty. But . . . I have a *lot* of stuff. Even if the statistical average holds, and I get my full 78.5 years of life, it looks like I'll need just about every day I have left to get through it all. So that's why I'm starting tomorrow. Or at least the day after.

IV. INTO/OUT OF THE CLOSET

"That's all you need in life,
is a little place for your stuff."

—George Carlin

Transitional Objects

Louise DeSalvo

The moment that our moving company delivered boxes to the home in Teaneck, New Jersey, where I'd lived for over thirty years, and dumped them onto the floor of our living room, the place I retreated to in late afternoon to drink a cup of tea and gaze out the stained-glass window to the trees beyond our neighbor's house across the street, I began to live in that liminal space that occurs when you move. Before I even expected it, that room had become transformed into the place that I was leaving and stopped being a space I cherished. I thought, not of all the good times this room had seen, the family that gathered here at Christmas for our ritual of opening one present at a time, the writers who drank tea and talked shop with me here, the guests who sat and enjoyed an after-dinner drink here after one of our home-cooked meals, but of all the opportunities for enjoying this room that I had missed, the fires I hadn't made on windswept days, the times I hadn't lingered to see the sun set through the stained-glass window, the journal entries I hadn't made while reclining on the sofa. After the boxes arrived, I entered what the composer and writer Allen Shawn has called the "huge crisis" of moving: "It's actually true," he's said, that when you move, "you are losing a part of yourself and you are going to have to rebuild a sense of where your center is."

On the night of the boxes, I had a dream, one of those heart-pounding dreams from which you awaken in the middle of the night that taint the next day and the day after that. In my dream, the boxes come, and there are so many of them, they fill up the entire living room, floor to ceiling. They are piled everywhere, on top of the furniture, in the spaces behind the furniture. Inside the room, there is no light, for the windows are covered over. In the dream, I see the boxes from the kitchen, try to walk into the living room, realize that this is impossible, know that I can never remove the boxes, that they'll be there forever. I know that I can no longer stay in this house, that I must grab my keys, climb into my car, get away. But once I start driving, I have nowhere to go, but I don't want to go back to that place I had, until now, called home. In the dream—and this is when I awaken—I drive and drive and drive.

What will I become in my new home? What will become of me?

On the day I begin packing, I realize I'll have to pack every single thing I own. And I think, *How can I ever do this?*

How will I ever pack every book I own, the ones by and about Virginia Woolf, Henry Miller, Sylvia Plath, Djuna Barnes, and all the other writers I adore, the art books, the knitting books, the self-help books, the cookbooks? Every note I've taken for all the books I've written? Every piece of correspondence (many, from well-known writers)? Every diary I've kept? All the office stuff, the paper clips, pens, staplers, reams of paper? Every knitting needle, every ball and skein of yarn? Every tool, every nail, every screw? Every shoe, skirt, sweater, pair of trousers; all the underwear and all the outerwear? Every painting? Every hand-knit sweater, every piece of needlework, every handmade quilt? Every piece of stained glass? Every piece of pottery?

I realize that I'll have to make a decision about every single item I own, whether to keep it and move it, whether to get rid of it and give it to Goodwill, whether to trash it. And this realization is so shocking that I stop what I'm doing and sit down and cry. It isn't the packing, I know, that will cause me pain: it's that, in packing, I'll be reviewing my life—the celebratory times, the painful times. Packing will be a full-scale life review thrust upon me when my psychic resources are at a nadir.

Nothing has prepared me for the agonizing choices I will now have to make.

Stored in our basement and attic, and in the nooks and crannies of several closets around the house, are all the objects that have come into my husband's and my possession after the deaths of his parents and my mother and my sister. Until now, we haven't thrown them away. We have coexisted with all this stuff without giving it too much thought. We've moved a box of his mother's personal effects off an extra chair in the basement and onto the floor when we've needed the chair upstairs to seat another guest. We've kicked aside his father's toolbox in the storeroom when we needed to open an old filing cabinet. We've pushed aside my mother's old clothes in the closet downstairs to get at our winter coats to bring them upstairs. We've lifted my sister's photograph albums off the top of a ream of paper when we need another. And each time we've moved something, there has been a moment of recollection, an elegiac pause in the day's passing.

But now, once and for all, I'll have to decide what to keep, what to let go.

Will I keep all my dead mother-in-law's costume jewelry, pack it up, move it to the new house, or throw it away? Keep the three hand-carved Baroque Italian chairs languishing in my basement, a wedding gift to my husband's grandmother by his grandfather? Is this the time to give away my mother's clothing? What about my dead sister's handmade doll's dresses kept so carefully by my mother, a reminder that there were good times in my sister's tragic life?

The sieve my grandmother took to America from Italy that has started to rust that I know I'll never use again? The ugly afghan she made me? Do I throw these pieces of my family's past away? My husband's father's tools? Do they go? But they are the only mementos, except photographs, that we have of his life. And what about my grandparents' marriage licenses, visas, passports, birth certificates, naturalization papers, work permits, each item, a small, irreplaceable piece of our family's history?

If I decide that I should throw away any one of these things, will I later regret it? For if anything goes, I can never get it back: another piece of my family's past, obliterated by me.

As I pack my possessions, I become ashamed of all the stuff I have because I pride myself on buying only what I need, turning leftover vegetables into soup or into a pasta sauce for another meal, making bread from scratch, saving chicken bones and vegetable parings for stock.

But. There are over two hundred cookbooks. Scores of books that I just had to have but that I haven't yet read. Nine bins of yarn. A stash of watercolors.

What shocks me most of all is the pasta. Forty pounds of it. Bucatini. Ditallini. Orecchiette. Farfalle. Spaghetti. Spaghettini. Orzo. Croxetti. Tubettini. Enough for over a year. I tell myself that I have all this pasta because, as a child, there was never enough food, not because my parents couldn't afford it, but because my mother's cooking habits were erratic and eccentric. As I survey all the stuff I have, I vow that I'll never again buy another book, not even another cookbook; never again buy another hank of yarn; never again buy another pound of pasta.

Still, this packing makes me confront all my unrealized desires. The recipes I haven't tried; the sweaters I haven't knit; the books I haven't read; the watercolors I haven't painted; the photograph albums I haven't filled. Makes me see, too, the "too-muchness" of my nature. Too many cookbooks; too much wool; too much pasta. Do I accrue all this around me because of my family's early history of poverty? Do I need all this to tell me who I am?

I know that much of what I own, much of what I have, will outlast me. And that, one day, my sons will have to go through my possessions and decide what to keep, what to throw away, too, just as I must, and that it will pain them as much as it has pained me. Perhaps, like me, they will hang on to a few totemic objects for a while, then, one day, jettison them from their lives. Just as Kathryn Harrison, in *The Mother Knot*, finally divested herself of her mother's "lingerie, old slips and camisoles," intermingled in a bureau drawer with her own; the "pullover; an evening jacket, two cardigan sweaters; a black velvet dress" she'd stored in her closet; and "a compact of rouge, a concealer stick, and three eye pencils" she hadn't parted with. Just as Paul Auster, in *The Invention of Solitude*, describes how he gave "an armful" of his father's ties to Goodwill; there were "more than a hundred" of them, and Auster describes how he remembered many of them, and how "the patterns, the colors, the shapes . . . had been embedded in my earliest consciousness, as clearly as my father's face had been"; and how this act of disposing of his father's ties made Auster understand, even more than the burial ceremony, "that my father was dead."

The day we move, I pack my car with my most precious possessions. Everything I don't want to entrust to the moving men. Thirty-five volumes of my writing journals. A framed photograph my husband's taken of me standing in front of the Dome on a trip to Paris when we were chasing Henry Miller's ghost. A few first editions of Virginia

Woolf's novels. A stained-glass lampshade made by my father. My son Justin's ceramic pieces; those of my sister. My son Jason's blown-glass pieces; his pastels. An herbal sampler embroidered by my mother. My hand-sewn quilt—five years of work there. My most beloved knitted sweaters. A few pieces of my mother's and mother-in-law's heirloom jewelry. Boxes of family photographs. My grandkids' paintings—volcanoes and rockets; flowers and fish. A clock that was my grandmother's, then my mother's, then mine—I stopped the clock, wrapped it in towels, found a safe place for the winding key.

I have persuaded my husband it's better if I go ahead, if he handles the move. He knows I'm lying. He knows I don't want to watch the house being dismantled, don't want to see it emptied. Can't bear to see the bed where I've read myself to sleep every night, where we've made love thousands of times, disassembled. Can't bear to see the desk where I've written my books wrapped up and carted away. Can't bear to see the kitchen stripped of all my cooking equipment—my "toys." Can't bear to watch the ornately carved antique wooden dining room table we bought at a junk shop for $60, wresting it away from someone who wanted to paint it white, broken down and wrapped in quilts. Can't bear to see our Mark Reichert painting of his wife, Sally, bought with money we didn't have when we were in our thirties, taken off the dining room wall where it has been silent witness to festive dinners too numerous to count. Can't bear to see my mother's gilded mirror with its scallop-shell pattern taken off my living room wall: it had hung there since soon after her death, when my father moved into his second wife's home, and getting that mirror assuaged some of my grief, because having my mother's mirror was like having a memorial to her in my home, and, each day, as I passed it to collect the mail, I could remember my mother standing in front of it when I was just a little girl, patting her hair into place before going out, could remember her adjusting her veil on her hat the day of my marriage, could remember her gazing into it the day she went to the hospital the last time, saying, "Mildred, you look like the wrath of God."

And so I'm not there when the men take all the furniture out of the house; not there when they take out all the boxes of books; not there when all the paintings come off the walls; not there when the rugs are rolled up; not there when my husband closes and locks the door to the house. And so I don't see what I don't want to see—the old house emptied of everything that has made it our home, the old house, transformed from being my home into a place that has lost its soul.

On the day after our move, I unwrap my grandmother's clock—it had traveled with her to America from Italy. After her death, it was given to my mother, and my mother had given it to my son Jason. But now he's given it to me.

"It should have been yours instead of mine in the first place," Jason tells me. But my mother had a special affection for her grandchildren, one that even transcended the special bond most grandparents feel. I was the daughter she couldn't care for; he was the grandson who gave her joy.

I know I will put this clock on top of my mother's china closet: it came to me soon after her death, when my father was getting married again. I get the china closet because my father calls me one day to tell me to come and get it if I want it, otherwise he's going to call a hauler and get rid of it and everything else from our family's life together—furniture, photographs, memorabilia. My father is moving on to a new life with a new wife. His new home—the home his new wife has lived in for years—has no place for the china closet my mother and he bought when they moved to the suburbs after World War II, no place for my family's photos, none for my sister's pottery, my mother's embroidered samplers.

"What a bastard," my husband says. And we hire a U-Haul and collect everything.

I had stopped the clock at 1:14, just before wrapping and moving it. The face of the clock was a burnished bronze with ordinal numerals that my father had etched onto it when he refurbished it for my mother after my grandmother died.

I am tired from the move. So when I take up the key to wind the clock, I drop it, and the key skitters over to the heat register, drops into it, drops down, far beyond the reach of any hand.

The key, irreplaceable. The clock, stopped, marking the moment when I left my old home behind and moved into this new place.

Closet Fantasies

From Thoughts from a Queen-Sized Bed

Mimi Schwartz

As always when the dogwood blooms pink outside our bedroom window, my husband, Stu, and I "do the clothes." That involves taking plastic lawn bags full of soiled winter clothes to the cleaners so when they come back we can hang them, with moth balls, in the new cedar closet on the third floor. The cedar alone doesn't work, we discovered last fall when moths ate three of my sweaters and eight of Stu's ties, some of which were not even wool.

Stu and I do all this so that we can bring down the summer clothes that have hung optimistically all winter. Half of these items haven't been worn in ten or twenty years, but we keep thinking "maybe this year" . . . so they don't land on the giveaway piles that we force ourselves to make every spring. On these piles go pants with cuffs worn away by a hipless husband whose pants keep slipping below his belly for lack of suspenders; my unbleachable blouses with indelible grease spots that are located below the pin/scarf camouflage line; bad buys that have served penance in the closet long enough; whites so bleached to yellow that no one can begin to debate their ever looking like new; and fabrics so thin, holey, and colorless that even though they are hard to part with, we manage. Only about four or five items per year for me, two for Stu, who keeps rescuing everything to wear "around the house."

I try to set him straight. "This should go," I say yearly, putting my fingers in the holes of his old MIT sweatshirt, ready to rip. We can always use new rags.

"Do it and *I* go!" he says, like Clint Eastwood in an ambush, and counters with my blue bellbottoms, the ones that I wore pushing the kids' stroller. "How about these? Nobody wears these anymore."

"They will," I say, grabbing them. "They're coming back."

The survivors, his and mine, get carried up and down the stairs, year in and year out, even though half of them never have the safety pins from the cleaners removed. No matter. They are vessels of hope, past and future, the way we imagine who we were and might still be—you never know—especially when they look expensively new, like my long chiffon skirt and matching shawl, last worn to my nephew's wedding, circa 1970.

I press the gay green and pink flowers against me as images of the Rainbow Room, us doing the tango, dance before me. I repeat the ritual with my blue-striped bargain knit dress that I bought at Loehmann's ten years ago. And the white slinky print with the military shoulders and wide Velcro belt. They all go in the closet, in back, next to my hermetically sealed wedding dress.

My husband's promise lies in his Bermuda shorts, the same ones he had on in the Grand Canyon snapshot on the mantelpiece. That was thirty years ago, before his midlife spread, and the madras looks like new because he hasn't worn them since. "I still like these," Stu says every year, sucking his stomach in, and I tell him to save them. After our diet, *I'll* wear them.

After our diet. These are the key words. Because two weeks before doing the clothes, we start Weight Watchers, the Atkins Diet, the Diet Center, whatever it takes to look good without a coat on.

By closet time, we are down a few pounds and anything is possible. The promise of youth, passion, old beautiful clothes, they are only ten more pounds away, twenty at the most. I am already picturing myself in my red, see-through sixties gauze dress as heads turn. Stu is seeing himself diving off the high board in tight Speedo trunks, unscathed. This is also the time when we linger in front of store windows, imagining new acquisitions for the new/old us: a black lace bodysuit like my daughter's, a sleek purple turtleneck for a man with no tire around his waist. Yes, this is the year. Watch!

After the clothes have been rehung or placed in bags and the bed is cleared again, I go to my unbelievably neat closet where, for a few days, life is under control. I pick something to wear for hauling this winter's rejects and survivors to their fates in the Salvation Army dumpster outside of Superfresh in the shopping-center parking lot. I will fondle the khakis I wore when I fell in love, the jeans I bought last June after Weight Watchers, and put on my black corduroy pants with the elastic waist. . . . Now there's an item I'll never give away.

Buddha in the Closet

Katy Brennan

*F*or me, the California Closets website is online porn. This is pure, unattainable fantasy. In this virtual realm, I'm promised "Space To Be" and a perfectly organized life. Here, even my "reach-in" closet can be a "Tranquil Space" where my color-coordinated jackets, skirts, and pants hang full inches apart and my four cotton sweaters stack perfectly on a small shelf. This is life as vacation—together my husband or boyfriend and I seem to have only one week's worth of clothing, and we must be somewhere like San Francisco, as all our clothes seem perfectly suitable for sixty-degree weather—no heavy coats, bulky sweaters, or lug-soled boots. There are just two pairs of sexy heels, a pair of flats, and gym shoes for me. For him, I see one pair of dress shoes, a pair of hiking boots, and some Top-Siders, presumably for when we go sailing. And even the seas must be perfect, because if we own foul weather gear, it's nowhere in sight. Everything is under control. Life is lived with confidence and security, always in lightweight cashmere and soft cotton jersey.

But as it is, I live in intemperate New York City, alone, with three small reach-in closets, each a Pandora's box of memories and regrets in the form of faded, stretched, ill-fitting, and seriously out-of-fashion clothes. Despite a few years of Buddhist meditation focused on reducing my attachments, I just can't seem to let these things go. There are suits I bought as a senior in college for my first job interviews, almost twenty years ago, and more jackets, skirts, and drab, practical trousers I accumulated over a decade of working in the publishing business. But after just as many years as a freelance writer, I never wear these things. I don't like them, but they were expensive. I fear that if my work dried up and I needed a job, I wouldn't have the money to replace them. But then I realize that no one would hire me if I wore these things to a job interview today. I can't rationalize keeping them anymore. Besides, they make me think of a comment a friend's mother made recently, answering for me when her husband asked why I "never got married." She nudged him and said, "She's a Career Girl!"

I should also toss the half dozen bridesmaid dresses I've got crammed in here, and the oversize sweaters and baby-doll jumpsuits I wore in college in the eighties and figured I'd wear again when I got pregnant. Somehow, as these things hung here alongside the cocktail dresses, shimmery tops, and short skirts I wore on countless nights with a seemingly endless stream of flattering, fleeting dates, I got to be forty-two years old.

"You're the most successful single woman I know," a friend marveled at the regularity with which I dated back in the 1990s, long before Match.com. I responded, "Yeah, right, successful at staying single!" and thought I was making a joke, not a prediction. Now I think maybe I'll give those sweaters a year or two longer before I give them away. I can still wear a few of those little skirts, too, but I'm not sure I want to. I'm growing less interested in being attractive than in being comfortable.

Even if I whittled my wardrobe down to what I'd actually wear today, none of the closet units I see on the California Closets website will fit into the small spaces I have. To make this dream a reality, I'd have to make my entire bedroom a closet. I'm tempted. In over a decade of trying to make my small, dark, rent-stabilized one-bedroom apartment work, I've never really tried to make it a home. I've seen this place as a staging area for my busy work and social life, one big dressing room for the glamorous show of being a single girl in the city. But as I face the prospect of my twentieth college reunion, I no longer feel so much like a girl, and playing dress-up feels like more of a chore than a game. Even *Sex and the City* is over, though not quite. Maybe that fantasy is just too seductive to die. Of all its perversions, perhaps the most painfully distorted was Carrie Bradshaw's walk-in closet, with plenty of room for hundreds of pairs of gorgeous shoes. As on so many sitcoms set in New York, the apartment itself is the biggest joke. Still, I've taken even some of Carrie's most irritating musings to heart. "Maybe," as one end-of-episode aphorism went, "you have to let go of who you were to become who you will be."

What I'd like to become is a bodhisattva. I'm just not sure how to dress for the part. I'm tempted to let go of all my possessions and escape the world of Western capitalism for a mountaintop retreat in the East. But I've recently learned about the Middle Way—the realization by the Buddha that the way to enlightenment lies neither in exaggerated asceticism nor in self-indulgence. "Remain natural," my teacher says. "Come to your own realizations through your own experience."

Though I'm instinctively skeptical of any language even vaguely redolent of religious dogma, I've come to believe that Buddhas actually do bestow blessings. Just looking at Buddhas makes me feel better these days—more peaceful, accepting, patient, loving, and loved. In the Mahayana tradition I've been studying, depictions of the Buddhas are more than idols or icons of worship; they are mirrors. Their images are meant to reflect the highest human potential, inspiring us to be more mindful, compassionate, patient, and accepting until we finally achieve the Buddha's Enlightenment. The idea is that we are each born with this potential, a Buddha nature and a pure, infinitely capacious mind. I'm not sure how many lifetimes I will need to become a Buddha, or if Buddhas even exist, but I'm enjoying developing bodhichitta—the desire to become enlightened for the benefit of all living beings. In this life, I think the wish itself is akin to Pascal's Wager: If by happily accepting life's challenges as steps in my spiritual path, I generate sufficient good karma to become a Buddha, great. But if this life is all I've got, at least I'm enjoying it more than I used to. For now, I don't see the downside to letting the Buddhas in. I just need to make some room.

I know I ought to create a shrine—a physical space for meditation—but can't imagine where I'd put it. I work from home these days and manage to cover every horizontal space with files, folders, and books. I meditate in bed and find Buddha in my mind— the only place I can actually find anything, according to dharma. In these teachings, I am told that the nature of reality is emptiness and all of what we perceive to be external and inherently existent is mere appearance to us, a projection of our minds. All the meanings and emotions we attach to people, places, and things are similarly projected, not intrinsic. On some level, I get that my bulging closets are not inherently problematic but that my mind makes them so. Like connecting a high-watt bulb of my consciousness to the old, poorly wired fixture of my brain, just considering that my mind could be so powerful blows it. I can't help but cling to the belief that I'd be happier living in another, bigger space, with more natural light, a bit of fresh air, and a big walk-in closet.

"Change your mind," we're told nearly every week in class, "and you change your life." While I'm sitting in a guided meditation, reducing my emotional attachment to people, places, things, and circumstances seems not only sensible and possible to me, but absolutely urgent. Drunk with bodhichitta on my mile-long walk home, I resolve to reduce my anger and my attachments, let go of the past, increase my connection to the present, and to finally clean out my closet. But by the time I get home and open the closet door, I feel drained. Tomorrow, I tell myself, I'll load up a bag for Goodwill.

For the moment, the sweaters on my dresser provide a good focal point for meditating on emptiness. In the winter, when I crave warmth, I perceive them as intrinsically good things to have. But now that the weather is getting warmer, I want them out of my sight. The objects themselves have no inherent value from their own side. They are neutral, empty. The more time I spend meditating on emptiness, the more useful it seems. In emptiness, anything is possible—even a clean closet, should I decide that's a virtuous goal.

Buddhas are those beings who have fully realized emptiness. The rest of us are nearly blind to our own infinite potential because we're so bound to our finite, present conditions—our bodies, our circumstances, and our stuff. I get the existential truth of death and impermanence. It's the "stuff" I can't seem to sort out. How can I begin to clean up my contaminated, deluded mind when I can't even clean up the clutter in my home? How can I meditate on the nature of emptiness when my closets are so full? Short of full enlightenment, I'd like to realize at least a little light between the hangers.

Resolved to let go of the past and transform my own closets into something closer to my ideal, I begin in the closet I use the least and realize that this will be as much an exercise in grief as release. I see that all my formal black-tie dresses are gone. I wouldn't have given these to Goodwill. I might have even passed these things on to my nieces. These were beautiful, expensive pieces—a dark green silk-satin halter dress with dark brown trim, a slinky deep purple scoop-neck covered in hand-sewn sequins—and must have gone with my summer subletters sometime last year. In the chaos of packing and unpacking, happy to have my rent covered while I took off for a sunny spot on the beach, I never thought to check on these things. I've had no reason to go looking for them, either, as weddings and fundraisers are more rarely on my calendar than they once were. In the far corner of the closet, I find some of my deceased sister's clothing I'd taken from her apartment and saved. I knew I'd never wear these things but wanted to have them for purely sentimental reasons. Now they serve to remind me I've survived worse losses than stolen designer eveningwear. Still, in those dresses, I was embraced, admired, and maybe even worshiped for a fleeting moment or two.

"Use your suffering to increase your renunciation of attachments," my teacher says. "Transform adverse conditions into the path."

As I clear out the stale business attire, I come across another empty hanger. Emanuel Ungaro, it says, and it once hung my favorite black suit, one I bought as soon as I had enough money to invest in something timeless. I lost the skirt on a business trip in the late nineties, and the jacket at the 2004 Democratic National Convention, where I'd gone with a boyfriend and his family, full of hope and excitement. By the time the election was lost, so was the relationship.

"This is the source of all our suffering," my teacher tells me, "attaching our happiness to externals—the people, places, or things in which we perceive intrinsic meaning." We find something attractive, and we see it as an object of happiness and a positive reflection upon ourselves. Inevitably, though, these feelings change; we become impatient, disillusioned, and unhappy. The object of attraction becomes an object of aversion. We create distance. We move on. So I think that maybe aversion is a corollary of attachment. Perhaps we are too hasty in throwing things away.

I come across a bunch of summer dresses I've worn only once in four years. Despite all my dharma teachings, these seem too intrinsically "good" to forsake. One is a stiff cotton with enormous ties on the shoulder that some Audrey Hepburn character might have worn to a garden party, and the other is a spandex lace number with dropped shoulders and a fishtail with which a Marilyn Monroe character might have turned heads wherever she went. Both the owner of the chic East Hampton boutique and the girlfriend I went shopping with insisted I buy these things because I was a "knockout" in them. They were made for me. Even as I handed over my credit card, I mused that I couldn't imagine where I would ever wear such things. It wasn't as though I ever attended polo matches in Newport. As it went, I was invited to a polo match in Newport the following week, and the man who took me there was knocked out, for sure. But he was stoned, too, and drank too much, and asked me to chip in for our room at the Motel 6. I think I only went away with him to have an occasion for my new clothes.

I've spent so much money on so many useless things, outfitting a fantasy. None of the outfits I have now seem to fit me anymore. All the good ones have been lost or taken.

"How many more times can I do this?" I find myself muttering nearly every time I dress to go out on a date. Although I repeat such Mantras of Despair less often than I used to, they remain almost as reflexive as exhaling deeply when I open my closet doors. "I can't do this anymore," I say aloud as I try on various combinations of things that don't work together, sometimes followed by the more desperate "I hate this" or the most frequent, "I've got absolutely nothing to wear!"

Now that I've done some cleaning, I can see what I actually do have to wear. But even with all that's gone now—by design, accident, or theft—I will likely never see actual inches between articles of clothing, at least not in these closets, not in this apartment, and perhaps not in this lifetime. As with so much of my housekeeping, cleaning my closets has been an archival exercise—deciding what things, if not immediately useful, somehow seem worth keeping and what truly needs to go.

What I've found in my closets is a reflection of who I've been and who I am, if not who I'd like to be. I am sentimental, confused, and conflicted. These are not intrinsic flaws or virtues, nor are they permanent states of being. I am bound to change. For now, I decide to practice patience with myself and accept my life as it is. More than inches between my hangers, this may be a true realization of emptiness. I may become a Buddha yet.

Spring Cleaning

Mira Bartók
(and, posthumously, Norma Kurap Herr)

*M*y mother, Norma, who had been a musical prodigy in her youth, became schizophrenic at age nineteen and homeless at sixty-four. Seventeen years after she took to the streets, I saw her for the first time, three weeks before she died. When I retrieved her things from the women's shelter where she had been living the last three years, I found a dirty sock filled with keys, one of which opened up a storage room at U-Haul. Among the boxes filled with canned tuna, family photos, books, maps of the world she made in five different languages, giant surreal collages, dozens of scissors, stuffed animals, and a 1950s Geiger counter for measuring radiation, I discovered seventeen years of diaries. I have taken the liberty of editing her lengthy journal entries from the spring of 1996 into these few pages. No matter where my mother lived those long years—cheap hotels, motels, shelters, bus stations, airports, and park benches—she always believed in keeping a clean "house."

April is the cruelest month, or so the poet says. It's a full moon at Hotel Chelsea and tomorrow I'll awake to half a sausage and a cup of bad coffee. The American tragedy was written long, long ago, so it's best not to travel late into the night. Most of my years I awoke to an empty house, now I have none at all.

On a more productive note, I washed the hotel's curtains by hand and continued work on scrubbing the dresser in the room. First, I tried to put a little bleach on a toothbrush and *swooshed* with warm water fast but I unfortunately learned that was not such a good idea to do on wood. It's what I do with my teeth, which are terribly stained and which I keep in a glass of water by the bed, when I have a bed and when I remember to put them there. Sometimes I hide them in my eyeglass case because they steal teeth, as you know. They would steal the shirt off your back if you let them. After the dresser debacle, I cleaned all the blinds and promptly forgot the day. Note to self: Sometimes a nap only brings dreams of sorrow.

What do I remember? That there are three boxes in the middle ear—the *malleus* (hammer), *incus* (anvil), and *stapes* (stirrup) that form a chain. The *stapes* transmits vibrations of the eardrum to the cochlea. It is 5 mm long and is smaller than a grain of rice. The body's smallest muscle, the *stapedius,* pulls on the *stapes,* the smallest bone. It works with the tensor tympani muscle to protect the ear from sudden loud noises, like the gunshots I heard in this neighborhood last night. Yesterday, I fell asleep on the wet ground in the park. I must have slept right through the rain. Later, I ate a cheese Danish, cold coffee, $1.49. Thieves, bastards—all of them.

Later, in my storage room at U-Haul, I washed the chair that had been in the pink bedroom at Grandma's house, the house that was stolen from me by criminals. I could apply a rose color binding at the base of the chair and attach with gel to create an accent color. I will make a note on that subject and return to it later. I made small repairs on various items, cleaned and scrubbed what I could see in the dark. Note on saving the planet: Always use low phosphate or phosphate-free cleaning products. Use chlorine bleach sparingly or switch to a nonchlorine bleach, like borax. For household cleaning, use these six simple ingredients: vinegar, soap, baking soda, washing soda, borax, and ammonia.

Afterward, I spent the afternoon sewing and reading poetry. It was cloudy, scattered showers. For dinner I ate beans at Taco Bell. I know now the beans were poisoned. The name of the game is not *Of Mice and Men* but *Of Rats and More Rats*.

The second of May in Chicago. I awoke hearing my curses, echo of a life under thieves. Think of something cheerful: a sweet pea. Draw a picture of it.

I miss my teeth very much. I haven't seen them in weeks. Translated: I feel quite beastly! They stole my memory, my teeth, my house, my childhood, and my children. What is left to steal? I had a spoonful of their "scrambled eggs" that had been saturated in Spanish oil that circulated privately and killed people in Spain and I feel like vomiting. Better get to the Laundromat and change my thoughts. *"For lo, the winter is past, the rain is over and gone; the flowers appear on the earth; the time of the singing of birds is come, and the voice of the turtle is heard in our land."* But if that is true, who the hell wants to hear the turtle?

How to be productive while your life is under siege: clean and make order, draw, draw, draw to stop the rage, file and label, and clean again. Note on Madame Dorsey's Household Tips: She is mistaken in writing that bond white correction fluid on fabric will dye out stains. Maybe if I caught a stain immediately it would wash but otherwise no. I would have to know the composition of the liquid before attempting a stain removal. Thus far, nothing has worked. Things to clean my next visit to U-Haul: trunk, cedar chest, clothing, Grandma's broken figurines.

McCall's Motel, Mother's Day. Today I crushed a bug with my foot. I could not dispose of it. Into the white glazed floor, it looks like a large burn stain! What is this bug? As they say, the days fly whether you are in or out of love. As far as I am concerned, this is the last trick in my lifetime. No one provides me with the necessities of life: clean air, food on the table, decent clothing, and a clean environment. We are still in the place of time passed, the forties, when I was a Baby of the War and everyone took a dive.

I spent the day at the library and when I came back to the motel, it was good to have an FM radio in lieu of a friend, man, sister, mother, child to greet me. Beautiful music, Violin Concerto #5 in A Major by Mozart. Right afterward there was report of a plane crash off the state of Florida. I washed the bathroom to regain my consciousness but did not leave as clean as my last departure.

Short feeling of well-being this afternoon. It made me suspicious so I did not go out. The highlight of my evening was antiphonal singing via FM but we won't talk about the dinner or lunch. I would forego the occasional pie if suppers were better in this world. There is something oppressive in my room. I will patch a hole in my blue blanket and wash the curtains again. Everywhere I go the curtains are covered with dirt. Afterward, I will review my vocabulary study: *etrog:* citron; *lulav:* palm branch; *purlieu:* bordered by a forest; *anabiosis:* revival of consciousness; *nelumbo:* lotus, plant or fruit, legendary for inducing a state of forgetfulness.

Note to your homemaker, if you are lucky enough to have a home: There are many nontoxic alternatives to chemical cleaners. For furniture and floor polish: There are several commercial products available that contain lemon oil and beeswax in a mineral oil base. Toilet bowl cleaner: A strong solution of natural acid, such as vinegar, will rid toilet of most limescale without polluting water. Glass cleaners: Firstly, don't wash windows when sun is shining directly on them. Cleaning solution will dry too fast and streak. To cut dirt, mix 2 T. borax or washing soda in three cups water and spray onto the glass using a pump sprayer. If you use a squeegee, like the kind they have at gas stations, your window won't streak.

Note to self: None of this applies because I am homeless.

I feel a bit like one of the Maupassant or Zola stories I read in childhood, about a woman who was compelled to go to a ball and had to borrow a necklace from another grande dame, and it was lost and she spent her life paying on this necklace and found out later in life that the whole story was false. Someone moved in on the floor of this gyp joint and dumped a lot of trash near the elevator. It's a dog's life.

We are still in May, birth flower Lily of the Valley. A stemless, *convallariaceous* herb, *Convallaria majalis,* with a raceme of drooping bell-shaped, fragrant white flowers. My radio is playing very lush piano music by Debussy. The morning headlines say that the United States will start testing babies for AIDS and I am ever so groggy—it must be the radioactive gas they send up from below. Another summer in this city will kill me.

There was arson in my room here at the hotel. Strong possibility of sabotage. A chair caught on fire and they blamed me. The walls were scorched black. Also damaged: one small electric clock-radio (theirs, not mine), my clothes, the few books I have brought here, which I will reshellac and cover in time. I wonder if the authors who wrote the books would take all of this as a bad omen: Mailer's *Naked and the Dead,* Heller's *Catch-22,* Chaim Potok's *In the Beginning.* And *War and Peace* by Tolstoy. There were others. All burned books, like in Hitler's time. The men who came just dumped the burnt debris into the bathtub. One of these things was my blue blanket I carry with me everywhere. Don't they know these are my belongings, not the hotel's? The loss of the blanket is too traumatic for me to talk about. I have carried it with me for the last six years.

I took three loads to the Laundromat and cleaned out the closet. There is a white powder everywhere from the extinguisher. This place is now an area of conflagration. And then there are the bugs. Nowadays, I find the little bugs that come in when the sun sets very unbearable. What are they? Beetles? Vermin sent by extraterrestrials? Outside, it is raining but there is not enough rain in the world to cleanse this filthy rotten city!

I washed my bookcase in my room at U-Haul, then covered it with brown paint. I went back to the hotel for TV viewing of the Hitler Machine and how they accumulated false teeth and eyeglasses, which is on a level with the rats in this city. I live or inhabit the same world with the same kind of monsters. The hotel said to me today that I was a walking fire hazard and I had to move out. I said—what about the bugs? They are a constant irritation as soon as it grows dark.

I did more arranging in my hotel room and cleaning, trying to obtain more cool. This afternoon I thought of buying a sleeping bag. I saved some money and could do it. I could camp out in front of my old house; wait for the so-called "owner" to leave. Once, the man left the front door open and I walked inside. Everything was different. Where were my pictures on the wall? The piano? The pink sateen armchair Grandma used to sit in? I left in a hurry. They have their camera tricks and I didn't want to get caught in someone's movie version of my life. In a pinch, I can use a lightweight blanket or rug on the ground. It beats the airport where I sometimes sleep in baggage claim, where it is noisy and everyone comes and goes.

At U-Haul, I finished my spring cleaning. I added a dab of bright blue paint to some of the more important objects I need to find in the dark and completed polishing all of my mother's silver serving trays. Later, I listened to Schubert's Violin Rondo and a Fantasia by Mozart. I will go on strike. I refuse to pay wasted dollars for some dirty room. Someone once wrote a book called *One Hundred Years of Solitude*. I've had sixty years of deprivation, six years of being without a home. From now on, until my house is returned to me fair and square, I will sleep beneath a tree.

For future notice: If you want to keep your drains clean and odor free, never pour liquid grease down a drain and always use a drain sieve. Once a week, mix one-cup baking soda, one-cup salt, and 1/4 cup cream of tartar. Pour 1/4 of this mixture into the drain, followed by 1/2 cup vinegar. Close the drain until the fizzing stops and flush with boiling water. As a last resort, use a plumber's snake, available at most hardware stores, but be aware—a snake can often damage pipes. Buy and eat less meat, be green, save the planet.

Hungry Heart
Branka Ruzak

When I enter my sister's apartment on the fifth floor of my dad's co-op building in Queens, I know something is very wrong. Her clothes are piled in stacks everywhere, with narrow passages left for walking between rooms. There are pots and dishes stacked precariously on the kitchen counters and stove. Even though there is lots of sunlight coming through the windows, it's dark, because all her things are blocking the light. I squint. I can't quite take it all in. And I'm finding it hard to breathe.

I haven't been here in a few years, since my sister moved to our dad's building after our mother passed away. When she had moved to her previous apartment, five or six blocks away, my sister had never unpacked her boxes. That was the year we took care of Mom and everything else fell by the wayside. The fact that my sister's former apartment had remained unpacked did not exactly surprise or perturb me in quite the same way. Because our mother had been very ill the last year of her life and had required a lot of care, I didn't take notice.

My mother, like my sister, used to collect things. The compulsion to hoard originally led my mother to collect Ann Landers newspaper clippings. They were held together by paper clips underneath the plastic doily on the dining-room sideboard in the house where I grew up in Ohio. There were also the stacks of empty cottage cheese and yogurt containers in the kitchen cabinets. She could never have enough of those for storage.

Then in her later years in New York, my mother took to hiding knives and wooden spoons, rolls of toilet paper and towels, stacks of supermarket vegetable bags rolled up and held together securely with rubber bands, boxes of cookies and chocolates, all stashed in her dresser drawers. They seemed to be anywhere she could find room—along with thousands of dollars in cash underneath the dishes in the china cabinet. It was as if she were preparing for hard times, much as in the Depression she had survived in Europe as a child. It wasn't until she was in the hospital the year before she died that I found this secret stash.

I read somewhere that women are more likely to hide cash than men. A mattress or sofa, a lingerie drawer or freezer, might feel safer than a bank, in case there is a depression or a war. And I have heard that it's actually a good idea to have some cash lying around in case of an emergency. But discovering cutlery and food in my mother's dresser was a find that made me feel queasy. It was as if my family had an embarrassing secret, a skeleton in a closet that I couldn't really talk about. I hope that whatever it is, it isn't genetic.

I've heard stories from friends about people they knew who quietly hoarded and accumulated things. There was the radical journalist who never invited friends over to the house because he lived with stacks of clothes piled up around the apartment. Then there was the boyfriend who had so much stuff lying around, he had created a nest for a rat that moved in under his bed. I had one close friend, a Yale graduate, who couldn't stop shopping on eBay. And recently, a friend sent me an article about New York's own legendary pack rats: the Collyer brothers. Somehow they had managed to accumulate 140 tons of junk in their three-story Manhattan brownstone, which included 25,000 books, fourteen pianos, a dozen chandeliers, the chassis of a model T Ford and bundles of old newspapers, magazines, and garbage piled to the ceiling.

What seemed like distant, isolated incidents of compulsive hoarding hit close to home when news of my elderly Aunt Franceska's (Francheska) death reached me a few years back. Sadly, she had stopped taking her blood pressure medications until it was too late for her. The police found her body in my grandparents' house where she lived alone, midst stacks of the newspapers, religious literature, family heirlooms, and clothing she had collected on every available surface of the house.

My Aunt Dusa (Doosha), or Teta Dusica (Doosheetsa), as we always called her, told me that when she cleared my grandparents' house to sell after my Aunt Franceska's death, a truck was needed to cart away the lifetime accumulation of things. My aunt had personally counted more than a hundred pairs of her dead sister's shoes, all like new, that she gave to local charity.

The little I knew about my Aunt Franceska was that she was a religious zealot who had alienated her siblings by suing them over the ancestral home they had inherited in Zagreb. I hadn't seen her since childhood. The recent revelation about her saddened and horrified me.

First it had been my mother, then my sister, now my eccentric aunt. Am I next? Can I escape the compulsion to amass things?

My sister spent the first few years of her life in Zagreb, surrounded by my mother's family and friends. They adored her. She was their little doll—their *lutkica*. Because immigration of entire families was dissuaded in then-communist Yugoslavia, my parents were forced to leave their daughter behind and apply for her visa from Austria. My sister stayed with her surrogate parents, my aunt and uncle. When my sister finally rejoined my mother in Vienna, at the age of three, it was only to be separated from her beloved aunt and uncle. A short time later, she and my mother were reunited with my father, who was already living and working in Ohio. She wouldn't see her European family for another fifteen years.

So perhaps it's little wonder that my sister turned out the way she did. I remember when I went into my sister's apartment to help her put together the old armoire that my mother's Slovenian uncle had made. It had arrived on a Lufthansa cargo plane, packed in many pieces, and was now lying in my father's apartment downstairs from her. At the time, I wondered about the practicality of transporting a piece of furniture this size, given the exorbitant cost and the lack of space in my sister's apartment. But for my sister, sheer sentimentality won out over any practical considerations. The only place we could assemble and place the armoire was the entranceway in her studio apartment. As she had somehow managed to squeeze her concert Steinway piano along with enough furniture for a one-bedroom apartment into her studio, there was barely any room for us to stand without feeling claustrophobic. Whenever I needed to get a breath of fresh air and sit for a minute, the only place I could go was the bathroom. As her plants occupied most all of the available space there, I had to sit on the bathtub rim with my feet in the tub.

Hoarding of this sort is an emotional response to not having. Once you begin to collect things, you can never have too much, because nothing is ever enough to make up for the loss or abandonment of one sort or another, physical or emotional. And once one need is satisfied, then you can always find another void to fill.

My parents had both known deprivation as young children. My mother was one of seven children who grew up in Europe during the Depression and WWII. There were a lot of mouths to feed on rationing and the family goat that provided milk and cheese. As for my father, his father abandoned the family at a very early age. His mother worked hard to support him and his two siblings by taking on a variety of jobs.

In adulthood, my mother grieved over the family, friends, and career she had lost when she immigrated to the States. As she had not really wanted to move, she felt she did so at great personal sacrifice. My father also missed the family and friends he had left behind, but he had a career and friends here, so he adapted more easily, while my mother felt alone and always yearned for her large family and home back in Europe.

When my mother died and he had a lot more free time on his hands, my father started haunting the 99-cent stores, unable to resist a bargain. He quickly filled their co-op with dolls, clocks, and glass figurines. While my mother invested in useful household items, which she hid deep in drawers, Dad specialized in sentimental tchotchkes that he spread around the house with wild abandon.

Much in the same way, my sister now haunts the thrift stores in her neighborhood, looking for bargains. Buying a silk blouse or skirt for under $10 is an opportunity not to be missed, and not having room in her closet doesn't prevent her from getting it. She is no better when it comes to collecting and using department-store coupons. And as soon as she has bought one thing, she finds something else that suits her needs better. And then I inherit the first item—the now discarded, changed-my-mind-for-a-better-one item. When I take things from her, I feel like I am doing her a favor. I am clearing some room in her apartment. And usually what I do is turn around and pass it along to someone else who may need it.

It wasn't just an accumulation of things that we grew up with, but an overabundance of food. My mother had been a compulsive gardener while living in Ohio. At the height of the summer, the garden was always overrun with lettuce and tomatoes, far more than we could ever eat. As a result, she was always giving vegetables away to the neighbors. When I moved to New York after college, I remember getting UPS deliveries of Italian prune plums and Bosc pears from the fruit trees in our back yard. To this day, I'm still surprised they survived their delivery, albeit a bit bruised. And during the winter months, my mother would send me care packages full of pounded and breaded chicken, pork chops, and schnitzels that she pan sautéed, packed, and froze, so they would arrive intact during the winter months, like ethnic TV dinners.

Although now I have to laugh at the memory of those food packages, at the time I remember being overwhelmed and dismayed by the constant stream of food arriving at my apartment building, as if I were some orphan living in a war-torn country. I felt as if I would burst from so much food. And it wasn't like I could say no. In my family, "no" even to food meant insult and rejection of love. So, I often gave the food away to anyone who would eat it, from appreciative friends to people at the local Catholic shelter for women.

It's no wonder I rebelled against my upbringing. Brought up with clutter, I aspired to minimalism. After constantly being inundated with heavy food, I yearned for a lighter, cleaner cuisine. And I learned to love things simply for their beauty instead of merely for their functionality. I could no longer live with clutter. To me, it constituted disarray and emotional chaos. Simplicity and order came to represent balance. In the absence of clutter, I could feel calm and think.

Just today, I go to the local post office with the peach-colored delivery slip I find in my mailbox. My Teta Dusica has sent me a package from Zagreb. The box is large and heavy. It takes two postal clerks to carry it to me. I'm glad I've brought my portable hand truck to bring it back home. Looking at it closely, I see that the box is a package my dad originally sent to Europe from Brooklyn, where my parents had lived for a while. I feel a surge of emotion when I see my father's neatly printed return address on the box in his beautiful calligraphy. I try to calculate how many years my aunt and uncle must have had this box in the basement of their stucco house in Zagreb.

I feel it is appropriate that now, with both my parents gone, the box is being returned to us, thousands of miles across the Atlantic Ocean. I stop a moment and breathe before I take my scissors and cut the tape. When I open it, I am overcome with the musty damp smell that emanates from it. I'm sure these things have been sitting in my aunt's basement for a long time. I find the clothes my mother left at my aunt's house nearly twenty years ago and a few of my aunt's things as well. I am barely unpacked in my new apartment and my closets aren't even organized just yet, so I don't know exactly what I'm going to do with all these clothes. They are an odd assortment of dark, Communist-era paisleys, woolens, and pastel polyesters from America. Once released, everything spills out all over the sea-grass rug in my apartment foyer. I start sneezing and can't stop—a reaction to the dust and mothballs. The scattered fabric brings up vague, unsettling family memories. The physical remnants of my family leap out everywhere like the entrails from a body. I feel as if I am looking at a corpse. The remains of my family.

I pick out the few things I want to keep, all handmade by my aunt—a red and blue polka-dot corduroy robe, a few tailored blouses, and two gingham dresses that my mother used to wear in the summer. I put everything else in a large bag to give to the local community center. I hope someone else can use it.

Meanwhile, as I write, my sister is in Zagreb visiting my aunt. Tomorrow, she'll be on a Swiss Air flight back to New York. She has bought extra luggage to bring back yet more of my mother's things from my aunt's house where my parents lived for a short while on the second floor. When my sister comes home, she'll deposit her luggage in my dad's apartment, where there are still piles of things left over from my mother's illness—a wheelchair, walker, and commode that never got returned; boxes of liquid nutrition that must surely be expired by now, just like the expired cans of decade-old canned vegetables and soups in the kitchen cabinets, surrounded by all of Dad's tchotchkes.

It used to be that my mother's family accumulated food and necessities in case of war and famine. But, nowadays, the hunger in our family is not in the pit of our stomachs. It is a gnawing ache in our hearts, the kind of hunger that can never be satiated.

I am purging my closets yet again. I now have one large bag ready to go out the door for the thrift shop. I look inside the foyer closet at the shoes lined up on my shelf. I think of my poor Aunt Franceska and all her shoes. I promise myself: The shoes. I must get rid of some shoes.

V. OTHER PEOPLE'S DIRT

Madam and Her Madam

I worked for a woman,
She wasn't mean—
But she had a twelve-room
House to clean.

Had to get breakfast,
Dinner, and supper, too—
Then take care of her children
When I got through.

Wash, iron, and scrub,
Walk the dog around—
It was too much,
Nearly broke me down.

I said, Madam,
Can it be
You trying to make a
Pack-horse out of me?

She opened her mouth.
She cried, Oh, no!
You know, Alberta,
I love you so!

I said, Madam,
That may be true—
But I'll be dogged
If I love you!

—Langston Hughes

The Color of Cinnamon

Janice Eidus

On a July afternoon, in a picture-book-perfect, colonial Mexican town, high in the mountains, my five-year-old daughter, who is adopted from Guatemala, draws happily with markers in the shaded corner of the otherwise sun-dappled patio of our brightly colored, art-and-plant filled Mexican *casa*. My husband and I bought this house six years ago, and we're deeply attached to it, although we're able to stay here just a few months of each year. Our demanding jobs back home in New York City, where we live in a two-bedroom apartment, approximately one-fifth the size of this house, preclude longer vacations. When we're not here, we keep the *casa* rented.

Across the large patio from my daughter, I sit lazily on a cushioned lounge chair, enjoying an occasional breeze and listening to the sounds of the two chirping parakeets above me. We inherited the birds and their roomy, wicker cage when we purchased the *casa*. My daughter has renamed them: The blue parakeet is Budgie; the green one is Gudgie.

I watch my daughter as she bends her head intently over her coloring book. Her long, black hair, loose and shimmering, falls across her heart-shaped face, and I note, not for the first time, how very much she resembles (far more than she resembles me) the sisters-in-law, *Señoras* Carmen and Silvia, who clean our *casa* and cook our meals. Like my daughter, the *Señoras* have skin the color of fresh cinnamon, and deep, black-brown eyes with long lashes, and shoulder-length hair that flows thick, black, and silky.

At the moment, the two *Señoras* are somewhere together in the *casa*, scrubbing and scouring, climbing and crawling, which they do without hesitation or complaint every day. They do this for us when we're in town, and for our renters throughout the year.

The two *Señoras* and my daughter could easily pass as family: Carmen, the grandmother; Silvia, the mother; my daughter, the grandchild and child. I, the Bronx-born Jew, fair-skinned and green eyed, with ancestral roots not in Central America but in Eastern Europe, am the outsider, the *gringa* who doesn't belong.

Whenever I'm in Mexico, I find myself worrying that I've become a kind of contemporary domestic version of the 1920s "Fat Cat," minus top hat and cigar, plus gender change—*una imperialista, puerca, capitalista*. Despite my worries, I sit here, reveling in my laziness, as Budgie and Gudgie sweetly and noisily serenade me. I don't lift a finger to help the two *Señoras* clean my house.

If my Brooklyn-born, lower-middle-class parents—both avowed, lifelong left-wingers—were alive to see me today, they would be horrified. They, who raised me and my siblings in a wonderfully integrated and diverse (sometimes dangerous) Bronx housing project, never wavered from their progressive social and political beliefs, which did not include "hiring others to do our so-called dirty work," as my unfashionably dressed, sensible-shoe-wearing mother had declared one afternoon after we'd returned from an awkward, never-to-be-repeated visit to the opulent home of her suburban Republican cousin, who employed a live-in maid, a gardener, and a cook.

Expanding upon my mother's words, my always loud and didactic father said, with great feeling, "All work in one's home is noble and honest! Grow up"—he looked hard at me and my sister and brother, although at me most of all, the sloppiest and most rebellious of the three of us—"and do all of your own work!"

Were he and my mother visiting me today in my Mexican *casa*, they also would bring up, with self-righteous passion, the fact that my daughter's ancestral history in Guatemala very likely contains numerous sad, and enraging, stories of cinnamon-skinned women who did all sorts of "so-called dirty work," for low—or no—pay and who were horrifically exploited by unfeeling, imperialistic *gringos* and *gringas* who very much resemble me.

My parents would be right, of course. But here's my dilemma: I hate doing housework. And so, despite my own progressive social and political beliefs, I can't stop myself from taking advantage of the fact that, here in Mexico, I can afford to pay someone else to do it for me.

As a child, back in the Bronx, in our claustrophobically small kitchen in the housing project, day after day, I watched my mother as she swept, dusted, washed, and wiped, while my father, despite his rhetoric about "noble, honorable work," never once lifted a finger to help her to do what to him was "women's work" and, therefore, beneath him. I swore to myself, like so many rebellious daughters before me, that I would grow up to be *nothing* like my mother. I assured myself that such pointless, trivial domestic tasks were beneath me, too.

I was wrong, of course. As an adult, I quickly discovered what the point was of all that seemingly endless sweeping, mopping, washing, and dusting: Living amidst filth is disgusting. Women's work or not, I didn't want to live surrounded by clutter, *schmutz,* and all the vermin that *schmutz* attracts. Fairly quickly, I came to see that there's nothing intrinsically demeaning about taking care of one's home and that, in fact, housework really *is* honest and noble work.

But, I still loathe doing it. I find it to be maddeningly boring, repetitious, and uninspiring. I'd rather do anything else: grade student papers, alphabetize my books, comfort a chronically whiney and depressed friend.

Therefore, for two fabulous months each year, I do no housework at all. *Señoras* Carmen and Silvia sometimes laughingly tease me, speaking slowly because they know how primitive my Spanish is: "*Señora* Janice, we don't believe that you know how to boil water or sweep a floor!"

In my grammatically flawed Spanish, I laughingly respond, "*En mi casa en Nueva York*," I do both of these tasks, plus more. "But not," I add honestly, "as well as you do them, *Señoras!*"

Casting their eyes to the floor, they shyly and graciously accept my compliment, and then they tell me how glad they are to be in my employ. "*Mucho gusto, Señora* Janice," they smile. Silvia adds that it is the money she earns working for me that enables her to send her son to college, a dream she never thought would come true.

Now it's my turn to cast my eyes downward, embarrassed by the power imbalance in our relationship.

"Mama!" my daughter suddenly exclaims, from across the patio, breaking my train of thought. She puts down her coloring book and crayons and comes to stand beside me.

"Yes, sweetheart?" I shade my eyes and look directly into her dark eyes, amazed, as I so often am, by the absolute ferocity of my love for her.

"I want to go help Silvia and Carmen," she says.

"*Seguro*," I say, nodding, speaking in my stilted Spanish, trying as best as I can, in my Jewish, *gringa* way, to keep her connected to the language of her birth country.

She turns from me and happily skips through the sliding glass door that separates the patio from the rest of the *casa*, to join the two *Señoras*, who are, by now, probably cleaning the master bedroom, dusting the lamps, sweeping beneath the queen-size bed, plumping the pillows and straightening the rose-colored embroidered bedspread, all the while talking nonstop to each other about their family's woes and joys, as they always do while working.

This isn't the first time that my daughter has helped the *Señoras* do their work. They've been showing her how to grill *tortillas con queso*, and how to clean silver so that it shines like the moon. "*La luna,*" she eagerly repeats, staring into the *Señoras'* eyes, waiting for their approval, which they give freely to her, along with *muchos* hugs and kisses.

Now, alone on the terra-cotta-colored patio, listening to the songs of Budgie and Gudgie, I sink even more deeply and lazily into the soft, cushioned lounge chair, happy to know that these strong women who look so much like her, and who speak her birth language, are in my daughter's life.

A delightful warm breeze ruffles my hair, and I close my eyes, envisioning my daughter all grown up, a high-powered, twenty-something businesswoman, living in a spacious, elegant Park Avenue apartment kept pristine and perfectly ordered by numerous housekeepers and assistants of various ethnicities and backgrounds.

In a flash the image changes, and I see her as a hardworking preschool teacher, living in a cramped, walk-up studio in downtown Brooklyn, a studio that she loves in all its cluttered, messy, dusty chaos.

A new image: Here she is in the same small studio, but this time it's pristine and meticulous, kept that way by no one but herself, a young woman who finds housework soothing and fulfilling.

But, wait: She's older now, in her forties. She has returned to her roots in Central America, perhaps to her birth country of Guatemala, or to our house in Mexico, where she is now the *Señora* in charge, the owner of this colorful, grand house, which is kept in tip-top shape by a couple of hardworking, cinnamon-skinned *Señoras* who very much resemble Carmen and Silvia.

At last, I open my eyes and rise slowly from the comfort of my chair. As I head inside the house, I promise myself that, whichever path my daughter chooses to take, I will be happy for her, knowing that, in housework and all things, she has found a way to be herself.

I also promise myself that, right now, I will make myself a delicious lunch of scrambled eggs and *tortillas*, with no help at all from the cinnamon-skinned *Señoras*.

We're Tired, She's Hired

Kayla Cagan

Here is a list of emotions I didn't want to feel and thoughts I didn't want to own when hiring household help: paranoia, guilt, responsibility, anxiety, shame, indulgence, happiness, entitlement, and fear. My husband didn't share any of these concerns. It's not that he was callous but simply relaxed, hopeful, and open-minded in a way that blew my highly strung mind.

When my husband and I finally decided to hire a housekeeper for the first time, I was both secretly devastated and quietly relieved. Noisy thoughts rushed in: Was I a horrible housecleaner? Could I not live up to my womanly duties? And wait, why were these my womanly duties? Did he think I was lazy? How much would we have to pay her or him? How do we tip? Does this make me spoiled and entitled? Do I have to sit there and watch someone clean our apartment? And what if I turned into my grandmother, who to this day was still paranoid that every maid she ever had in her life was stealing from her? And then, would I become the kind of person who defined our help as "a maid" instead of a housecleaner, housekeeper, domestic assistant? In short, would I be not only the messiest wife on earth but the tackiest as well?

I should back up and say that the reason that we considered hiring someone was that we had a shift in our finances, which provided us with the ability to hire a cleaning person, while living in Manhattan, as freelancers. This almost never happens and certainly never happened to anyone in our circle of friends, including struggling artists, musicians, writers, etc. We were so used to odd jobs, temp positions, unemployment, and occasional writing gigs that we never expected help of any kind. We always just helped ourselves. I had no idea how to let anyone help us.

But when our workload started picking up, we stopped picking up around the apartment. I had to admit we needed help of some kind. I mean, we were not filthy or dirty people, and our clothes or books or magazines were in somewhat neat piles. But one of us, or maybe both of us, was becoming too busy with work and too exhausted after work to work. And our exhaustion was not going to help us execute our plans to clean on the weekend, or on a weeknight, or before our families came to visit us.

So, we hired a cleaning service, a very well-known, nationally recognized service, to deploy a cleaner to our complex, walk up the three flights of prewar stairs with her portable-backpack vacuum, and enter our apartment. When we opened the door to greet our new housekeeper, I thought there must be some mistake, because in front of me were two cleaners. This sent me into the first of many internal tailspins. Did they think I was such a crazy mess of a woman, a woman who obviously couldn't keep her house together, a woman who doesn't even have kids or pets but can't seem to scrub the tub, isn't some totally spoiled and/or very possibly insane nut job? I'm pretty sure the cleaners were not judging me, but I am quite sure of how hard I was judging myself. I had to remind myself that normal, sane people hired doctors, drivers, decorators all of the time. I'm sure some of them also hired cleaners. But I was reared by my mother to have a strong work ethic and an independent streak. I imagined two very tarnished angels sitting on my shoulders, whispering in my ears that they would have been sparkly angels had I bothered to polish them before having guests over to our apartment. One angel owned the voice of my mother, the cleaner-perfectionist, *harrumphing* at my need for another woman to come into my home to manage and Swiffer our lives. She had three jobs at one point in her life, while raising our family, and never once hired help. In the other ear, I heard the voice of my southern grandmother, warning me to watch over my shoulders. "Don't let them take the sugar pots. They'll slip the silver spoons into their pockets. Where are my linen napkins?"

I so didn't want to be a martyr like my devoted mother or paranoid like my intense grandmother when it came to keeping house. I wanted to define myself as a totally competent, damn fine domestic goddess, but it wasn't, and isn't, the truth.

The truth is and was that I am an average housekeeper, at best. I do not spend most of my day cleaning our home, dragging my finger over the back of a lampshade or across the television monitor on the hunt for dust. I feel guilty, angry, and resentful about it. Does this make me less of a woman? Possibly. Does this make me more of a modern woman? Maybe. I'm not sure. But I do know that all of these complex feelings and thoughts that race through me are not shared by my husband. He sees it very much as business, a fair deal, an exchange of money for services. (He insists, however, that after our first housecleaning visit, he was very, very careful about how he peed into the toilet. I had never realized this was such an issue before, which grosses me out on a whole other level, but apparently he realized he had a little habit of missing the bowl.) But getting back to business, I wanted to agree with him—it was just supply-and-demand business. I want to be that pragmatic, not emotional. And I sucked it up and forced myself to mentally repeat my new mantra, "This is a luxury, just like a car. I am making this choice because it will make our lives easier. And that's good for us, for our marriage, for our health. I can't have another night of doing dishes alone, with my good friend, Regret, to keep me company. I have to admit it. We, and I, need help." But a little part of me still saw it as failure on my part. I felt guilty that we were paying someone for services that I could perform, and it felt wrong that 99 percent of the time, the person cleaning our house was probably making a lot less than we were. I was desperate for jobs many times in my past, and I could certainly empathize with earning a living that did not connect with my girlhood hopes and dreams.

Nevertheless, we gave in to this craving for cleanliness, and the women washed and tidied our apartment (we never once had a man sent from the agency), and we paid the expensive fees and relevant tips (I found out that 25 percent is considered a very good tip), and we felt thankful and appreciative of the tremendous job these two had done. Our tub gleamed, there was no soot on any windowsill, our kitchen linoleum floor reflected our smiling faces back to us. Most important, I never once had an emotional breakdown while the cleaners were there. In fact, I was at ease almost immediately. We continued to use the service for six more months, until we moved to Brooklyn, where we decided again to hire a service. But this time, through a friend, we located an independent contractor. We paid her in cash, she was in our home-sweet-home weekly, and she did a better job than the nationally recognized chain.

I finally and peacefully accepted the fact that there would be a third person in our home, a person who refreshed and reinvigorated us with a sense of order and purity, by just allowing it. Allowing my insecurities to reside within me, not our home, allowed the whole cleaning system to work, and I wondered why we had waited so long to hire someone in the first place. All of my initial worries and concerns had now disappeared, like so many swept-away dust bunnies.

I was finally at home, in our home.

Disinfect to Protect

Jessica Shines

*T*hey say that to be a good writer, you have to be willing to examine the dark corners of your mind. I have put off writing this essay about cleaning in the same way that I do actually clean my house. I don't like to look at the mess in my house, and I hate to revise essays. Every day I become a little more depressed as living in a dirty house or cluttered mind will do to you. In that sense, writing and cleaning are both spiritual practices that help to clear negative energy and see what is going on inside oneself. It is almost as if the house is a metaphor for the soul, and indeed they say a messy house is the first sign of mental illness. There have been many teachers in my life—intentional and otherwise—who have shown me the value of cleaning and its spiritual importance. Let me tell you about a few.

When my last roommate moved in, I asked her if she was clean. Not an especially tidy person myself, I had lied in response to the question a year earlier when I was being interviewed for the apartment. Many fights and written compromises later, I was a woman who knew how to take care of herself. Sometimes I even enjoyed it. Allowing oneself to forget the laws of karma is never a good idea, but I was hoping that the new girl would not bring her own drama or mess—emotional or physical—into what was finally a harmonious home.

I was wrong. Resistant to any formal division of chores, other than random acts of kindness, the new girl forced us to take care of her simply by not doing it herself. She never said she wouldn't clean, but she did do it in her own time. She was like the stereotypical man who intentionally ignores the mess around him until the woman in his life—or vicinity—breaks down and cleans out of sheer exasperation. Far from being grateful to us for not letting her suffocate in her own filth, Aziza seemed proud of the fact that she would not know where to find the broom if asked. It took me months to realize that she was manipulating us and that we were serving her as surely as if she were writing us a check for our services.

Teresa, the one who had unwittingly let me move in the previous summer, was a little wiser than both of us and could see the dynamics of the situation clearly from the start. She was also into new age spirituality and saw the messiness that I had moved in as metaphor for the depression and emotional confusion that I was also suffering from, not as the problem itself. It was almost as if our apartment was a metaphor for our psyches and the material things represented feelings. It is a metaphor, in that when people are disturbed, it is easiest to see it in the way that they keep their houses. While Aziza was prone to alternately throwing our things or denying us access to her things, Teresa would keep hers clean and insist only that others who used them do the same. I, on the other hand, usually kept my things to myself, as I did not yet have the nerve to demand that people respect them. I was private, Aziza angry, and Teresa appeared to be on some sort of drug that made her ooze vulnerability. I mean, Teresa was open-minded. In addition to scouring our apartment as if it were her paid job, Teresa also enjoyed playing the guitar, beating her African drum, and practicing tai chi in common spaces. It was this last habit that bothered Aziza, our Haitian roommate, who'd cultivated a temper to match her nationality's stereotype. One summer evening as I was bathing in the glow of the TV and Teresa was attempting to unblock some energy by doing her impression of the Karate Kid just outside my field of vision, we were startled by the sound of our third roommate opening her door. A few months after she moved in, Aziza had turned into something of a rarely spotted creature emerging only to cook, eat, and have the opportunity to slam her door shut. It was not dinnertime yet, so this was an unexpected sighting. On her march to the bathroom, she offhandedly remarked that "something stank." Neither of us gave much thought to this comment until a moment later, when she returned with a can of Lysol and a look of mischief in her eye. She proceeded to sanitize the air around Teresa, who had, as usual, elected to forgo deodorant. Though Teresa continued to move through her poses, Aziza's can slipped a little, covering our sage roommate in chemicals. As I reposed on the couch, wondering how this display would interrupt my primetime viewing, Aziza disappeared into her room under cover of a cloud of disinfectant, and Samantha called the police to report an "assault."

As my first housemates, Teresa and Aziza taught me a lot about how to interact with people—namely never to live with strangers. My struggles in that loft also brought home the lesson that cleaning is hard work that has to be done on a regular basis. It is necessary in order to stay sane and in touch with one's environment. When I was the one leaving Teresa's rice cooker dirty, I became a believer in the interconnectedness of life. Most important, cleaning, like most spiritual processes, is something that will make things a whole lot worse before they get better. When Teresa would walk into my room to find me swimming in piles of paper that would indicate the beginnings of a personality disorder to some, she understood that I was in the midst of looking at my things (and consequently looking at myself). In the process of cleaning out my junk, I threw a lot of things away, and I also remembered things I had forgotten, accidentally and not.

My mother never taught me to clean. A quartet of Polish women would appear at our house once a month on Saturdays with, in my mind, the express purpose of waking me with their vacuums. When I moved out, I hired these same women to clean my own apartment. After they happily chirped away in an unintelligible language, they billed me for over $200 and I realized that I was resigned to my filth. Then my first roommate taught me to clean, and I began to charge my mom $50 for cleaning her house on my weekend visits. At first, I considered myself to be doing her a favor. After all, I was offering her a heavy discount, even when one accounted for the blood ties. It was no secret that I needed the money, but I also wanted to help my mom, who I perceived to be throwing money away on services that she could easily perform for herself. After a while, it became clear that I was not the one with the power in the relationship. One weekend after my mother tried to cajole me into cleaning her bathroom for $5 instead of $15, I came home and remarked to my housemate that there was a remarkably small difference between caregiving and slavery.

Growing up, I always thought that freedom was the power not to have to clean or do any chores. My parents were divorced, and in my father's house no one did anything they didn't want to do . . . including my father. It was enough for him that we were going to school and he didn't want to weigh us down with the trivialities of domesticity. Besides, with no woman on the premises, excepting an elderly landlady who came by monthly to cluck over the mess, no one cared enough to raise an objection. When I was born, my father had firmly told my mother that they were going to raise me just as they had my two older brothers. Far be it from him to implant silly ideas of keeping house in my head. No, I was to be as "free" and filthy as a man. Whenever I would offer to help with the dishes, he would shoo me away by asking whether I was done with my homework.

My father's well-intentioned negligence, combined with my mother's preference to pay people to clean rather than actually do it herself, convinced me that doing one's own dirty work must be abhorrent and vaguely anti-intellectual. Like most children born to the middle class in America, I had perceived my power to lie in my laziness. I thought that having to do one's own work was noble in that it instilled humility, but the word humility was too close to humiliation for my taste. The fact that it was women's work did not make it any more attractive. Cleaning requires an attention to detail and a concern for the superficial that women are both pressured to internalize and then despised for possessing. Thus I learned that tidying up was a concession to appearances, a weakness that women were particularly subject to because of their underdog status in society. They didn't have the power to say no, unless they had enough money, and even then they had to be discreet about their housekeeping methods lest someone accuse them of being unwomanly.

As a woman, I understood that it was important to put on a face, but I resented this social mandate and decided that I would rebel by being dirty in my private space.

My next home turned out to be a ten-by-twelve-foot dorm room that I had to share with another young woman, who was, of course, anal retentive. My messy ways did not go unnoticed by Samantha, who requested a change of quarters after I spilled a glass of Kool-Aid and let it sit for a weekend. Hey, no one ever said freedom was pretty. But I always maintained that she really wanted to leave because of her discomfort with my sexuality. I was as open about making out with people in our room as I was about tossing dirty clothes on my bed. Much like overeating and promiscuity, which have been linked in young women and may both stem from a genetic or personal disposition, slovenliness is another behavior that smacks of a lack of self-control. These traits, considered to be sins in the Judeo-Christian tradition, are particularly troubling in women. After all, who wants a woman who can't control her sexuality, her emotions, or her waistline?

Fiery feminist that I was, I chafed when I read the results of a 2004 CDC study that found a high correlation between adverse life events and overeating, promiscuity, illicit drug use, and just about every other behavior that I would have considered an exercise in personal choice. Here I was preaching to my friends to relax and stop lying about both the numbers on their scales and notches on their bedposts, that it wasn't necessary to conform to ideals of femininity and self-control that mandated they Lysol anything in their dorm that wasn't paying tuition. As it turned out, self-restraint and concern for the appearance of things were actually the more beneficial, if regressive, traits for a woman to possess. I was torn between feeling proud of women who refused to let society inflict self-inhibition on them, and genuinely concerned for vulnerable young women who find it hard to control their lives because they have no control over their bodies. As a Black woman, I know that HIV/AIDS, obesity, and diabetes disproportionately affect women of color for several reasons, not the least of which is economic inequality. Cleanliness, proper nutrition, and safe sexual behavior are all necessary to survive in our world. A white woman living in Beverly Hills might have access to psychotherapy when others find out that she is binging and purging. A woman who sleeps around with men in an affluent area is a lot less likely to contract HIV than a girl living in the ghettoes of D.C. And a Black woman who refuses to clean her house, watch her weight, or pretend that she and her boyfriend are simply "hanging out" all night is not seen as a radical feminist. She does more than fall short of the feminine ideal; she proves the racial stereotypes to be true, the ones that say that we are overweight, overly interested in sex, and incapable of being obedient to our men. Nonetheless, it was when I read this article that I began to grasp that having control over oneself, even though it might not be "natural," might actually be desirable. After all, when people do not have control over themselves and their environment, it has control over them. They drift every which way and let things happen.

So it is that I've realized cleaning up after oneself is, too, a primary, powerful act, an instrumental part of life, regardless of gender or class. When I wipe out my bathtub, I feel proud in a way that I cannot from hiring a service, even could I afford one. A thorough cleaning helps me to see many things that I cannot when I am standing up. Ironically, I now look down on women who don't know how to keep their house. (With men, I only shake my head in resignation.) During the second wave of the feminist movement, from what I've been able to piece together, some women became convinced that domestic work was without value and would hold them back from a career. As a consequence, many women take pride in having no ability to cook, a distaste for cleaning, and a general malaise in the private sphere. However, to be at an advantage, no one should depend on another for one's well-being.

You may wonder whether I have given up on being able to live in someone else's space. I just graduated from school, and I am packing for an internship this summer, where I will have to share a room with another student. My room looked so bright after I cleaned it yesterday. The sunlight bounced off the covers and the space looked bigger. In addition, I had to go through all of my things, and self, to decide what to keep and what I don't need anymore. This has become a lot easier now that I don't save the task for once a year. Constantly changing my address does ensure continual clean-out, which is very unsettling but necessary. Cleaning makes me tired. It brings up too many emotions, makes things dirty and messy. However, when I saw a major part of my life fit neatly into luggage and waiting for the next chapter in my story, I saw who I really am, underneath all the mess—and that was worth all of the work and exhaustion. For me, cleaning house is not so much a war against dirt or a compulsion to control my environment as it is a journey of discovery.

Cleaning Ambivalence:
A Personal and Political Reflection

Julianne Malveaux

As I sit to write this essay, there is a load of clothes churning in the washing machine. When words stick to my fingers, I pry myself away from the keyboard to work at other unfinished tasks, like the three unpacked suitcases piled up from the last two weeks of travel. As concepts weave themselves through my consciousness, I wander through the house, righting misplaced items, dumping dead flowers, collecting glasses carelessly left here or there. There are people who will help me with many of these tasks, but I have cleaning ambivalence. Part of me thinks that if you mess it up, you ought to pick it up. Part of me puts the whole issue of housework in a sociopolitical context, viewed through the lens of race, class, and gender. Even as I attempt to place scholarly constructs around the issue of housework, part of me wants to say, "It ain't that deep—just pick up your stuff."

Not everyone picks up their own stuff. According to much research, men don't do their share of picking up and cleaning up. From a class perspective, upper-class people are more likely to afford people to pick up their stuff than others. And from a racialized historical perspective, an entire Southern economy was based on the free labor of slaves, both in the house and in the field. Most African American women have the memory of a mother, aunt, grandmother, or great-grandmother who did "days work." Those memories, along with the professional work my foremothers did, have contributed to my cleaning ambivalence.

My great-grandmother Addie Hawkins was a maid. I keep a picture of her in my home office as a reminder of black women's work history. My home office also features a batik print of African women working, stirring pots, and grinding nuts, under the shade of a tree. There is an Annie Lee print of black women picking cotton on another wall. I surround myself with images of black women working to remind me of both my personal and professional roots. Addie Hawkins, the mother of eight children, five of whom were college graduates, did housework so that her children and grandchildren wouldn't have to. My early professional work focused on African American women in the labor market, and one of my first published academic pieces was on private household workers.

Ma Moo, as we called great-grandmother Hawkins, was the rule rather than the exception for the black women of her era. From 1900 through 1950, the majority of African American women served as private household workers. The remainder mostly worked in agriculture or in other service jobs. Precious few were professionals— teachers, nurses, or social workers. African American women did not enter clerical occupations in large numbers until the passage of the Civil Rights Act in 1964.

African American women did housework. We cleaned up after other folks. Race and class determined the ways we made a living; in some ways they still do. While fewer than 5 percent of African American women now work as private household workers (with a larger proportion of Hispanic and other immigrant women doing such work), there is a range of service jobs where we are overrepresented—home health workers, licensed vocational nurses, and other jobs that provide essential services that are typically female and do not pay well. Even as fewer African American women do private household work, housework remains a personal, professional, social, and economic issue for most people and families.

Housework is a dreaded chore for some, a cheerful obsession for others, and a fact of life for most of us. Economists and sociologists study the division of housework among spouses in married-couple families, concluding that women do more of the work than men do, but also noting that some women claim "ownership" of household tasks and do not delegate them because their spouses' method of housecleaning may not meet their standards. The unequal division of housework seems as persistent as the pay gap and will probably take as long to eradicate. Some families have the means to purchase a solution and use paid housekeepers to do the work in their homes. Others argue over it. Still others simply ignore it until it becomes a crisis.

Put me in the last camp. Perhaps in utter rebellion against the historic roles of African American women, I cultivated a studied indifference to housework. I used to joke that I had a dust ball that had grown so tall that I might date it one day. And I had been known, once upon a time, to purchase new underwear or towels rather than take the time to wash the items I already had. No amount of parental nagging could push me to develop anything more than a passing interest in housework. In my early twenties, as a cash-strapped assistant professor, I still managed to pay someone to clean my home at least once a month.

Rarely did I think about the contradictions implicit in the housework pass-along I was participating in, and about the relative privilege I experienced by bringing another woman (or sometimes man) into my home to do cleaning. I rationalized that I was too busy, too bored, and that it was "worth it" for me to pay someone else to do my dirty work. And, I rationalized that I was not as bad as those bosses who had been memorialized in fiction and nonfiction—the white women who hired African American women and paid them little or nothing, gave them old clothes or leftover food in lieu of wages. I prided myself on paying more than the market wage, on being an affable and friendly employer. If there were twinges of guilt, there was also the knowledge that I observed "best practices" for the people who cleaned my home.

I had, after all, studied private household workers as a labor economist. In the 1980 volume of *Black Women in the Labor Force* (MIT Press), I contributed an essay on domestic workers. In the essay, and in subsequent work, I wrote about the role that race and class played in the work black women had to do. Too, work as a maid or private household worker was woven into my family's work history. Not only did my great-grandmother Addie Hawkins work as a maid, but my grandmother Rose Elizabeth Nelson majored in home economics at Tuskegee. She migrated to San Francisco from Mississippi during World War II to work in the shipyard, an African American "Rosie the Riveter." After she retired, she was housekeeper for a wealthy family in Marin County. She was a phenomenal cook and one of those housecleaners who would run the white glove over a surface that should have been dusted before sniffing, disdainfully, at jobs poorly done.

My mother, Proteone, was a social worker with a focus on gerentology. As a college student, she worked as a maid for white families during her summers. As a social worker, she was responsible for finding helpers for elderly clients, and through that work she got involved with the National Welfare Rights Organization. Founded by Dr. George Wiley, the organization had more than twenty-two thousand members at its peak. Economic justice for the poor was a key focus. Johnnie Tillmon, the organization's president, wrote an essay, "Welfare Is a Women's Issue," that was published in *Ms.* magazine in 1972. My mom, an activist social worker, brought her clients home and encouraged her children to be involved in helping with organizations like the National Welfare Rights Organization (NWRO). Mrs. Helen Little was a leader in the Bay Area chapter of NWRO. I'd often stuff envelopes and run errands for her to help with her organizing work. Before I'd begun to study labor markets, Mrs. Little told me that private household workers were exempt from the minimum wage and would be paid only what they could bargain for, when many had little bargaining power.

Race and class affected the prism through which women viewed private household work. When the first Commission on the Status of Women was convened by President Kennedy in 1961, the members actually asked that the government do something to train more private household workers so that they could be freed up to work. The Department of Labor provided several grants to train women on how to be better private household workers. It did not, apparently, occur to anyone that training women for such low-wage work might empower the women who would employ private household workers but would do little to empower the private household workers themselves!

The recommendation to increase the number of private household workers was not the only recommendation of the president's Commission on the Status of Women. Still, it was historically myopic, given the history that African American women, especially, had with private household work. From fiction and non-fiction accounts, it is clear that the African American women who had few options but to clean other women's homes often spent less time with their own families so that they might attend to the families of others. Generations of African American children endured the absence of their mothers so that white children could be cared for.

Class played as much a role in the occupational status of women as race did. In other words, working-class white women would not benefit from the increased availability of private household workers. Only those women with means would be beneficiaries of government involvement in the training of private household workers. When the issue of housework is viewed through the lens of race, class, and gender, it is clear that women are most likely to do housework both in their own homes and in the homes of others, that poor women are most likely to be employed in low-wage work, and because of the legacy of slavery, until very recently that African American women were more likely than others to be employed as private household workers.

For all of my professional study of the field, there have been personal experiences that have jarringly reminded me of the way black women's role as mammy and maid is inextricably woven into our national consciousness and forced me to question my own attitudes. About a decade ago, I traveled to Moss Point, Mississippi, my mother's home. As I went to board my plane to leave the area, I noticed an elderly white woman with far too many packages (pre–September 11, 2001) who seemed to have difficulty navigating. She was traveling unaccompanied, and I was traveling lightly, so I offered to help her with her packages. I assisted her onto the plane and put her packages in the overhead bin before taking my seat in the first-class cabin of the plane. A few minutes later, one of the flight attendants brought me a $2 "tip" from the woman with a question about whether I did "day's work." I was outraged, both at the woman I'd attempted to simply offer a kindness to, and by the flight attendant, who surely must have known that I did not do day's work. She indicated she was simply passing along a message, but I upbraided her for her ignorance and for her assumptions. It was only after the plane landed and I'd gone home to reflect that I realized how bonded I was to my own class status and to the fact that I did not do day's work. My mother did. My grandmother did. My great-grandmother did. I could argue that they did such work so that I wouldn't have to. But history argues that my extreme reaction suggests some distance from, and ambivalence about, my roots, the roots of most African American women.

The housekeeping tradition has provided lucrative fruit for some women, though few of them are African American. An industry has organized around gracious living and a group of gurus who promote the finest food, distinctively set tables, and elegant entertaining. Martha Stewart, Mary Emmerling, and Rachael Ray are among the best known of the "domestic divas" with the former model and restaurateur B. Smith the best-known woman of color in the bunch. These women have taken the domain that has been typically female, given it an upscale twist, and profited mightily from it. While African American women are disproportionately represented among those who are poorly paid private household workers, they are underrepresented among the icons of gracious living.

It was gracious living that so many women were taught when they majored in home economics. They were training in the art of home management, learning about nutrition, textile care, entertaining, household management, budgeting, and other skills that may now be "lost arts" for young women and men. It was never reasonable or fair that women should shoulder the burden of household management, but it is possible that in an effort to move toward gender parity, some of the art and science of household management and gracious living have been lost. Why? Partly because people don't have time to daily set the fetching table and sit down, as a family, at a meal. Partly, too, because we live in a graceless, fast-paced age where tradition has less value than it once did.

I am president of Bennett College for Women, a small liberal arts college in Greensboro, North Carolina. The college had a home economics major from 1927 until 2006, when, due to declining demand, the major was discontinued. Dr. Louise Guenveur Streat, who served as professor and chair of the Department of Home Economics from 1947 through 1984, visited the campus in May 2008 to present a pictorial and historical study of the home economics major at the college from 1945 to 1970. The large scrapbook, painstakingly maintained, was a gift to the college archives, a request that an illustrious past not be forgotten. Headlines and clippings of awards and accomplishments of former students had been compiled, along with pictures of students immersed in their studies. While the presentation itself was historic and rewarding (Dr. Streat is more than ninety and still an impressive speaker), the more notable aspect of the presentation was the amazing grace of the former students and their evident pride in their affiliation with Bennett College and with the home economics program.

The gathering plucked at my cleaning ambivalence, an ambivalence about training women in home economics, not physics, chemistry, or accounting. At our ceremony, my ambivalence was tempered by an appreciation of the contribution that gracious living, the study and practice of home economics, adds to our quality of life. The setting was replete with tradition, as is Bennett College, one of two historically black colleges and universities (HBCUs) that focus on women. As I appreciated the accomplished alumnae women—professors, social workers, decorators—who majored in home economics, I wondered how to combine an appreciation for tradition with the tools young women need to compete in the twenty-first century.

A generation ago, Bennett College students were assigned "duty work" or "beauty work" on the campus. They were involved in campus upkeep, polishing brass, picking up trash, serving meals in the cafeteria, and performing other duties. The tradition of "duty work" was abolished sometime in the sixties, as parents complained that they did not pay competitive tuitions for their daughters to do cleaning. There are alumnae who long for the "good old days" of dress codes, mandatory chapel gatherings, and duty work. They suggest that duty work teaches young women to value the blessings they have at Bennett College and also reinforces values like discipline and hard work. While I cannot imagine having been required to polish brass as a condition of college matriculation, I can certainly appreciate the importance of caring for one's campus. Can one combine tradition and core values with contemporary expectations of a college experience?

If we all had to pick up our own stuff, how differently would we order our lives? What if we could delegate the whole enterprise out, as many do? How would we use the time freed up by the fact that someone else orders our lives? Each of these questions must be viewed through the lens of race, gender, class, and history that are shared by many women. There is, perhaps, no resolving the ambivalence that comes from the fact that cleaning and household maintenance are ever-present realities. Still, we all ought to know how to pick up our own stuff. When we can't, or won't, we ought to acknowledge those who help us manage our lives. And we ought to pay them fairly.

I am all but dressed this morning, when I notice that the entire left sleeve of my blouse is wrinkled, so wrinkled that it clamors for ironing. So I drag my ironing board out, set it up, and tackle the blouse. I think of the opening of Tillie Olsen's story "I Stand Here Ironing," in which ironing is a metaphor for the protagonist's attempt to iron out her relationship with her daughter. I think of Lutie, the maid in Ann Petry's *The Street,* of the household work she did and its role in African American women's history. I think of my Grandmother Rose, who might have risen up from her grave to shake me had I dared wear the wrinkled blouse (*Young'un, I know you haven't lost your whole mind—do something about those wrinkles*). I am ironing, and thinking, and I find myself humming for connection, for contentment, for joy, and for ambivalence. I can run, I suppose, but I can't hide from this legacy. From both a personal and a political perspective, I must shift and sort it out.

A Clean House, a Sad Home
Michael Hill

People told me to get a cleaning woman after my wife died, and I did. Pat is her name. I'd put her in her midforties. She shows up every two weeks with her mother, who is about twenty-five years older. They go about their business in a no-nonsense way. Minutes after they arrive, the kitchen floor is wet with soapy water.

I told Pat not to even try with the two boys' rooms. Even if they weren't still asleep in there, the mess is such that you would not be able to get to a surface to clean it. But that first time they came, the rest of the house got the full treatment. Objects were dusted. Rugs were vacuumed. Bathrooms sparkled.

It's not as if I had done no cleaning at all during my twenty-seven years of married life. I washed plenty of dishes, wiped off counters and the stovetop, worked on the stubborn stains in the kitchen sink. The bathrooms were always my responsibility. So was the cat litter box. I knew how the vacuum cleaner worked. Still, I couldn't figure out where all this dirt was coming from, this grunge gathering in the corners, this layer of dust over everything. I guess Nancy had taken care of that with a style of cleaning that called for constant attention, not the limited directed attacks I conducted. How could I do this without her?

There were all these cleaning chemicals underneath the sink that I had never focused on before. Murphy's Oil Soap. Hmmmm. I knew that was for the wood floors, but how exactly do you use it? The clothes, okay, I knew how to make the washing machine go. I had not done it that often, but I found you could get a lot of loads done fairly quickly. Still, it was Sisyphean, especially when the boys got home from college. Piles and piles and piles of dirty clothes, new ones every day it seemed. Not to mention the sheets.

What about that stuff that gathers in the corner of the stairs? And under the bed? Nan always gave the DustBuster a good workout on those, but she had told me its batteries were going, not holding a charge like they used to. And there was enough to do without trying to find new ones. I did like this Swiffer thing—I had bought it—but it was hard to tell when its cloth pads got filled to the max with dust, when they could take no more. Still, the Swiffer was good for running under the bed, where the dust gathered in layers that an archaeologist could love.

Nancy's mother had what we called the clean gene. It was an obsession with her, those sparkling bathrooms, those polished floors, those well-vacuumed rugs and dust-free corners. Saturday was cleaning day when Nancy was growing up. It was a forced march for the two daughters in this Italian American family. Though there were many things they would rather be doing than dusting and scrubbing, they were not allowed to go out until the house was spotless. The mother directed their efforts. Every week, the background music was a weekly broadcast of the Metropolitan Opera.

Not surprisingly, Nan rebelled a bit. It was not that she came to like a messy house; on the contrary, she wanted things to be clean. But she was an intellectual and, as a result, collected books and papers to excess, fretting about the unruly piles but leaving them be. And her remembrance of things past (she actually read Proust!) meant that she refused to clean on Saturdays. And that she really did not like opera very much, other than having a soft spot for *La Bohème*.

As for me, I grew up with a meticulous mother and maids. The cleaning happened. I didn't pay much attention.

It was a Wednesday when she told me she had a sore throat. Nancy had to teach that day and forced herself to get her voice through a lecture. When she signed on to instant messaging in the afternoon, I congratulated her on making it through the last lecture of the week. "Yeah!" she replied.

On Thursday her sore throat turned into laryngitis. That was an old bugaboo of Nan's. In fact, she had laryngitis when we first met. She was a college freshman. I was a junior. So our conversation, the one where we fell in love, was put off for a couple of weeks. That was over thirty-five years ago.

The only problem with the laryngitis that day was that she got a call from a good friend, a younger woman, now the mother of two boys—just like Nancy—who was about to head to South Africa where we had once all lived. That time in South Africa was one of the reasons I had hesitated about hiring someone to clean the house. We inherited a servant with our house there. It was horrible. Nancy felt like a prisoner in her home. The relationship was complicated, exploitative on both sides, layered with the generations of South Africa's racial history. We finally came to a mutual parting of the ways. The day that woman left was one of Nan's happiest in Johannesburg. I concluded that I don't mind having employees, but I don't like having servants.

On that Thursday, Nan forced her damaged voice into action and had a wonderful, enjoyable long conversation with our old friend. But it meant another night of soup for dinner.

Friday morning, it appeared that Nan had fought off the flu and was feeling better. But then that afternoon, she told me via IM that it was back. There were even typos in her message. That was not like her. I knew she was feeling bad. More soup for dinner. A DVD for distraction.

She threw up just before we went to bed. Ugh, a real flu. She kept throwing up all night and was badly dehydrated the next morning. I talked to my doctor. I tried to get some fluids in her. Then I took her to the emergency room for rehydration. The doctor there knew immediately something was wrong. An infection had taken over her body, flowing through her bloodstream. It was the meningococcal bacteria. She had sepsis. Her immune system was going crazy. About eighteen hours later she was dead.

At her sister's suggestion, a soprano sang a selection from *La Bohème* at her memorial service.

I now look forward to my biweekly visits from Pat and her mother. When I come home from work those days, the kitchen and bathrooms shine, the rugs are well vacuumed, the dust has disappeared. They leave out the cleaning supplies that are running low, and I fill their orders.

But just like me when I pick up a rag, Pat and her mother only clean the house. They do not clean the home. Nancy did that.

The Intimate Lives of Houses

Louise Rafkin

During my first few years as a professional housecleaner, I made a lot of mistakes. Times were lean. I said yes when I should have said no. I cleaned for people with dogs. I cleaned for people with gaggles of kids, even babies. Actually, babies are fine. It's only after they try feeding themselves that the trouble begins. I developed this equation: If there's a toddler, there has to be a dog—the dog will surely shed, but at least the food on the floor will be taken care of.

I know the floors of many homes intimately—more so than the people who walk them daily. The floors are the flesh of the home, the exposed skin. Pulled tautly across the foundation, they take the brunt of the living, are first to expose dirt. I know which marks are dried peanut butter and which are knots in the woodwork. I know the scuffs, the divots, the chips in the linoleum. I know burns in the carpets; a dropped cigarette necessitates the careful arrangement of a chair. Hairline cracks in the bathroom tiles of the homes of near strangers are as familiar to me as the lines on my lover's face.

This preoccupation is not new. As a young girl playing with my Barbie dolls, I only wanted to set up the house. I arranged Barbie's

Day-Glo cardboard furniture and carefully made her double bed, neatly folding sheets of tissue over a cigar box, placing cotton facial pads for pillows. I made sure to smooth the creases, ironing the Kleenex to make it lie flat. I placed each item in its proper position, inserting tiny plastic food onto the shelves of the Dream House fridge. Then I had no idea what to do. I couldn't make Barbie talk, or answer the phone, or pine for Ken. For me, the game was over as soon as the house was decorated, straightened, and cleaned.

Even then I knew the story was in the house. The naked intimacy of an empty home is itchingly enticing. The story in the objects on a bedside table is even more telling than a love letter. A tube of K-Y jelly, crumpled and aging, forgotten and fallen behind the headboard, is an obvious clue. Other clues: self-help books with bold titles claiming answers to all marital difficulties. Dueling TV clickers, one for each side of the bed. Porn. Sex toys. Whips. Childproof canisters of sleeping pills. A Bible, its black, cracked cover always dusty, untouched from month to month, perched optimistically beside the bed. Post-its with scrawled messages, numbers, names.

Elsewhere in the house are more clues. At a gay man's house a shopping list on the counter is headed "Penis Butter." At a drug dealer's home there is every modern appliance but, pointedly, no answering machine.

Over time, I have become attuned to the emotional feeling of homes. In looking for good jobs, I am alert to a cleanness of spirit in a place. I look for a home that I am drawn to clean. Every house has a feel to it: angry, sad, cheerful, even optimistic. Sometimes the loneliness in a house can be palpable, uncomfortable. While cleaning these homes, I turn on the radio or television to fill the silent rooms with chatter.

In the calmest of deserted homes, the emptiness may connote clarity, suggest transparency or even openness. A sunny room may actually claim a sunny disposition. And in some houses there is a feeling that is not happiness, as such, but an energy that is neither draining nor overwhelming.

The Japanese word *ma* suggests this kind of fullness of space. *Ma* is best described in metaphor: the area between stepping stones, the gap between musical notes, space revealed when a door is slid open. In cleaning a house with *ma*, I am part of the rightful order of things. I contribute to the continuation of the story. My presence, and the effect of my work, is like the draw of a good fireplace, effective and sure.

And when I close the door behind me, check in hand, I am refreshed.

But this is not always the case. After a hiatus of several months, one of my regulars called again. (I nicknamed this couple the Shedders, because from the evidence in the bathroom, they had to be losing fistfuls of hair on a daily basis.) With a voice full of sadness, Mr. Shedder informed me of his impending divorce. Though I had cleaned for these people for several years, I rarely saw them and hardly knew them. Still, I took the news hard. They represented an ideal: childless academics with progressive politics and soaring careers. I had dusted photos that testified to their commitment, both to each other and to a bigger picture. Snapshots lined the den. In these they were hippies, longhaired and be-jeaned, among throngs of people protesting against something. In one, dressed in fancy caps and gowns, they radiated hopefulness and looked hungry to take on the world's problems. Pictures of each other graced the desks in their side-by-side offices.

But the next time I cleaned this house, the desks were cameo-free. The hinged frame on the bedroom dresser was empty and stark, like the square of whiteness that flashes abruptly at the end of a home movie. The husband had moved downstairs, into a spare bedroom. A yellow Post-it stuck to the wife's bedside table read, "It's all yours."

For the next few months, I could hardly bear cleaning this house. At any given time, only one of the Shedders was in residence. Still, there was evidence of the separation everywhere: a plethora of empty wine bottles when previously there had been only a few; a stack of worn, curly-edged paperbacks from the seventies, each advocating a different brand of be-here-now philosophy. A wide-screen TV. Then one week I noticed *his* shaver in *her* bathroom. The next week, the desktop photos reappeared.

When the Shedders reunited, I was more eager to clean their house. It is not only dirt that makes a job easy or hard.

Once while I was dusting at a one-time-only job, I found a letter taped onto the back of a picture frame. It was unsealed and addressed to a man I vaguely knew. Of course, I couldn't resist: I read a long confession of obsessive love from another man who had previously lived in this house but had long since left town. I couldn't imagine how the letter had come to be stuck to the back of the picture, or why it was there.

"I hope someone will send this," it closed. "I am not brave enough to accept my passion."

Later that day I mailed the letter. Sometimes I want my presence in a house to have an effect beyond that of a well-mopped floor.

Ecstatically Cleaning the Toilet

Nancy Peacock

*T*he Hamiltons were old hippies who still lived in the woods and fixed a lot of pasta for dinner. They had two young boys and worked long hours, and getting dinner on the table seemed to be the day's crowning achievement. Cleaning up after dinner clearly was not. There were always strands of cooked spaghetti stuck to the kitchen counter and long sticks of uncooked spaghetti that had fallen to the floor. My vacuum cleaner could not suck up unbroken sticks of hard spaghetti. It would clog or spit it out, or else the spaghetti would hover at the vacuum cleaner's mouth as if it were gagging. Before vacuuming the kitchen, I had to sweep, and I hated that.

I also hated the fact that the two boys, El and Lee, had not been coached in the art of using a wastebasket. They were allowed to drop their trash everywhere they went. Wads of Kleenex littered the bathroom counter. Used Stridex pads covered the carpet of Lee's room. And candy wrappers were everywhere. In the days following Halloween I could map the movement of El and Lee by following the wadded-up candy wrappers. They were along the stairs, in the hallway, in their rooms beside the beds, and next to the chairs facing the TV. Candy wrappers were something else that my vacuum cleaner would gag on.

Before I did anything else at the Hamiltons' house I made an all-inclusive exploration with a plastic grocery bag in my hand. Stray candy wrappers, Stridex pads, and Kleenex were picked up and put in the bag. It was a lot of bending over, and I'd always work up a nice backache by the time I was finished. I'd also work up an attitude, because by the time I'd picked up all the trash my real job hadn't even begun.

I was tempted to give it a go with the vacuum cleaner and the candy wrappers. I knew vacuums could handle a lot of things. I'd heard coins go up in mine, and I had a housecleaning friend who made it a policy never to pick something up. He told me about sucking up his client's underwear with his client's vacuum cleaner. "Bikinis," he said when my eyes widened. But bikini or boxer, this was my vacuum cleaner, and I decided not to risk it. Getting a clog out during a workday was hell.

First I would have to take the wand apart and if the clog wasn't in the two hollow metal pieces, where it could easily be blown or pushed out, then it was in the hose. Getting a clog out of the hose involved turning the vacuum on and squeezing up and down the hose, trying to loosen the clog. And if that failed, it involved taking the vacuum outside, turning the blower on, and spraying dust all over the rose bushes. I worked hard at finding all of the dropped candy wrappers at the Hamiltons' house, but I didn't always succeed. They had a habit of getting kicked under furniture or hiding behind bedskirts and chairs.

Other than the pasta issue and the inability of two family members (possibly more) to use a trash can, I liked the Hamilton job. I liked the location, I liked the woods surrounding the deck, I liked the boys' rooms, which were full of interesting things like rocks and sticks and birds' nests. But best of all was my recent discovery of books on tape. The Hamiltons were never home, so I could listen to a tape without any interruption.

I'd always thought the ideal job would be one that allowed me to read books. I felt a pang of envy whenever I passed a parking deck with its attendant sitting in the little glass booth. Mostly the parking lot attendants, when they weren't taking money from exiting cars, seemed to be reading. The lucky stiffs, I thought.

I once worked in a hardware store and called in sick three days in a row so that I could finish reading James Michener's *Centennial*. The thing about calling in sick three days instead of just one, I realized, was that it was very convincing. After the second day my coworkers assumed I really was sick, and pretty damned sick at that. When I returned to work they asked me if I felt better, and I answered truthfully that I did. I'd had a wonderful three days sitting by the woodstove, drinking hot tea, snacking on popcorn, and reading. I felt tremendously better.

Now that I had books on tape and my Walkman, I suddenly had the perfect job. Every week I went to the library and checked out two books on tape. It was a small library, and soon I had gone through all the novels and all the memoirs and was starting in on the self-help. I didn't enjoy the self-help books much, and listening to them only meant one thing. My supply was running low.

Every week the search for suitable books became more and more difficult. I was down to some flaky new-age books when I discovered that my local video store rented books on tape for $1 a day. This would cost me $5 a week, roughly $20 a month. I added it into my budget. It was worth it.

But there were other problems besides my supply of tapes. It was difficult to turn a tape over or punch the buttons with rubber gloves on. And the earphones fell out of my ears constantly. And if they didn't fall out of my ears, my clients, seeing me with headphones, became extra talkative. But worst of all was that my Walkman went flying off the waistband of my blue jeans far too often.

It happened mostly during vacuuming, when the headphone cord caught on the edge of a chair or a table. It also happened when I leaned over, which I did frequently, especially at the Hamiltons' house, where I picked up lots of candy wrappers.

It was at the Hamiltons' that my Walkman took its final dive down a flight of stairs. I was halfway through Annie Dillard's novel *The Living*, leaning over to pick up a candy wrapper, when the cord caught on the stair rail and yanked the headphones out of my ears and the Walkman off my jeans. I watched it fall. Hardwood stairs all the way down. Pieces were springing loose along the way. It made a terrible clunking noise against the stair treads. I knew my Walkman was a goner, but what most concerned me was the vase of tulips in the hallway. I prayed that my Walkman wouldn't launch itself off that final landing and into those tulips, and thankfully, it didn't. Instead it bounced once on the hallway rug and settled peacefully against the base of the table that held the tulips. I picked up the pieces on my way down and added them to my plastic grocery sack full of candy wrappers.

On the way home I stopped at RadioShack and priced another Walkman. Mine had been cheap, and I wanted a good one this time. I wanted one with headphones that would stay on. I wanted one with large chunky buttons that would be easy to push. I wanted one that might be a little weather resistant so I could safely wear it while cleaning a shower. And I wanted one that would automatically reverse the tape direction, saving me the trouble of flipping the tape. Forty-five dollars. The price had gone up, and I couldn't afford it right then. I told myself to forget about it. It had been a fun fling, but my tape supply had become problematic again. I was almost through all the books on tape at the video store, and I hadn't scouted out a new dealer. I went back to turning on the TV while I cleaned. I went back to *I Love Lucy* and *Unsolved Mysteries*.

A few years later the local library moved to a larger building and expanded its selection of everything, including books on tape. On my first visit I noticed whole shelves full of white boxes. In the old library the tapes had been housed in plastic bags and hung on a rod. Now the books on tape had white boxes and dignity and, more important, five shelves of their own. Suddenly there were hundreds of authors available to me. Bailey White, Alice Sebold, Jane Goodall, Charles Dickens, Mark Twain, Natalie Goldberg, and Anne Lamott. Just to name a few. I checked out two, then went to RadioShack and bought a new Walkman.

I told the salesman that I cleaned houses for a living and I needed a sturdy Walkman. One that could take a beating but hopefully wouldn't have to because it would stay in place. I remembered to tell him all the other features that I wanted. He showed me a white one, with a cover that flipped over the tape to keep it dry in a light shower. The buttons seemed good. The earphones hooked around the ear, holding them in place. It was still $45. I bought it.

Recently I listened to a series of tapes called *The Language of Life,* featuring readings by different poets and interviews with Bill Moyers. This was a wonderful experience. As I listened and worked I became happier and happier. The red rug, which I took outside to shake, seemed as bright as a flower, and the dust motes shimmered in the sunlight. The white tiles in the kitchen were blinding, like fresh snow in bright sun. Even the dryer sheet did not feel so offensive to me when I put it in with the towels. I'd made it to Coleman Bark's translations of Rumi by the time I hit the bathrooms.

Of course I'd heard of Rumi, but I had never paid much attention. Now I was on my knees, scrubbing a toilet while Coleman Barks read Rumi to me, and I was ecstatic.

> *Birds make great sky circles*
> *of their freedom.*
> *How do they learn that?*
> *They fall, and falling*
> *they're given wings.*

While I listened to Coleman Barks read his translations, my movements became more fluid. Housecleaning was a dance. I scrubbed. I sprayed. I sponged. I wiped the mirrors clean of streaks, and there was not one cell in my body that resented the work I was doing. I was making "great sky circles of my freedom."

On my way home that day I made my usual stop at the Thrift Shop. I perused the writing books as I always do, and in one of those amazing intelligent-universe moments that I believe both Rumi and Coleman Barks would appreciate, I found a hardback copy of the very book I had been listening to on tape. It looked as though the book hadn't even been opened, but if it had been dog-eared and falling apart, I still would have purchased it. Clearly it was waiting for me.

In this book Coleman Barks tells me that the word dervish means "doorway"—"an open space through which something can happen." Now when I clean a house, I check the dervishes for spiders. How lucky, I think, to live in the corner of a dervish. But of course we all do. It's just that spiders know a good thing when they see one.

The Language of Life tapes kept me happily cleaning houses for two weeks, because once I was finished with the series I started it all over again. One of my favorite poets is Naomi Shihab Nye. She said into my ear, as I scrubbed a stovetop, ". . . poems hide. In the bottoms of our shoes. / They are sleeping."

Suddenly I remembered the Hamiltons' house. They were long-gone clients. I'd dropped them. The abundance of spaghetti and candy wrappers had finally gotten to me.

But once while cleaning their house I had missed a little mountain of candy wrappers during my initial garbage sweep. The pile was between a wall and a chair and next to a pair of shoes. I was vacuuming by the time I found them, and I was pissed off to see them there. Instead of turning the vacuum off and making a trip to the trash can, I scooped up the candy wrappers and stuffed them into the shoes. *Take that,* I thought. But now, years later, cleaning a stovetop, I wish I had been more respectful of the shoes. I did not know that poems might be hiding there, sleeping.

The Walden Pond Cleaning Service

Richard Goodman

> "*Housework was a pleasant pastime. When my floor was dirty, I rose early, and, setting all my furniture out of doors on the grass, bed and bedstead making but one budget, dashed water on the floor, and sprinkled white sand from the pond on it, and then with a broom scrubbed it clean and white. . . . It was pleasant to see my whole household effects out on the grass, making a little pile. . . . *"
> —Thoreau, Walden

"Alright, so who referred you again?"

"Emerson."

"Emerson? Is that an employment agency or something?"

"No. Ralph Waldo Emerson. The celebrated poet and scholar. I live with him."

"You're gay? I mean, I don't mind. Gays are incredibly clean. Fastidious. *Everyone* knows that."

"Gay I am when the sun shines over the dew's sparkle in the morning."

"Well, your sexual preference is of no concern to me. Now, this Roger Emerson. Can he provide a reference?"

"Ralph Waldo. I can, I am certain, call on him to vouch for my qualities."

"That's fine. Because it's quality cleaning we want here. Now, looking at your resume, I see you spent time in jail."

"That was a matter of conscience."

"Well, I have a twelve-year-old daughter. I hope your conscience will stay away from her. She's very impressionable. Not to mention she just started wearing a training bra. I also see you lived in the woods by yourself for a number of years. What was *that* all about?"

"I lived there two years and two months. At present I am a sojourner in civilized life again."

"Sojourner? Is that a cult of some kind? I can't stand cults. Ruthie, my sister's daughter, is somewhere out in Oregon. They won't even let us text message her."

"No—I am a sojourner, a temporary guest."

"Nobody said anything about you staying here. You won't be a live-in. The ad was clear about that."

"I have understood."

"Henry David? Such a nice name! You're not Jewish, are you? No, not with that last name. *Unless you changed it?* Don't tell me— were you ever Thorowsky? Thorgold?"

"I am of French Huguenot descent."

"*French?* Do you cook, too?"

"I eat at the meanest table. I prefer the simplest fare."

"Okay, we'll skip the cooking. Now, I also see you made pencils."

"As did my father before me."

"Can you make a *living* doing that?"

"I seek not riches. I seek only to provide myself the bare necessities."

"I pay seven dollars an hour. That's more than McDonald's."

"That will suffice."

"And for that I expect you to scrub the floors and clean all the counters. And scour the bathtub. Now, I read in that crazy book of yours how you like to take all the furniture and put it outside on the grass. I don't like that idea, Davy. I've got picky neighbors. I don't want my lawn to look like some trailer-trash yard sale. So let's just leave the La-Z-Boy indoors. Anyway, Herman would be furious if you moved it even one inch. He's spent years getting it to exactly the right distance between the television and the refrigerator. You don't smoke, do you?"

"I have a faint recollection of pleasure derived from smoking dried lily-stems before I was a man. I have never smoked anything more noxious."

"Good, because Herman can't stand the smell of smoke on his La-Z-Boy. Drives him bananas. You like coffee in the morning? I drink decaf."

"I take no stimulants."

"What gets you going, Davy?"

"Morning air! If men will not drink of this at the fountainhead of the day, why, then, we must even bottle up some and sell it in the shops, for the benefit of those who have lost their subscription ticket to morning time in this world."

"Wow. Maybe you should be in sales. Well, each to his own. I need my cup of coffee in the morning or I am a *witch*. Anyway, back to the job. I expect you here at nine sharp."

"I arise before the dawn."

"And I expect you here until five."

"I will give an honest day's labor for an honest day's wage."

"You know, I like you, Davy. I thought you might be some kind of kook from your wacky book, but you're alright. Those clothes, though. Did you get them at a sample sale for the homeless?"

"I fashioned them myself."

"*Fashioned?* Stay with cleaning, Davy. A tailor you're not."

"Most men live lives of quiet desperation."

"In the garment industry they do, Davy. You got that one right. So—can you start Monday? And just write down what solvents you need. I buy organic. They work just as well, and I like to do my bit to save the planet—you know what I'm saying? I'll pick them up over the weekend. Oh, one more thing. I'd like you to clean the lawn furniture. I hate it with a passion, but my sister-in-law Shirley got it on sale, thought she was doing me a favor, so what am I gonna do. That you can leave outside—forever."

VI. A CLEAN NEW WORLD

"My mother had no end of tragedy in her life. She would make herself get up and take a deep breath and go out and do laundry. Hang up sheets. She told me that when she looked at the laundry, the sheets flowing in the wind, and the sun, it was like a fresh start."

—Patti Smith

Waxing Poetic

Laura Shaine Cunningham

My relationship with wood, especially my wide boards, has lasted for decades and been charged with erotic overtones and undertones of subjugation, drudgery, and ecstasy. I confess—my floors have brought me to a place no man has ever done: to my knees.

The history goes back two generations, to the floors of my childhood in the Bronx. In that distant time (the late fifties, early sixties), women remained at home doing "housework." They wore outfits, called housedresses and dusters. Often they were shod in pragmatic footwear, orthopedic sandals. In the culture of the first-generation Jewish lower middle class, these women, so uniformed, were called "Balabusters," a word that struck me, as a child, as apt, for I imagined "ball busting." These early urban housewives cleaned with ferocity; they wielded mops, brooms, rug beaters. They pounded dirt from their homes; they climbed ladders to wipe down venetian blind slats. They hung from windows with throw rugs. Their hands and knees (housemaid's knees) reddened and roughened from their endless toil. As fierce as their labor was, so was their pride—"I cleaned my shower stall today," one might boast. "You would not believe the slime."

They found dirt in unlikely crannies—the grooves of shower stalls and rubber Frigidaire seals. They heaved appliances away from walls and found plumes of dust and upturned amber husks of roaches. They were foot soldiers at war against dirt.

These women were both impressed by and competitive with one another: "I saw her cabinets" was the sort of remark I might overhear. "The shelving paper has not been changed in years. . . ." Or, "Her house is clean, but she needs a paint job."

Balabusters busted each other, but they needed the camaraderie— "I found a better cleanser for the toilet." "Did you try Carbona on that carpet stain?"

There were arenas in which these stocky women, in dusters, did battle—swiping at those infernal venetian blinds, draperies—all, dust magnets—wiping and scrubbing any porcelain tile area but especially tub and sink drains (gummy with mold and mineral deposit, bleeding with rust). From them, I learned the acid tests: You could tell if a woman's house was clean by looking behind her toilet bowl or under her kitchen sink. But the ultimate test was . . .

Waxing.

"My floors glow," my next-door neighbor said. "Come see."

Demonstration was part of the process. Someone had to see and had to know—how many hours, perhaps days, had been spent on those floors.

My relationship with floor wax, as best as I can recall, started at age three, when I was ordered onto a couch for three hours, while my aunt waxed, polished, and "let dry." She then proceeded to buff. I bore witness. My aunt "watched" me and I watched her—wax.

She was, in retrospect, a mediocre waxer—she used a liquid floor polish, applied with a long-handled brush, with a soft cream-colored fleecy applicator. Her motions were not graceful but determined as she made her way round the parquet. Her apartment was crowded with furniture—overpopulated by heavy near-black breakfronts. Most of her furniture seemed to have heavy, footless bases, so she had to "wax around" the upright piano, the mahogany bookcases, the breakfronts and armoires.

At one crucial crevasse between a bookcase and the piano, my aunt had to wedge herself sideways, the floor wax pole pressed against her. She applied the wax, then used a new little fleece hood to buff. She buffed with woman power (no engine), and this was executed as an aerobic feat, her arms moving fast and hard, as she circumnavigated her Junior Four apartment. After the application, inhaling the pungent lemon scent, she would wait, standing against the wall, in an unwaxed hallway, until the next step—the buffing. But this reprieve offered a sensual aside.

"Smell it!" she would cry.

And I would inhale, and—I admit—I got hooked. As some children might enjoy whiffs of airplane glue, I got a discreet high from floor wax.

Later when I was older, and would return from school to find the apartment already waxed, I would sniff in appreciation—"It smells so good!"

And my aunt, an unsmiling woman (and what did she have to smile about?), would almost beam. "Yes, I waxed all morning." She often reported on the hours—"It took three hours." But it was never quite done. "Next time, I will do the halls."

From her, I learned to appreciate not just the wax but the wood. Her wood "deserved" this treatment. "Real parquet," she would say, and I would bend to study the herringbone patterns of the oak flooring. Indeed, unlike lesser floors, which might have been cheap, flat tongue and groove or, worse, linoleum simulated parquet, my aunt's floors were the real deal. The fact that she had a "sunken" living room added to the drama: One stepped up, as onto a stage, to reach her dining area, which she took particular pride in. There the parquet was fully exposed, no area rugs to interfere.

My mother died when I was eight years old, but not before demonstrating her own approach to waxing. She was, unlike my aunt, her sister, a "career girl," not a balabuster. She never wore a housedress or a duster or orthopedic sandals. She owned one "cocktail" apron, a tiny black chiffon affair that she donned on the infrequent occasion she had company for dinner. She didn't cook either. But she did clean and wax—fully attired, in a business suit, on high, open-toed heels.

But my mother also appreciated wood, and the wax it deserved. We did not have the coveted parquet in our tiny "efficiency" apartment, but she did comment on our "hardwood." She bought a dark lemon oil-scented polish, also applied by long handle. However, she had invested in a newer, more expensive product—self-polishing wax. It hardened to a high shine without any buffing.

The effect was glossy, but now, with hindsight, I am appalled. I know better than to use such self-polishing stuff, any spray-on, or the ultimate anathema, polyurethane.

As I grew up, I grew into a deeper love affair with wooden floors, and at thirty-four, I bought an old house with 1849 "pumpkin pine" wide boards. I was instructed by a country wood floor restorer in the *only* way to really treat good wood—with paste wax that requires buffing. I waxed this way once and have never looked back to "easier" or more modern methods. There is nothing like Butcher's orange (not the clear bowling-alley finish) paste. It melds organically into the wood, protects it, and, when buffed, emits a spiritually satisfying warm glow.

The aroma of Butcher's is perfume to a wax-a-holic.

Admittedly, applying the paste is masochistic exercise—one assembles soft clean rags, falls to one's knees, and just starts to rub, and rub, and rub, essentially crawling, as a pilgrim would on some sacred route . . . until one reaches the end. Dragging along my center hall, I look like an indoor *Christina's World*. The process is hard on my knees. Yes, I consider knee pads, but I have never gone that far—I wear my own domestic uniform: heavy sweatpants and thick socks (inevitably discarded as they get waxed, too—ending up with hardened orange heels). I do play classical music while I crawl around, with the wax rags. And the experience has a humbling sensuality as I feel the paste soften in my hands, warmed through the rag. As I am never subservient to anything but my wide boards, I can live with this periodic (two times a year) experience on my knees.

The wax itself has an erotic property and recalls the hormonal pastes of good sex. I do get a nostalgic thrill from this, I suppose, recalling human experiences—with similar moistness and circular motion. And like my Balabuster aunt, I enjoy the post-wax inhalations, the sighs of successful waxing ("I got in the corners!"). In the ritual, I stand back, eying the drying opaque floor from many angles, watching as light beams may illuminate a "missed" spot. On a good wax job, I can see the arclike design of my wax-swiping and note that I have achieved "full coverage."

In the beginning, I buffed by hand as well, which may be the most arduous physical act I have ever performed. If a caloric burn rate was applied, I would guesstimate that floor waxing and buffing by hand might equal performing in a decathlon. I soon graduated, however, to an electric buffer—there are some devices that can do the job better—and a buffer is far superior in achieving the longed-for high but "soft" shine: the post-wax glow. So I work with an upright buffer, with two magical spinning fleece-covered "heads" that not only shorten the buffing time but provide a near-mirror finish. This is more overtly pleasurable than the crawling phase: The buffer has its own energy and can lead one on a merry chase, like a car with a misalignment—I may be somewhat tilted and dragged in one direction or another, for the wild ride across the wide board. I enjoy exerting pressure on the chrome staff and pressing so the buffer heads achieve maximum friction. I manage to gain control of the powerful machine and make it do my bidding, until we are both done.

At the climax, I might cry out an actual "Ahhh!" This is Balabuster bliss.

The waxed floor is one of domestic art's greatest wonders. I never walk across or even gaze at my wide boards without a thrill as residual as the paste itself—yes, the wood is catching the sunlight, I note, and my spirit soars up each reflected beam.

Sweet Sheets

Juliet Eastland

*I*n my early twenties, my sense of self depended on a few factors. It was critical, for instance, that I be able to fit into my black jeans. It was important that I be reading a Good Book. And I had to have a sumptuous bed: in this case, a satin-smooth wooden futon frame, with a bouncy spring mattress, fluffy pillows, shams (standard *and* European), and 400-thread-count—minimum—sheets. The whole poof was covered with a fuchsia satin comforter cover I'd bought in Chinatown on one of my first solo New York field trips. It screamed bordello, and it was a far cry from the Laura Ashley flower-sprinkled meadows of my childhood. I had several deluxe sheet sets, the extras of which I kept carefully folded and enshrined on their own shelf in the closet. I tended to favor neutrals, but even though I had several sets of what an untrained eye would deem identical bedding, I could tell at a glance whether I was picking up the ecru sateen with the tiny swiss dots or the cream percale with the slightly bigger swiss dots. I never, ever got them mixed up.

Not that I had many nighttime visitors at that point in my life. To the contrary, my bed was a private defiance, a luxury all the more extravagant for being witnessed by so few other than myself. My bed was my reminder to self, every day when I got home from work, feeling anonymous and bruised after a day in the city, that I was more than the sum of my sweat-stained pits: I was *Woman!* A Woman deserving of pampering, a Woman in tune with her sensuality. A Woman ripe for the plucking, if not now then certainly in the near future. The rest of my housekeeping could go to hell, and often did. But not my bed. I'd pick up my Good Book; slide into my satiny, butter-smooth, cool, freshly laundered, lightly scented, high-thread-count sheets; and think: *There's hope.* God, did those sheets feel good.

My apartment at that time didn't have laundry, so my dealer, a saleswoman at Schweitzer Linen on the Upper West Side, recommended the Laundromat a few blocks down Broadway. It was a hole in the wall, but she knew the couple who ran it, and she vouched for the cleanliness of the place. Like any addict, I had my rituals. Each Friday afternoon, I loaded my sheets into my granny cart—carefully, so as not to rip them on the metal hooks—and toted them to the Laundromat, where I washed them (in the third machine from the end if I could, the newest one), on delicate cycle (warm wash, cold rinse), using an organic, hypoallergenic, extra-gentle, supremely expensive detergent. Once clean, the sheets were removed immediately from the washer, lest they sit in their own moisture a moment longer than necessary, then transferred to the dryer, where they were dried on low heat in ten-minute cycles until they were almost—*almost*—completely dried (too dry, and they get crispy). They were loosely piled into the granny cart, then rushed home, stat, to be draped on a drying rack in the living room, close enough to the window for a final blast of fresh air, though not so close that exhaust from the passing buses would blow in. The whole venture took several hours, longer if my sheets and I encountered unforeseen crowds or broken machines. No wonder I never had a social life.

Thinking about the time I lavished on those sheets, I have to laugh. I have a two-year-old now, and in my fantasy game of What I Would Do with Four Straight Hours to Myself, laundering does not figure in. It's not that I don't still have those sheets. I do. My husband and I sleep on them, and they still feel wonderful, soft and flannelly. But that lustrous, sensual feel of satin against my skin— that feeling of promise—is gone. The fabric is worn and pilled from being thrown, willy-nilly, in with the other laundry. There are—oh, unthinkable! —stains. And I don't spend time matching sheets and pillowcases the way I used to. Whatever I grab first from the linen closet, that's what's going on the bed.

To my surprise, I don't care. I remember one evening, about four months into parenthood, when the postpartum fog was beginning to lift and I was finally starting to look around again and take stock of the world beyond my baby and me. Exhausted and unshowered, I stared at the bed—unmade, a patchwork of faded, mismatched sheets and pillowcases—and thought, *I've given up. I'm appalled.* Then I thought, *No, I'm not.* I'd given up something, yes, but it didn't feel like a loss. Rather, it was a defeat in the rapturous sense, as if I'd surrendered to a higher power. My rumpled, rather homely bed was a concession to an utterly new world, full of utterly new realities: spitup and sleeplessness, yes, but also a passion so intense and raging that just touching my baby's cheek, I would feel my stomach knot. This was a far, far messier world I had entered. A disheveled bed seemed appropriate.

I feel lucky that I view my youthful relationship with my bed with tenderness rather than with disdain. When I'm reaching into the linen closet, my daughter close behind ready to "help Mommy," I do say a silent thank-you to those sheets. They helped me nurture a part of myself that hadn't yet bloomed. And now, they're delighting my daughter, in a very different way, as she throws them with abandon off the shelves and onto the floor so that she can practice her "fowding" (folding). Maybe someday, when she's older, I'll recommit to a bed of luxury. Maybe not. Maybe *she* will discover the happiness of a high thread count. The important thing now is to help her make sense of her own life, to help her make her own bed, so to speak, so that when she lies in it, she feels only joy. Impossible, I know, but isn't that sense of promise, that feeling of wild, possibly unrealistic hope, an essence of parenthood? In fact, it's a theme in my life. I have the sheets to prove it.

Green, if Not Clean

Pamela Paul

*A*long the neat vs. clean divide, I have historically fallen into the neat camp. As long as things appear orderly on the surface, it's generally been okay by me if a fine layer of dust lies on top. So when I had my first child, I swore I wouldn't become one of those purifier-wielding neurotics who zap binkies and rattles in one of those ludicrous nursery germ-killing devices and refuse to return a fallen lollipop to a child's quivering lips. Who's afraid of a little grime? Life is dirty, I figured; better that kids get used to it. I'd even convinced myself that the four-inch-high dust bunnies lurking in my house were good for my daughter. "She'll grow up accustomed to dirt and won't develop allergies," I reasoned.

But at a certain point, I had to face reality: My house was filthy, and the fact that my desktop displayed relatively neat piles of manila folders didn't obviate the fact. Though I hadn't had time to clean the house myself (or, let's face it, cared to devote myself to the task) and was too stingy to hire someone else to do it, ten months after my daughter's birth, I'd run out of excuses. Besides, the image of her actually confronting one of the bunnies was enough to get me to Costco.

Once there, I found the familiar Donna Reedish brands of my orange-carpeted, Lysol-scented youth oddly soothing. It was as if the good old-fashioned scrubbers and solvents on display could magically transform my home along the lines of my rosiest nostalgia. I grew up in a sparkly environment, back in the seventies suburbs, when normal people could afford live-in help. I imagined an efficient housekeeper buzzing around my house with Ajax, telenovelas humming in the background—something financially impossible but worth fantasizing about nonetheless.

Now that I'm my own matriarch, I told myself, it was time to spruce up. I was even eager to begin a life of responsible motherhood: clean, yes—but not neurotically so. Isn't there something magical, after all, about swiping a truly grimy bathtub or crusty kitchen counter and seeing it turn sparkly clean within seconds? Ah, the satisfaction of fastidiousness—easier than ever in our era of turbo disinfectants, HEPA filter-equipped vacuum cleaners, and Handi Wipes. I unloaded the rediscovered cleaning products of my youth and set them down to study the labels, as any responsible mother would do. Like most other new moms, I had become hyperconscious of everything that could potentially be mouthed, chewed, or suckled in the roving maw of my teething, crawling child.

But here was a mystery: Where were the ingredients? There was nothing but an ominous series of *Caution*, *Warning*, and *Danger! Keep Out of Reach of Children*. I turned the bottles every which way but found nothing other than references to harsh-sounding materials like bleach, ammonia, chlorine, and the ever-present "disinfectant." With cereal boxes detailing everything from trans fats to soluble fiber, I expected there to be some description of what I would be spraying on my countertops. Heaven forbid I didn't rinse the bathtub thoroughly—what kind of residue would my daughter's bottom be resting on?

Surely, Mr. Clean could tell me more. I logged onto the Procter & Gamble website, where I found lots of handy tips about usage but nothing about what made the stuff work. It turns out manufacturers aren't required to list ingredients; there is no FDA regulating what goes in and what must stay out of soap-scum spray. It's not easy to get a hold of ingredient lists either. The government hosts a website that lists components of many cleaners, gleaned from Material Safety Data Sheets (MSDS), which are posted by law in the factories where products are manufactured, but the Mr. Clean Antibacterial Multi-Purpose Cleaner I held in my hands didn't even show up. Companies frequently update their products, rebrand and rename them, and tweak the formulations. Still, I was able to click onto his all-purpose cleaner, and the results weren't encouraging. Some ingredients were unspecified, and the MSDS provided "no information about the [product's] potential for carcinogenicity." I was able to follow the trail of one ingredient, diethylene glycol monobutyl ether, which has an intimidating ring but appears in everything from brake fluid to hair dye. Though the MSDS measures workplace exposure, which can be far greater than the amount one would encounter at home, the foreboding Hazardous Substances Data Bank warned that "results of limited repeated-dose oral work reported suggests that material may be rather toxic when inhaled or absorbed through skin in repeated small doses." Eek. And that was just one ingredient.

Further research didn't assuage my concerns. Companies say they conceal ingredients to maintain trade secrets. It's almost impossible for a trained chemist, never mind the average consumer, to keep up. Environmental organizations and producers of "eco" products told me, not surprisingly, to be wary. A 2005 study by Clean Production Action, an environmental group, found traces of six classes of chemicals in dust taken from seventy homes in seven states (California, Maine, Massachusetts, Michigan, New York, Oregon, and Washington). Chemicals such as phthalates, alkylphenols, polybrominated diphenyl ethers (commonly know as PDBEs), and others linked to adverse effects including hormonal and sexual development impairment were found in every sample evaluated.

When I called the Soap and Detergent Association, a spokesperson for the industry assured me no tests had proven cleansers to be carcinogenic and that alkylphenols, which can imitate estrogen in the body and are commonly used as surfactants, have a "negligible" environmental impact. "All chemicals are toxic at some exposure, including salt and water," he told me, emphasizing, "the most important thing consumers can do to ensure the safe and effective use of a product is to read the label."

"But that's what I did . . . ," I insisted, feeling part angry adult, part chastised child. With Beatrice now a cautious toddler who weighs each step to preempt a tumble and her younger brother a fastidious one-year-old ("Uh oh," he'll intone dramatically when spotting a stray crumb on the floor), I see myself reflected in them. Perceptive, wary, even a bit suspicious.

Yes, I like to think I'm a skeptic. Contradictory information abounds: Environmentalists cite risks while industry groups emphasize the sketchy science that proves them. Mostly, the answer is: We don't yet know. Not enough solid research has been done. But the way I see it is this: In a courtroom, you're innocent until proven guilty. When it comes to my family's health, I don't want to wait to be proven wrong after the fact, twenty years from now when my son is unable to impregnate his wife or my daughter suffers from a new strain of cancer. Instead of becoming crazy Purell Mom, I've turned into an environmentalist neurotic. (Why must we all seemingly end up some variant of maternal extremist?) Dirt may not scare me, but potential toxins do.

It seriously ran against my cheapskate instincts to dump the Costco cache and worse, to bid adieu to the admittedly whitewashed fantasy of my Fantastik childhood home. Life in a house stocked with Seventh Generation and its ilk never emits that strangely intoxicating scent that so many of us have come to associate with "clean." Though my house is regularly cleaned, my bathtubs rarely shine, the countertops are sometimes streaky, and the floors need to be washed in vinegar solution rather too frequently. In the end, there are still dust bunnies beneath the stairwell and under my bed. But I figure, hell, if I don't kill them, they won't kill my kids.

The Road to Vacuum Glory

K. M. Lyons

I have a confession to make. I haven't told many people this, because I felt too self-conscious, and the sad truth is that once I tell, I have a tendency to get overexcited, if not to appear big-eyed and downright zealous. But believe me, I've wanted to tell. It's a relief to share something about your inner self, and this seems like the perfect time to open up. I'm keenly aware that, depending on how you look at it, it's possible I have a problem.

I have always dreamed about, even fantasized about, spending big bucks on a really nice, high-quality vacuum. Yeah, I know. Crazy, huh? Or maybe you're my kind of people, and you're feeling a tad overexcited yourself right now? Miele? Dyson? Oreck? What does that do for you?

In the beginning of what became a twenty-year relationship with my husband, I realized quickly that through his eyes this desire for a fine-quality dirt-sucking machine made me seem not only foolish about money but downright obsessive compulsive about cleanliness. Truth be told, I felt apologetic and sheepish about both, on the surface anyway. Deep down, I knew I was right about the value of a great vacuum, and I've always thought being a *little* compulsive about cleanliness just makes good sense.

When I've put myself in the role of a therapist around "my vacuum issue" and asked myself when I remember beginning to feel this way about cleaning, I can't come up with a clear shift in perception. There is no beginning. It could be said I was born with good taste and a desire for clean. Or maybe it was my mother's insistence that we drag out the big old canister vacuum every weekend to give the house a mandatory, albeit brief, "once-over"? Maybe it was the repeated mantra "You get what you pay for" that flowed easily from her lips, so often that I began to look at every item I purchased with a furrowed brow, anticipating that this would be the one to let me down because, shamefully, my pocketbook wasn't fat enough to trade up for the more expensive and therefore more effective model.

I suppose I don't have to know where the desire originated from. I do know that somewhere along the way, as a young wife, mother, and multipet owner who liked vacuuming and keeping the house clean, I realized I was caught in a crazy-making bind. I simultaneously squelched my desire for a real vacuum by buying Dirt Devils for less than $100 (and purchased every year like clockwork because the devilish things predictably lost their suction) and nurtured my instinct to hover over our carpet, which needed constant maintenance with a steel-willed determination (as if I'd been brainwashed), trying to convince myself that spending money on appliances wasn't the solution.

Truth be told, we never really had enough money for me to justify indulging my desire anyway. For us, spending $500 on a vacuum might as well have been $5,000. After all, I told myself, my husband was the primary breadwinner, and there were plenty of other priorities for our money, namely preschool, daycare, bills, and, well, food.

As time passed, my husband stopped being the primary breadwinner, and we moved to a house with hardwood floors and zero carpeting in the state of California, a much more expensive place to call home. So despite the fact that the money was more "mine" to do with as I wanted or as we needed, there were more things competing for those dollars. Despite the logic you'd think would be associated with this economic shift, earning the money didn't change the feeling I'd worn for so long that an expensive vacuum was indulgent and frivolous, not to mention silly for the carpetless.

So I swept that pet hair—*a lot*—and I mopped the wood floors with Murphy's Oil Soap. *A lot.* I continued to buy cheap vacuums just to deal with the pet hair on the furniture, as well as the bare floor, and they—bless their little consistent plastic hearts—lost suction. That never changed.

I longed to buy a rug for our little house with the hardwood floors, but my husband said that carpets and pet hair didn't go together. He insisted that rugs weren't pet friendly, and of course, ironically, without a good vacuum, this seemed logical. Furballs, or dust rats as my husband almost lovingly referred to them, are a peculiar enemy. You can watch them roll around on a hardwood floor. They're easy to spot once they appear out of nowhere, but you have to be quick if you're going to sweep them up, because each one has a will of its own, rolling around easily and running from you with every breeze that blows into the room. My husband made jokes about those balls of hair. He looked at them fondly, even going so far as to create stories about them hiding under the beds like impish little monsters just trying to have fun eluding us. He wanted cleaning to be playful—and me less zealous, I think.

And yet, he didn't care so much about cleaning. I was the one who wanted the floor to be clean. I didn't like the cute, anthropomorphized furballs (or the pets, for that matter). I earned the majority of the money, I wanted the rug for the living room, but still, I resisted my growing, primal urge to scrap the fourteenth crappy vacuum for the gold-standard Dyson I'd heard so much about. *He won't approve. I don't need it. Rugs are overrated. Mopping is better.* Still, no one mopped but me.

It probably comes as no surprise that when my husband and I decided to separate in our twentieth year of marriage, one of the first things I did was go out and buy a rug for the living room. I love how the whole room changed, and the house seemed to soften and breathe a sigh of relief with the addition of that little square of fabric on the floor. But what I'll admit here, since I'm already confessing, is that that sucker is getting hairier by the day. I tried the lint roller, my hand-vac, the dog brush, the combo dog brush and *then* the hand-vac, but it's no use. I need another vacuum. And to rub something painful all over this annoying rash of a problem, when my ex-husband comes by now, he says, "The living room looks great, but what are you going to do about that hair?" I've been quick to defend my actions.

"The hand-vac works great on that hair."

Right. As if he's going to believe that. That little devil-guy hand-vac is strong, but it's no match for the hair that comes from a golden retriever/German shepherd mix dog, and a Himalayan/Siamese cross cat who lie—no, make that revel in smearing their hairy bodies all over that rug *every* day. Throw in the dirt and the cat litter and detritus from two budding teenage boys who are in and out constantly, and well, my DustBuster is just not up to the challenge.

And so I ask you, what's my next step? It's logical, right? Don't I hear the golden ultra uber vac calling my name?

And guess what? I feel proud. Almost giddy. I'm going to do it. Does this mean I've arrived? It feels that way to me. And so, I'm preparing myself for a major purchase. The expensive vacuum. My glory day in the hot sun.

As I see it, it's not just that I'm taking the leap, moving toward the instinct I've always had. I'm preparing myself for making my own decisions, for *listening* to my own instincts. I've more than arrived at the cusp/threshold/door to a living room without pet hair. I've arrived at spending my money the way I feel it should be spent. I've arrived at accepting that sucking up dirt is a priority to me—and one that makes me feel good.

At the age of forty-one, I can finally admit that I can't relax in my own home until the floors are clean, dammit. Call me not practical. Call me a woman who doesn't spend money on the right things. Call me a woman who would rather eat at home for three months than have a dirty floor. But whatever you call me, whenever you call me, I might not be able to hear you. I just might be using my new Animal Dyson while listening to my iPod and grinning from ear to ear.

The House We Keep, the Home We Make

Rebecca McClanahan

*T*here was a time, not so long ago, when homemaking was the ultimate taboo, at least within my circle of artist friends and colleagues. And housekeeping? No self-respecting, upper-case Woman (as in *I Am Woman, Hear Me Roar*) would dare stoop to conquer the dust bunnies, the errant Cheerio beneath the baby's high chair, the cigarette ashes flicked by a sultry lover's hand. We had better things to do with our time. Paintings to paint, photographs to develop in basement darkrooms, protests to organize, poems of rage and blood to write in the late-night hours.

And as for the rest? The cooking, mending, laundering, shopping, stacking, sorting, all that is required to keep a house and make a home? That, too, was beneath us, like the dust bunnies and Cheerios. Or behind us—a generation, or two or three, behind us. For many women artists and writers of my generation, homemaking was some faraway, forgotten place, the country of our mothers and grandmothers, and we would never visit that country again. Certainly we would never take our daughters there.

I wrote, just a moment ago, "a time, not so long ago," but now it occurs to me that that time has not passed, perhaps will never pass. This thought, to my surprise, makes me terribly sad. I also wrote "we," when in truth this Woman never truly Roared against making a home, keeping a house. You have no idea how difficult this is to admit. We live in a time when the values of courage and honesty, particularly for women writers, equate to confessing only the darkest, most painful parts of our lives. "How brave you are," my students say to each other over workshop tables, "to expose that." Meaning, to uncover this family secret or that heinous act or to openly confront the demons of alcoholism, promiscuity, substance abuse, incest, infidelity, illness, betrayal. "Thank you for your honesty," they say, and I understand their sentiments. In over three decades of writing and publishing, I have also wrestled many dark angels, and continue to do so, so I acknowledge the price such writing exacts. But more and more I have come to respect the honesty and courage required to recognize the bright angels when they appear in our memory, and to allow them equal space in our narratives.

So, here goes. I will now take a cleansing breath, and, at the risk of marring any image I might have achieved as a serious artist, one who attempts to plumb the deepest depths, who keeps Faulkner's dictum "the human heart in conflict with itself" taped above her writing desk, who fears that this confession will align her not with Little Women's Jo but rather with her sisters—the housebound Beth or the frivolous, overly feminine Amy or, Goddess forbid, the domestic goddess Meg—I will confess, to all those within hearing distance of my shaky voice, my cleanest dirty secret: I love making house, making home, keeping house, keeping home. From my first miniature cake pans (acquired at age six) to my first whiff of lemon furniture oil to my first whipstitched hem of a calico curtain, I was seduced by the warm, sweet world of home, and the seduction has only increased through the decades. I am lured toward domesticity the way some middle-aged women are lured toward Botox, affairs with young men, or overseas travel.

"I think you always had that tendency," my mother says, and the way she says it doesn't sound like a compliment, but neither does it sound like a putdown. After all, a tendency isn't something you have much control over. You're either born with it or you acquire it early on, like a stutter or slightly crooked teeth or an attraction to small reptiles or birds. "It's just the way you are," she says. "You were always my helper, my right hand." This must be true, for I remember those earliest years when I was tied, by choice and often against her wishes, to my mother's apron strings. And I remember the later years: sewing the aprons to which I sewed the ties that bound me even more tightly to her and to the world her hands created. My mother no doubt wondered at my infatuation with domesticity. Like many other women of her generation, she had assumed the role of homemaker less by tendency than by fate and circumstance. After a bit of college (a bit being all her family could afford) and a brief business career, she met a man, fell in love, married, and later followed him wherever the U.S. Marine Corps deemed to send him. First, there was just the two of them, love-nested in one-room quarters or upstairs apartments where my mother made dinner each night on a one-burner hot plate, until it was time to repack their few possessions for the next place, and the next. Soon the first child arrived, then another, and every few years another, and my mother would pack us all up, once again, to begin our next tour of duty.

I hated every move, every loss of neighborhood, friends, house, and school. The only thing that made moving bearable was knowing that no matter where we landed, from the moment the movers lifted the first piece of furniture from the truck, my mother would start making home. And despite the difficulties life pressed upon her—the constant care of six children, the juggling of budgets and schedules, her homesickness for faraway relatives, and her longing for the husband who was flying yet another mission in Korea, Japan, or Vietnam—she would continue making home. Each day as I dragged back from school, missing my old life and having made no friends yet, or maybe one, usually a military brat like me, the home she kept making would be waiting. I'd open the door to the *thrum-thrum-thrum* of the Singer sewing machine or the *whoop-splat* of fresh sheets being folded or the creamy smell of vanilla and coconut sifting from beneath the kitchen door, and everything else would fall away. The world she made within our walls was the warmest, safest, brightest world imaginable. Who could want or need more?

Lest you are becoming worried about me, let me assure you that I am relatively sane and that I possess an above-middling IQ. And I do not lack a sense of independence. I survived my share of sleep-away camps, later venturing three thousand miles from home and family to support myself while earning two graduate degrees. Those were rough times, the proverbial lean years all former graduate students brag about, but the roughest year was when I was finishing my dissertation. Writing, need I state the obvious, is difficult work. Extremely difficult work. Especially when one is operating under someone else's restrictions. To this day, the recollection of that year brings tightness to my shoulders, a violent kick to my gut, and the resurgence of the tic that grabbed my right cheek and did not let go for months. What eased me during those difficult times was not scotch-on-the-rocks (my budget would not allow it) or sex (I was between commitments) nor television (my borrowed black-and-white died after the first week). What eased me was the thought of the reward that awaited me. If I drafted this paragraph, rechecked that footnote, if I was finally able to clearly state my conclusion, I could do what I loved to do most: make home.

Home, at this time, was what my landlord called "a garage apartment without the garage." It consisted of two uninsulated rooms accessible by a rickety outdoor stairway and tilting, precariously, on four thick wooden stilts. The rent was $65 a month, including heat. Except there was no heat, as the furnace spewed a choice of black soot or nothing. I chose nothing. Luckily, South Carolina winters are generally mild, mild enough to support cockroaches so impressive as to have acquired their own stately moniker: palmetto bugs. But not even the nightly armadillo-like marches across the linoleum, nor their occasional surprise flank attack from the shower drain, could dampen my spirits. My own apartment! To do with it as I will! To vacuum, to polish, to arrange, and rearrange. Eight walls to paint. Three windows to clean until they squeaked. An oven in which to bake lasagna and oatmeal cookies. Two chairs, a card table, a bed to spread with my grandmother's quilt, photographs of nephews and nieces to hang, right there, beside the front door, curtains and dust ruffles and tablecloths to sew (for of course I had packed my Singer), and a wooden dresser to rub with lemon oil until it shone.

At this point, I must pause and take a break. Writing is such hard work.

I'm back at my desk now, feeling more than a little guilty. No, I haven't been checking email or crawling onto our quilt-covered bed for a nap. In the ten minutes I was away, I fluffed the sofa cushions, added fresh water to the yellow roses to extend their fragrant lives one more day, and concocted a marinade for the pork tenderloin I will serve our friends tonight. I've already scrubbed the potatoes, shredded the cabbage for the slaw, and grated the orange zest to sprinkle over the baked carrots. Orange zest! The smell takes me back forty years, to the California orange groves surrounding the house where we lived the year my father was serving in Japan, the year I baked miniature cakes in miniature cake pans and mailed them off. At the time, I was blissfully unaware that it would take weeks for the cakes to reach him; my mother was not the kind of mother to spoil her children's excitement with cold, hard facts. If baking the cakes made me happy and connected me to the father who had been gone for months, that's all that mattered.

Making a cake, a house, a home, for someone you love: What could be finer or more important? My painter friend, who keeps a lovely house but not eagerly, says she would rather be painting, any day. "Painting stays done," she says. "Housekeeping doesn't. The next day you just have to do it all over again." Of course she is right. Art does stay done. She is also right that few pleasures top the pleasure of having created a piece of art, in whatever form it finally emerges. Every now and then I take my books down from the shelf, wipe off their dusty covers (housekeeping, for me, does not always entail dusting), and enjoy the knowledge that not only are the books finished but that I had a hand in their making. True, I can't always recall just how that line of poetry got written or how that character's monologue came through my pen onto the paper, but I recognize the name beside the author photo and claim it as mine. This is a nice moment, but it passes.

Sometimes, of course, the rewards for writing go further. I receive a note from a grateful reader and am reminded that the words we write don't always stop inside our book covers, that they go on to live other lives. You might even say that they nourish our readers, or warm them, or give them a glimpse of a world beyond their window, a world ablaze with light. But truth be told, words go only so far and so deep. A poem by Wendell Berry ends with the lines, "The way of love leads all ways / to life beyond words, silent / and secret. To serve that triumph / I have done all the rest"—*the rest* including the writing of the very words that compose his poem. Art supports life, not the other way around. So, when my husband asked me what I wanted for my fiftieth birthday, I answered, "*The Oxford English Dictionary*. And a new clothesline."

Yes, I am grateful beyond words for the words other writers have given me and for the words that have passed through me onto the page. But to my mind, the making of a home is as worthy a pursuit as the making of a poem. Perhaps more worthy. Which leads me back to the dinner I am making for my friends tonight. Dearer friends no one could wish for, and I believe they feel the same way about my husband and me. They have shown their love in countless physical gestures: in trusting us with the care of their daughter; in offering their blood—not metaphorical blood but real, type O-positive—when I was facing major surgery and might require a transfusion; in the meals they have served us, the bread they have baked and delivered, still warm, though its delivery required three subway stops. The four of us share a love of the arts; each, in our own field, is a working artist. Yet, though we try to support each other's work, our deepest connections lie elsewhere. So, rather than reading a new story to them tonight, I will carve the pork tenderloin, which is a story in itself, as are the sofa cushions fluffed for them and the yellow roses spreading their sweet scent.

Once, a long time ago, I entered a time and place where I was so thoroughly broken I knew I would never find my way out again and didn't care if I did. Literature played an important part in my recovery, poems and stories I read and fought desperately to write. And music, threading its bright strands into the darkness. But finally it was the small, domestic gestures—some would call them trivial—that brought me home to myself. The wind-dried sheets I removed from the line and pressed close to my pale, aching face. The banana bread that I slathered with butter and placed on the blue china plate an extravagant friend had brought me. Gesture by small gesture, the world came back to me. The trivial, domestic daily world.

The art of housekeeping and homemaking reaches deeper than dirt, thicker than the dust that collects on my writing desk, dresser top, and on the top cabinets no one sees. To make a home and to keep it requires great stores of creative energy and is not for the faint of heart, nor for the heartless. Our mothers and grandmothers knew this, among other important things, which is why I still visit their faraway country as often as I can and why I hope that my nieces and nephews will visit, too, once I am gone. Yes, my painter friend is right. Unlike art, the making of home does not stay done. Every morning, every evening, the mess awaits us. The messy, hungry, beautiful world, wanting and needing our touch.

ABOUT THE CONTRIBUTORS

Teena Apeles keeps toned with a daily regimen of scrubbing, vacuuming, wiping, and mopping every surface in her home. She is the author of *Women Warriors: Adventures from History's Greatest Female Fighters* (Seal Press, 2004), and her work has also appeared in the anthologies *Father Poems* (Anvil, 2004), *Bare Your Soul: The Thinking Girl's Guide to Enlightenment* (Seal Press, 2002), and *Geography of Rage: Remembering the Los Angeles Riots of 1992* (Really Great Books, 2002). She is currently working on a graphic novel about a young woman who inspires dejected WWII veterans to battle the ills of their urban community.

Mira Bartók is the author of thirty children's books on the art and history of world cultures. Her essays, book reviews, and poetry have appeared in *Another Chicago Magazine, The Bellingham Review, Kenyon Review, Tikkun, Fourth Genre: Explorations in Nonfiction*, and *LINK Magazine*. Her work has been nominated for a Pushcart Prize and has been cited as a "Notable Mention" in *The Best American Essay* series. Mira is currently at work on *The Memory Palace: A Memoir in Words and Pictures,* an illustrated memoir about her relationship with her schizophrenic and homeless mother.

Katy Brennan, a graduate of Smith College and The London School of Economics, is a freelance writer living in New York City. Her work has appeared in several Hearst and Condé Nast magazines, *The New Yorker*, and *The New York Times*. She is currently at work on her first book, *Our Proudest Moments: A Memoir of Sisterhood.*

Kayla Cagan lives in a moderately clean apartment with her moderately clean husband in moderately clean Los Angeles. She writes moderately dirty plays on her moderately clean desk. Her plays can be found in the following anthologies: *The Best Ten-Minute Plays for Two Actors 2005*; *The Best Ten-Minute Plays for Two Actors 2006*; and *The Best Ten-Minute Plays for Three Actors 2006* (Smith and Kraus).

Rand Richards Cooper is the author of a novel, *The Last To Go*, and a story collection, *Big As Life*. His fiction has appeared in *Harper's, The Atlantic, Esquire,* and many other magazines. A longtime writer for *Bon Appétit*, Rand lives in Hartford, Connecticut, with his wife, Molly, and daughter, Larkin, and writes a column about fatherhood, "Dad on a Lark," for Wondertime.com.

Kathleen Crisci considers herself, first and foremost, a storyteller. She has been a featured reader at the Nightingale Lounge and the Cornelia Street Cafe. Currently an MFA candidate in nonfiction writing at Sarah Lawrence College, she is completing a collection of personal essays.

Laura Shaine Cunningham is the author of eight books, including the memoirs *A Place in the Country* (featured as a *New York Times Notable*

Book) and *Sleeping Arrangements* (now in its twentieth printing). Ms. Cunningham's fiction and nonfiction have appeared in *The New Yorker, Atlantic Monthly, The New York Times, The London Times*. She writes frequent essays for *The New York Times* and is a contributor to many magazines, including *The New Yorker, More, The Ladies' Home Journal, Harper's Bazaar, Metropolitan Home, Organic Styles*, and *Child*.

Patty Dann is the author of the novel *Mermaids*, which has been translated into many languages and made into a film starring Cher, Winona Ryder, Christina Ricci, and Bob Hoskins. Her novel *Sweet and Crazy* is about a widow with a young son. A respected writing teacher, Patty is also author of *The Baby Boat*, a nonfiction book about her experiences adopting her son. Patty's most recent book is *The Goldfish Went on Vacation: A Memoir of Loss (and Learning to Tell the Truth about It)*.

Lisa Selin Davis is the author of *Belly* (Little, Brown, 2005), about a man returning to his small town in the age of Wal-Mart. A freelance writer covering urban planning and environmental issues, she has written for *The New York Times, Salon.com, Interior Design, OnEarth, This Old House*, and lots of other publications.

Louise DeSalvo is the Jenny Hunter Endowed Scholar in the MFA Program in Creative Writing at Hunter College. She has edited *Virginia Woolf's Melymbrosia*, and coedited *A Green and Mortal Sound, Vita Sackville-West's Letters to Virginia Woolf*, and *The Milk of Almonds* and is the author of *Virginia Woolf: The Impact of Childhood Sexual Abuse on Her Life and Work, Writing as a Way of Healing* and the memoirs *Vertigo, Breathless, Adultery*, and *Crazy in the Kitchen*. She has just completed *On Moving: A Writer's Meditation on Old Houses, New Haunts, and Finding Home Again*.

In addition to being a messy mom, **Juliet Eastland** has written for *Bitch, Bust, Health, AlterNet, Geez, Planned Parenthood, Tricycle* and has contributed to several print anthologies: *Secrets & Confidences: The Complicated Truth about Women's Friendships* (Seal Press, 2006), *If Women Ruled the World* (Inner Ocean Publishing, 2004), *A Matter of Choice: 25 People Who Transformed Their Lives* (Seal Press, 2004), and *Tribute to Orpheus: Prose and Poetry about Music or Musicians* (Kearney Street Books, 2007).

Janice Eidus's recent novel, *The War of the Rosens*, won an Independent Publisher Book Award in Religion and was a finalist for the Sophie Brody Medal, an award for the most distinguished contribution to Jewish Literature for Adults. Her other books include the short story collections *The Celibacy Club* and *Vito Loves Geraldine* and the novels *Urban Bliss* and *Faithful Rebecca*. Her forthcoming novel, *The Last Jewish Virgin* explores myth, Jewish identity, and mothers and daughters.

Brian Gerber is a retired librarian who divides his time between a house in rural Dutchess County and an apartment in New York City. Before becoming a librarian, he was a computer programmer and mathematics teacher. He grew up in a Long Island suburb in a time when power household tools were uncommon. He has written a number of unpublished short stories and children's books.

Richard Goodman is the author of *The Soul of Creative Writing* and *French Dirt: The Story of a Garden in the South of France*. He has written on a variety of subjects for many national publications, including *The New York Times, Harvard Review, Vanity Fair, Saveur, Commonweal, Creative Nonfiction, Louisville Review, Ascent, French Review*, and the *Michigan Quarterly Review*. He teaches Creative Nonfiction at Spalding University's MFA in Writing Program in Louisville, Kentucky.

Penelope Green is a reporter in the home section of *The New York Times*. She lives in the East Village with her daughter and spends an inordinate amount of time dusting her baseboards.

Mindy Greenstein is a clinical psychologist and psycho-oncologist. She consults for the Psychiatry Department at Memorial Sloan-Kettering Cancer Center, where she was formerly the Chief Clinical Fellow. Mindy's most recent psychiatric papers were published in the *American Journal of Psychotherapy*, and she's written personal essays for *More* and *Self*, as well as other publications. Mindy lives in New York City with her husband and two children. And she actually likes cooking chicken, but don't tell anyone.

Michael Hill has worked in Baltimore at *The Evening Sun* and *The Sun* for over thirty years. He has held a variety of jobs, from police reporter to television critic to foreign correspondent in Johannesburg, South Africa. He currently writes for *The Sun*'s news analysis section, "Ideas." He lives in Baltimore with his two sons, Albert and Owen.

Ann Hood is the author of seven novels, including, most recently, *The Knitting Circle* (WW Norton); a collection of short stories, *An Ornithologist's Guide to Life*; and a memoir, *Do Not Go Gentle: My Search for Miracles in a Cynical Time*. Her essays and short stories have appeared in many publications, including *The New York Times*, *Tin House*, *The Paris Review*, *Bon Appétit*, *Food & Wine*, and *Good Housekeeping*. She has won two Pushcart Prizes, a Best American Spiritual Writing Award, and the Paul Bowles Prize for Short Fiction.

Sonya Huber is an assistant professor at Georgia Southern University in the department of writing and linguistics, where she teaches creative writing and composition. Her first book, *Opa Nobody* (University of Nebraska Press, 2008), presents a portrait of her anti-Nazi activist grandfather in fiction and memoir. Her work has appeared in *Fourth Genre, Literary Mama, Passages North, The Chronicle of Higher Education*, and many other journals and magazines, and in anthologies from Seal Press, University of Arizona Press, and Prometheus Books.

Formerly the editor-in-chief of *McCall's* magazine, **Sally Koslow** is the author of the novels *Little Pink Slips* and *The Late, Lamented Molly Marx*, which will be published by Ballantine in 2008. Formerly a writer at Conde Nast's *Mademoiselle* magazine, Sally developed *Lifetime* magazine for Hearst and Disney. She has written for *The New York Observer, More, Ladies' Home Journal, Better Homes & Gardens, Redbook, Self, Town & Country, Harper's Bazaar, Glamour, O at Home*, and *O, the Oprah Magazine*, as well as many others.

K. M. Lyons is a writer and professional editor who is taking a break from cleaning up after others to get back to the work she loves (besides vacuuming): writing nonfiction. She lives in Berkeley, California, with her two teen sons, a dog, a cat, and a blue-tongued skink.

Julianne Malveaux is president of Bennett College for Women in Greensboro, North Carolina. She is a writer, economist, and columnist whose commentary on race, gender, the workplace, and national affairs has appeared in *USA Today, Diverse Issues in Higher Education, Essence*, and *Ms.* magazine; daily newspaper credits include her work as editor of *Voices of Vision: African American Women on the Issues* (1996), coauthor of *Unfinished Business: A Democrat and a Republican Take On the 10 Most Important Issues Women Face* (2002). At Bennett College, her priorities are global education, entrepreneurship, leadership development, and communications excellence.

Joyce Maynard (www.joycemaynard.com) is the author of five novels, including *To Die For*, and the bestselling memoir *At Home in the*

World, translated into nine languages. Her essays have appeared in numerous publications and collections. She performs regularly with The Moth in New York City and with Porchlight in San Francisco, and she runs the Lake Atitlan (Guatemala) Writing Workshop.

Rebecca McClanahan has published nine books, most recently *Deep Light: New and Selected Poems 1987–2007* and *The Riddle Song and Other Rememberings*, which won the 2005 Glasgow Award for nonfiction. Her work has appeared in *The Best American Essays, The Best American Poetry, The Kenyon Review, Georgia Review*, and numerous anthologies; awards include a Pushcart Prize, the Wood Prize from *Poetry*, and the Carter Prize for the essay. She lives in New York and teaches in the MFA program of Queens University (Charlotte) and the Hudson Valley Writers' Center.

Karen Salyer McElmurray is the author of *Surrendered Child: A Birth Mother's Journey*, recipient of an AWP Award for Creative Nonfiction. Her debut novel, *Strange Birds in the Tree of Heaven*, was winner of the Thomas and Lillie D. Chaffin Award for Appalachian Writing and a recipient of grants from the National Endowment for the Arts, the Kentucky Foundation for Women, and the North Carolina Arts Council. Her newest novel is *The Motel of the Stars* (Sarabande Books, 2008). She teaches in the MFA Program at Georgia College and State University, where she is creative nonfiction editor for *Arts and Letters*.

Kyoko Mori is the author of two nonfiction books: *Polite Lies* (Henry Holt, 1998) and *The Dream of Water* (Henry Holt, 1994) and three novels: *Shizuko's Daughter* (Henry Holt, 1993); *One Bird* (Henry Holt, 1995); *Stone Field, True Arrow* (Metropolitan, 2000). She grew up in Kobe, Japan, before moving to the American Midwest at twenty. She now lives in Washington, D.C., and teaches creative writing at George Mason University.

Nancy Peacock graduated from Chapel Hill High School in 1972. Her first novel, *Life Without Water*, published in 1996, was chosen as *New York Times* editor's choice. A second novel, *Home Across the Road*, soon followed. Her latest book, a humorous collection of essays about her life as a self-employed housecleaner, is titled *A Broom of One's Own: Words on Writing, Housecleaning, and Life*. She now works as a writing teacher and lives with her husband in Chatham County, North Carolina.

Pamela Paul is an author and journalist for numerous publications. Her most recent book, *Parenting, Inc.*, was published by Times Books in spring 2008. Her previous book, *PORNIFIED: How the Culture of Pornography Is Transforming Our Lives, Our Relationships and Our Families*, published by Times Books/Henry Holt in September 2005, was named one of the best books of the year by *The San Francisco Chronicle*. Pamela is also the author of *The Starter Marriage and the Future of Matrimony*, published by Villard/Random House in 2002, and a contributor to *Time* magazine.

Alissa Quart is the author of *Branded: The Buying and Selling of Teenagers* (Basic Books, 2004) and *Hothouse Kids* (Penguin, 2006). Her books have been translated into eight languages. She is currently working on a third nonfiction book on subcultures for Farrar, Straus & Giroux and a regular media column for *Columbia Journalism Review*, where she is a contributing editor, as well as writing for *The New York Times Magazine* and many other publications. She teaches at Columbia University Journalism School and Teachers College, Columbia University, where she is a senior fellow.

Louise Rafkin is the author of *Other People's Dirt: A Housecleaner's Curious Adventures*, published by Algonquin Books (1998), reissued in paper by Plume (1999), and translated into three languages. She is now a Bay Area journalist who still loves to clean—but just her own house.

Markie Robson-Scott divides her time between London and New York. In the United States she has written features for *Vogue, Harper's Bazaar,* and the *ABA Journal,* and in the United Kingdom she has worked as an editor, writer, and book reviewer on many publications, including *The Guardian, Harper's Bazaar, The Sunday Times, Vogue, Elle,* and *Good Housekeeping.* She has also written a collection of short stories and is at work on a memoir about her father.

Thaddeus Rutkowski is the author of the novels *Tetched* (Behler Publications, 2005) and *Roughhouse* (Kaya Press, 1999). Both books were finalists for an Asian American Literary Award. He teaches fiction writing at the Writer's Voice of the West Side YMCA in New York and lives in Manhattan with his wife and daughter.

Branka Ruzak is a writer, producer, and editor for commercial and corporate advertising. As a child she spent many hours listening to her father's stories and playing Croatian folk music. Always an avid traveler, her studies in Hindustani classical music, as well as her enthusiasm for Indian novels, textiles, and a good cup of chai have taken her to India and other destinations. She is currently working on a collection of essays about family, identity, culture, and travel.

Mimi Schwartz has published five books, most recently, *Good Neighbors, Bad Times—Echoes of My Father's German Village* (University of Nebraska Press, 2008). Other books still in print include *Thoughts from a Queen-Sized Bed* (2002; paperback, 2004) and *Writing True, the Art and Craft of Creative Nonfiction* (with Sondra Perl, 2006). Her short work has appeared in *The Missouri Review, Creative Nonfiction, Fourth Genre, Calyx, The New York Times, Tikkun, Jewish Week, The Writer's Chronicle, Florida Review, Brevity, River Teeth,* and *Writer's Digest,* among others. She is professor emerita of Richard Stockton College of New Jersey.

Jessica Shines is a Chicago native and a recent graduate of Bennett College for Women. She is also a beneficiary of the Civil Rights generation and plans to advocate for others. When she's not being pampered by her bourgeois, feminist family, she enjoys dancing and taking late night walks. One day, she plans to work in international development.

Nancy Stiefel is a writer and psychoanalyst living in New York City. She is a self-proclaimed expert on the theory and practice of clutter and teaches a workshop on the topic for the Mid Manhattan Institute for Psychoanalysis. She's currently at work on a second novel.

Rebecca Walker is the author of several books, including the bestselling and critically acclaimed memoirs *Black, White and Jewish: Autobiography of a Shifting Self* (Penguin, 2001 and Riverhead, 2002), and *Baby Love: Choosing Motherhood after a Lifetime of Ambivalence* (Riverhead, 2007). Her latest book, *One, Big, Happy Family: 18 Writers Talk about Polyamory, Open Adoption, Mixed Marriage, Single Motherhood and Other Realities of Truly Modern Love* (Riverhead, 2009), celebrates American families living and loving outside the box of the traditional nuclear family. Rebecca writes for many magazines, blogs, and journals, lectures at universities around the world, and lives in Hawaii with her own very special twenty-first century family.

Lisa Solod Warren's anthology, *Desire: Women Write about Wanting,* was published by Seal Press in November 2007 to wonderful reviews. Her fiction and nonfiction has been widely anthologized and she has published dozens of short stories and essays in literary journals, magazines, and newspapers. She is currently working on a new novel.

ABOUT THE AUTHOR

© Patrick Jeannes

*M*indy Lewis is a writer and visual artist. Her memoir, *Life Inside* (Washington Square Press, 2003), was named a "Book of the Year" by *The American Journal of Nursing* and an *Elle* magazine "Must-Read." Her essays have been published in anthologies and in *Newsweek, Lilith, Body & Soul,* and *Poets & Writers* magazines. She enjoys leaving her creatively cluttered New York City apartment to teach writing at The Writer's Voice of the Westside YMCA, Brooklyn College, and intensive workshops in beautiful locations.

ACKNOWLEDGMENTS

*F*irst and foremost, I wish to express my gratitude and appreciation to the authors of these wonderful essays, without which
this anthology would not exist.

I am grateful to literary agent Tracy Brown for his responsiveness,
enthusiasm, and commitment to this project. My thanks to Krista
Lyons, my editor at Seal Press, who waited patiently for someone to
come up with this very anthology topic and whose generous support
and expert guidance helped bring the book smoothly to fruition.

I'm indebted to Deborah Siegel for generously sharing her
knowledge—and her agent—and for suggesting a key four-letter
title. Special thanks to Glenn Raucher and my inspiring students
at the Writer's Voice of the West Side YMCA. Thanks, too, Pamela
Paul, Katy Brennan, Connie Sommer, Peter Bricklebank, Charles
Salzberg, Jo Ann Miller, Jennifer Prost, and others who were there
to network, brainstorm, and offer feedback and to Ann and Preston
Browning for the quiet retreat of Wellspring House. My thanks to
Ruth Ferris for referring Attila and Rita, who know that cleaning,
like writing, is a "purification process for the soul."

Finally, I wish to thank my mother, Florence Teitelbaum, for
always keeping a fastidious home and for never failing to offer her
love and support.